D1418149

Other books in the Jossey-Bass Public Administration Series:

The Spirit of Public Administration

The Spirit
of Public
Administration

H. George Frederickson

Jossey-Bass Publishers • San Francisco

For sales outside the United States, please contact your local Simon & Schuster International Office.

(Copyright credits appear on page 273.)

Manufactured in the United States of America.

Library of Congress Cataloging-in-Publication Data

Frederickson, H. George.
　　The spirit of public administration / H. George Frederickson.
　　　　p.　cm. — (The Jossey-Bass public administration series)
　　Includes bibliographical references and index.
　　ISBN 0–7879–0295–0
　　1. Public administration.　I. Title.　II. Series.
JF1351.F735　　1997
　　350—dc20　　　　　　　　　　　　　　　　　　　　　　　　　96–19553

FIRST EDITION
HB Printing 10　9　8　7　6　5　4　3　2　1

The Jossey-Bass
Public Administration Series

Consulting Editor
Public Management and Administration
James L. Perry
Indiana University

Contents

Part One: Governance, Politics, and the Public

Part Two: Issues of Fairness

Part Three: Ethics, Citizenship, and Benevolence in Public Administration

Acknowledgments

Although I take primary responsibility for *The Spirit of Public Administration,* many people contributed both directly and indirectly in the book's content and completion. For direct contributions, I gratefully acknowledge the help of Richard W. Hug, Charles Epp, Ralph C. Chandler, David Kirkwood Hart, and David G. Frederickson. Each of them contributed some ideas, some words, and more than a little spirit to *The Spirit of Public Administration.* James L. Perry, who capably edits the Public Administration Series for Jossey-Bass Publishers, provided many splendid suggestions as well as needed encouragement. Hal G. Rainey and Kenneth J. Meier performed thorough, thoughtful, and very helpful evaluations of the initial draft and made important suggestions (some of which I followed) for improving the substance and spirit of the book.

Several friends and colleagues provided hallway seminars, e-mail exchanges, telephone conversations, and face-to-face talk that stimulated my thinking and sharpened the *Spirit.* They include Barbara Romzek, John Nalbandian, Phillip Cooper, Scott Fosler, Gary Wamsley, Todd La Porte, John Kirlin, Chester Newland, Ross Clayton, Laurence Lynn, Charles Goodsell, Donald Kettl, Julie Bundt, and Steven Maynard-Moody.

I am grateful to the University of Kansas for its support of the Edwin O. Stene Professorship and to the loyal alumni members of the Kansas University City Managers and Trainees, who contribute generously to the support of the professorship. Without such support, *The Spirit of Public Administration* would not have been possible. In addition, my colleagues and students in the Department of Public Administration at the University of Kansas have been encouraging and supportive. More important, they cheerfully sustain the scholarly environment and collective good will that has daily provided me an example of the spirit of public administration.

Alan R. Shrader, David B. Horne, and Susan R. Williams at Jossey-Bass have been helpful not only with the details one expects from a good publisher but also with the insight and judgment of editors who know the field of public administration.

I especially appreciate the skill, loyalty, and dedication of my assistant Thomas Michael Rundle. He guided the book's production through several drafts of the manuscript and expertly made the endless changes that improved it.

Finally, I am grateful to my wife, Mary, both for her support and for her editorial suggestions. I am the better for it, and so is the book.

The Author

H. George Frederickson was appointed Edwin O. Stene Distinguished Professor of Public Administration at the University of Kansas in 1987. Prior to that, he served for ten years as the president of Eastern Washington University at Cheney and Spokane. He has also served as dean of the College of Public and Community Service at the University of Missouri and as associate dean of the School of Public and Environmental Affairs at Indiana University. He has taught at the University of Maryland, the University of Southern California, Syracuse University, and the University of North Carolina. He holds a master's degree in public administration from the University of California at Los Angeles and a Ph.D. from the University of Southern California.

Frederickson is the editor in chief of the *Journal of Public Administration Research and Theory*. He is a fellow of the National Academy of Public Administration and an honorary member of the International City/County Management Association. In 1990, he received the Distinguished Research Award given jointly by the American Society for Public Administration and the National Association of Schools of Public Affairs and Administration. In the same year, he served as Distinguished Fulbright Scholar in the Republic of Korea. In 1992, he received the Dwight Waldo Award given by the American Society for Public Administration for distinguished contributions to the professional literature of public administration.

Understanding Public Administration

> *Energy in the executive is a leading character in the definition of good government. It is essential to the protection of the community against foreign attacks: It is no less essential to the steady administration of the laws, to the protection of property against those irregular and high combinations, which sometimes interrupt the ordinary course of justice to security of liberty against the enterprises and assaults of combinations of faction, and of anarchy. . . . The ingredients which constitute energy in the executive are first unity, secondly duration, thirdly an adequate provision for the support, fourthly competent powers.*
>
> ALEXANDER HAMILTON, *THE FEDERALIST*, NO. 79

This book is about the spirit of public administration. It takes a big broad-brush approach to the study and practice of public service. *The Spirit of Public Administration* has to do with immediate and pressing questions of how to do things effectively, efficiently, and equitably—this is management. But the bigger questions of public administration have to do with the beliefs, values, and customs of those who practice it. *The Spirit of Public Administration* brings the pertinent issues of public management to the big questions of how to define the public; how to conduct effective public administration in a democratic political context; how to balance efficiency, economy, and equity; how to be an ethical public administrator; and why it is essential for public administrators to also be representative citizens.

The purpose of this book is to further not just our knowledge of the subject, but also our understanding of public organizations and public work in public settings, which is described in this book as *point of view*. This point of view begins with an abiding belief that, on balance, public administration has contributed importantly to the quality of American democratic government. But this is a time of harsh criticism of our public institutions and those who manage them—in other words, bureaucrat bashing. In the contemporary context of hostility toward public employees, downsizing, contracting out, privatization, and load shedding, it may seem improbable to suggest that public administration could be a key element in improving the quality of governmental and other public organizations for all of us. But that is exactly the point of view of *The Spirit of Public Administration*.

To the individual, that spirit is a deep and enduring commitment to the calling of public service and to the effective conduct of public organizations and their work. Those of us who practice public administration (or who prepare people for its practice) know that spirit in many ways: in our individual views and beliefs about the purposes and prospects of government (particularly democratic government); about the nature of collective human enterprises and how to make them effective; and about ethics and morality in public life.

In the entire, that spirit accounts for the collective views and beliefs expressed in the professional associations of public administration as well as in the curricula and pedagogies of the schools and colleges that prepare people for public administration, and most important, as reflected in the customs and cultures of public administrators in units of government and in public nonprofit organizations.

The spirit of public administration is both outward and inward looking. It looks outward because it pertains broadly to the context of public administration, and particularly to the changing nature of the field. It has to do with the interaction between the changing context of public administration and its practice. Bureaucratic attitudes, beliefs, norms, values, and behavior spring from context. The spirit of public administration is also inward looking—a mirror on the behavior of individual public officials and on the values, norms, and beliefs that guide that behavior. It is also inward in that it reflects the conduct of public organizations, including whom they serve and how effectively they provide that service. To capture the spirit of public administration, both outward and inward perspectives are required.

The spirit of public administration combines rational and empirical forms of knowledge or ways of knowing with an understanding of the field built on experience, wisdom, and judgment. Rational assumptions and the traditions of social science research are essential to the creation of reliable and replicable theories of public administration. But theories that are derived solely from rational assumptions and social science methods may be unable to account for important forces in the field, such as compassion, courage, and benevolence. The aim of *The Spirit of Public Administration* is first to guide the reader to a knowledge of the field, and second and more important, to attempt to further an understanding of the field.

This description of the spirit of public administration begins with an examination of the meaning of *public* in public administration, followed by a consideration of the issues of fairness and social equity in public administration, as well as by a treatment of ethics in the field. Following that is a discussion of the unique connection between the public in public administration and the noble concept of citizenship in democratic government. Finally, *The Spirit of Public Administration* brings together the concepts of citizenship, patriotism, and ethics for an examination of the treatment of European Jews in the Second World War.

The phrase *public administration* was first used prominently by Woodrow Wilson when he was a young professor, long before he was elected president (W. Wilson, 1887). He used the phrase to describe the age-old conduct of public affairs—the implementation or "carrying out" aspects of the public's business. Laws and constitutions, he wrote, do not carry themselves out; someone must make it so (Rohr, 1986). In the complexity of modern times, the effective carrying out of public responsibilities requires knowledge, expertise, and experience.

It has been more than a century since Wilson called for a public administration that is distinct from politics and based on a merit-appointed civil service. Much has been gained in that time. The administrative parts of public affairs in the United States as well as in all other "advanced" nations is huge. In the United States there are approximately 20 million people directly employed by governments at all levels, compared with about 100 million who are employed by private business (*Statistical Abstracts,* 1993). It is estimated that another 10 million persons are employed indirectly, by contract, with the government; these are the "shadow" bureaucrats. In addition, there are an estimated 16 million employed in the nonprofit sector (Schervish, Hodgkinson, and Gates, 1995), and we have no way of knowing how many people are volunteers in public affairs. It is safe to estimate that one of every six or seven Americans is engaged in some form of public service. As Dwight Waldo (1949) tells us, ours is an administrative state.

The efficiency and effectiveness of the organizations in which these Americans work is widely debated (Osborne and Gaebler, 1992). There is no debate, however, as to the giant range, scope, and influence of the organizations and individuals that constitute public administration. Woodrow Wilson would be impressed with the modern administrative state.

But much has been lost. The first casualty of the administrative state is the gradual loss of the concept of the public in public administration. Although in our time the phrase *public administration* is usually used to describe government administration, it was for good reason that Wilson and others called it *public* rather than *government* administration. Chapter One of *The Spirit of Public Administration* describes how public administration has been impoverished by substituting *government* for *public* to describe our field. We have been deprived of the richness and vitality of concepts of the public and what it means to take public responsibilities.

The public is a broad, pregovernmental concept (Mathews, 1994). It manifests itself in many ways—neighborhoods, voluntary associations, churches, clubs, events, and the like—and it divides to become many publics. Government is an important manifestation of the public, but it is just one aspect of the public (Bozeman, 1987). To understand public administration, it is essential to find the public again. This should begin with a broad conception of what the public is.

Unfortunately, much of the literature of public administration is based on a narrow (and essentially governmental) definition of the field. When linked to a governmental definition of public administration, the practices of government—voting, politics, budgets, personnel management, and service delivery—become the subject matter. When public administration is defined as all of the means by which the public functions, including government, the subject changes to patterns of human organization: the values of groups and organizations and how these values are expressed; how voluntary organizations, nonprofit organizations, businesses, and governments function; and how governmental, nongovernmental, and business organizations interact. We live in a world of shared power in which governmental, quasi-governmental, nonprofit, and private organizations engage in policymaking and policy implementation (Kettl, 1993a; Smith and Lipsky, 1993).

Narrow definitions of public administration tend to assume management values such as efficiency and economy. Broader conceptions of the public in public administration include these values but add the values of citizenship, fairness, equity, justice, ethics, responsiveness, and patriotism. While managerial values are important in public administration, the values associated with a broadened definition of the public are what ennoble the day-to-day practices of public work. The broad definition of the public in public administration given in Chapter One suggests changes significant in both the subject matter of the *study* of public administration and the values that inform and guide the *practices* of the field.

Modern public administration is a network of vertical and horizontal linkages between organizations *(publics)* of all types—governmental, nongovernmental, and quasi-governmental; profit, nonprofit, and voluntary. Citizens participate in these publics in many ways and at many points. It is for this reason that the core values, or spirit, of public administration include a knowledge of a commitment to the public in a general sense, as well as a responsiveness to both individual citizens and groups of citizens in the specific sense.

Several years ago, in a prescient observation, Herbert Kaufman (1985) constructed a cyclical explanation of the relationship between private interests and concerns on the one hand and public action on the other. He described a wide-swinging arc between concerns of efficiency, economy, and good management at one end and concerns for "responsiveness" (particularly politically defined responsiveness) at the other end. Certainly, the reform movement and the Progressive Era were a strong response to an earlier time of bossism, spoils, and corruption—especially in the affairs of American cities. During the reform movement the pendulum was swinging from responsiveness to efficiency.

But the reform movement is over. In the past twenty years we have seen the pendulum start to swing back in the direction of responsiveness. Most of the cities that adopted the council-manager form of government as part of the reform movement have modified it to include directly elected mayors, election of council members by district, full-time paid mayors and council members, and staff and other support systems for elected officials (Frederickson, 1995). Put another way, council-manager government these days is not completely preoccupied with efficiency and economy and is increasingly concerned with political responsiveness.

There has also been a dramatic increase in contracting out and privatization. In some ways this trend runs counter to Kaufman's argument for the cyclical nature of public administration. Much of the justification for privatizing governmental functions is to make them more efficient or businesslike. It is also argued that privatization, particularly when associated with special district governments or authorities, removes public functions from the vicissitudes of politics (Burns, 1994). In the movement toward contracting out and privatization, the rhetoric is driven by management and efficiency metaphors rather than responsiveness values.

A second version of the cyclical argument is a nuanced and sophisticated description of "shifting involvements" between private interests and public actions. Albert O. Hirschman (1982) defines *public* to include "public action, action in the public interest, [and] striving for the public happiness—these all refer to actions in the political realm, to involvement of the citizens in civic or community affairs" (p. 6). By contrast, writes Hirschman, *private* means "the pursuit of a better life for oneself and one's family, 'better' being understood primarily in terms of increased material welfare. This is, of course, today's commonsense meaning of the contrast between pursuing the public interest and attending to one's private interests" (p. 7). Hirschman then accounts for the cycles of movement from public to private and back. It is, he claims, the role of disappointment that accounts for people's changing preferences for public and/or private activities. He describes it this way:

Acts of consumption as well as acts of participation in public affairs, which are undertaken because they are expected to yield satisfaction, also yield disappointment and dissatisfaction. They do so for different reasons, in different ways, and to different degrees, but to the extent that the disappointment is not wholly eliminated by an instantaneous downward adjustment of expectations, any pattern of consumption or of time use carries within itself, to use the hallowed metaphor, "the seeds of its own destruction" [p. 10].

Disappointment, *pace* Hirschman, is a better explanation of shifting involvements between things private and public than the usual rational explanations given by economists and sociologists. Hirschman challenges the rational view this way:

Now this seems to me a mistaken view of the way men and women behave. The world I am trying to understand in this essay is one in which men think they want one thing and then upon getting it find out to their dismay that they don't want it nearly as much as they thought, or don't want it at all, and that something else of which they are hardly aware is what they really want [p. 21].

In public administration, people see the limitations of all forms of collective action. Indeed, we often ask governments to do "impossible jobs" (Hargrove and Glidewell, 1990). It is no surprise, then, that people become disappointed. All collective action, for either private or public purposes, will at some point fail or not be fully satisfactory. We will be disappointed and grope for "new" alternatives. If our disappointments lie with corporate or private interests (market failure), we will likely reach out for public solutions. If our disappointments are with public activities—particularly governmental activities—(nonmarket failure), we will reach for corporate, nonprofit, and voluntary solutions.

Both the Kaufman and Hirschman models mask a more fundamental fact. Our way of carrying out public responsibilities is now so completely mixed as to render a public-private dichotomy or an efficiency-responsiveness cycle less useful as an explanation. This is not to suggest that there are not cycles that approximate Kaufman's and Hirschman's descriptions; rather, it is to suggest that the context within which these cycles occur softens their effects and diminishes their explanatory power.

One thing is clear, however: the public-versus-private and efficiency-versus-responsiveness issues are played out in the political arena. Politics is understood to be the authoritative allocation of values. An understanding of politics is essential to an understanding of public administration and especially to the values that link them. Chapter Two of *The Spirit of Public Administration* is a treatment of politics from a public administration perspective—and particularly from the Dwight Waldo perspective (1949) that public administration is in fact a form of politics.

The New Governance

Harlan Cleveland (1972) pointed out twenty-five years ago that what the people want and need is not necessarily more government, but more *governance*—meaning the full range of governmental, quasi-governmental, parastatel, nonprofit, contracting, voluntary, and other organizations that participate in the conduct of public affairs. In Chapter Three of *The Spirit of Public Administration,* we take up Cleveland's contentions regarding governance.

In the so-called new governance model (sometimes connected to Steven Skowronek's description of the new American state, 1982), we do not assume that things are governmental or private; rather we assume, in fact, that public means that they are both. The most interesting description of the new governance model comes from Gerald Garvey's persuasive *Facing the Bureaucracy: Living and Dying in a Public Agency* (1993), in which Garvey sets out two competing theories of public administration: the old theory and the new theory.

The old theory is particularly associated with the building of the administrative state to include not just the national government, but state and large local governments as well. At the core of the old theory is specialization and hierarchy. The development of a merit-based civil service with classification systems was the formal means by which specialization has been brought to government. Personnel administration was the scientific means by which merit could be determined and the very best people selected to work for government. Theories of scientific management were applied to the day-to-day operations of government; in this way, a firewall was built between the daily practices of administration and the winds of politics. Budgeting systems, purchasing and auditing systems, and a range of other management specializations were brought to government. The council-manager plan, essentially a corporate model, was also brought to American local government and is now the statutory system of government used in approximately half of U.S. cities. The focus of the old theory was executive in nature and fixed on an administration that broadly served the president at the national level, governors at the state level, and mayors and city managers at the local level. Most of the major reforms in American public administration, from the Brownlow Report and the Hoover Commission recommendations to the "reinventing government" movement, sought to expand the powers of executives to control and direct the administrative arms of government and to reduce political meddling on the part of legislators.

The new theory describes the notion of governance. The first principle in the new theory is taken from the work of Herbert Simon and his seminal concept of bounded rationality (1947). Rational behavior, Simon contended, was seldom possible, and most public officials engage in satisficing, doing the best they can in the context of what is known and what is politically and bureaucratically possible. Through time, the concept of incrementalism has provided a nuanced version of Simon's satisficing (Lindblom, 1959, 1965; March and Olsen, 1995).

The second principle is that new theorists are heavily influenced by the logic of economics, especially the notion of transaction costs. New theorists argue that individuals in their natural state tend to be rational and self-interested and to prefer to function in a free market. All transactions in the marketplace have costs: simple transactions cost very little in time or energy, while complicated or large transactions require information, labor, and time. Rather than viewing an organization as a hierarchy of relationships between superiors and subordinates, new theorists favor seeing it as a pattern of relationships that are the equivalent of transactions between principals and agents who each act in their self-interest or in behalf of institutional interests. Needless to say, this view presents a particularly unflattering image of public officials and portrays public administration in a spirit of self-service and greed.

Any understanding of modern public affairs recognizes the existence of the formal government-employed bureaucracy. Equally important, however, is the *shadow bureaucracy*.

> Although private contractors are outside the classified service, they often become insiders in the conduct of the day-to-day work of the government. Contractors frequently spend most of their day in government buildings working as fully integrated participants in project teams. Their fellow members may include civil servants on the federal payroll and even contractors from competing consulting firms. Practically speaking, many members of the shadow bureaucracy function as full members of federal officialdom [Garvey, p. 37].

What Gerald Garvey describes as the relationship between the formal and shadow bureaucracy in the federal government also holds true for state and local governments (Milward and Provan, 1994; Milward, Provan, and Else, 1993). The important point here is that both directly employed public servants and shadow bureaucrats are on the public payroll. The former have job security, benefits, and a permanent continuing position in government; the latter work for nonprofit as well as profit-making organizations, most of which operate primarily on the basis of contracts with government. They could be described as public administration once removed.

Patterns of contracts and subcontracts—particularly in large-scale complex tasks such as those engaged in by NASA and the Department of Defense—occur in which there is a very long-standing connection between the same contractor (for example, Thiokol) and a governmental agency (for example, NASA). The same is increasingly true at the state and local level, especially in fields such as mental health (Milward and Provan, 1994). And now it is common for governmental agencies to contract out administrative work such as budget preparation, data processing, inventory management, and the like (Kettl, 1993a). In addition, a large group of individuals that Garvey describes as "day-trippers" work for profit-making and nonprofit organizations or universities to provide policy advice or engage in research on a short-term contractual basis for government. Often they are quite specialized and work for relatively technical parts of government.

The new theory—that is, the governance model—is very favorably inclined toward this contracting or outsourcing approach to the public's work because it provides for more flexibility than does a large-scale civil service approach, which tends to be hierarchical, permanent, and continuous. The governance model also presumably reduces or holds the potential for reducing transaction costs. But the advocates of contracting and outsourcing seldom ask if contractors are as committed and public-spirited as are public employees. And they seldom ask whether contract management can ensure generally positive results for citizens. Even when government is a smart contractor (Kettl, 1993a), there can be no guarantee that private firms holding government contracts will not act primarily on the basis of the profit motive.

In Chapter Three of *The Spirit of Public Administration,* we set out an elaborate treatment of these newer approaches to public administration. We label this new set of theories "public administration as governance."

Social Equity

In Part Two of *The Spirit of Public Administration,* we address the fundamental purposes of public administration.

In the traditions of American public administration, efficiency and economy are the primary rationales for our work. Beginning in the late 1960s, the concept of social equity was added to our stated objectives or purposes. This emphasis on fair and equal service to citizens (or customers) significantly enhanced the spirit of the field.

The emphasis on social equity has been an effective instrument for conveying to both policymakers and policy implementors that issues of fair distribution of costs and benefits are often as important as those of efficiency and economy (Lineberry, 1977; Mladenka, 1981). One could, for example, argue that the health care issues of the mid-1990s, led particularly by President Bill Clinton, are primarily issues of fairness or equity. The United States has first-class health care, but the health care system is extremely uneven and unfair in the allocation of both costs and benefits among Americans.

Chapters Four through Six explore the perspective of social equity in the field. We first consider the challenging issue of administrative discretion, because if it does not exist, much of the social equity argument is rendered moot. We conclude that broad grants of administrative discretion are both theoretically correct and empirically accurate. We then turn to fixing the place of social equity in the literature and theory of public administration. Following that, we treat both contemporary and intergenerational applications of the theory of social equity. Finally, we reconnect social equity theory to earlier subjects in *The Spirit of Public Administration*—the public and citizenship.

Citizenship

When the public in public administration is found, it is often in the role of citizens. In the American experience with government, particularly at the state and local level, there has always been a unique connection between the citizens and those who engage in public work (Tocqueville, [1835] 1985). In a simpler time, citizens functioned through town meetings, raised a militia for defense, engaged in Midwestern barn raisings and other examples of direct collective action. Nearly 175 years ago Alexis de Tocqueville described Americans as an organizing, congregating people who tended to put together local groups to deal with collective problems. These groups were public but not governmental; the citizens acted together but were reluctant to cede to formally established governmental responsibility for services. In this setting, Americans were an energetic, active citizenry operating through a mix of governmental, nongovernmental, and quasi-governmental organizations, all of them closely held.

In 1835, Tocqueville described America this way:

> Americans of all ages, all conditions, and all dispositions, constantly form associations. They have not only commercial and manufacturing companies, in which all take part, but associations of a thousand other kinds religious, moral, serious, futile, general or restricted, enormous or diminutive. The Americans make associations to give entertainments, to found seminaries, to build inns, to construct churches, to diffuse books, to send missionaries to the antipodes; they found in this manner hospitals, prisons, and schools. If it be proposed to inculcate some truth, or to foster some feeling by the encouragement of a great example, they form a society. Wherever, at the head of a new undertaking, you see the government in France, or a man of rank in England, in the United States you will be sure to find an association [(1835) 1985, p. 198].

As the United States became more urban, specialized, and industrial, the characteristics of citizenship changed. From direct involvement through nongovernmental and quasi-governmental groups and organizations, citizens moved to politics, including voting, political party activity, and governmental job seeking. Citizenship as direct involvement in collective public activity gradually evolved to become citizenship as the connection between individuals and units of government—cities, counties, school districts, states, and the national government. This increasingly occurred through the mediation of political parties rather than through citizen-based nongovernmental organizations. Government was growing—particularly at the state and local levels. Patronage, spoils, corruption, and local bossism flourished. Traditional American forms of public expression and citizenship diminished and were replaced by governments, governmental jobs, political parties, and politics.

By the end of the nineteenth century, Americans reacted to politics, corruption, and spoils with the reform movement and the Progressive Era. This was the seedbed of modern American public administration and provided an energizing spirit for the field. This era of public administration brought specialization, professionalism, merit-based appointment and promotion, and the application of management sciences to government. It also established a public administration that was insulated from politics and political parties. The public and the citizens strongly supported the reform movement; indeed, in the earliest versions of its study, the academic field of public administration was presented as "citizenship and public administration."

As government professionalized, becoming more efficient and effective and less corrupt, public administration was challenged to understand and articulate the relationship between a professional public service and the citizens—the public. Citizens continued to organize in that unique American way, but they did so less and less to solve problems or provide services and increasingly to form interest groups to influence government. By the 1950s, the best way of describing relations between governments and citizens was *pluralism*—the tendency of citizens to organize interest groups to influence government. The traditions of citizenship as energized and self-directing publics had essentially been lost. Studies of citizenship increasingly focused on voting, participating in interest groups, and receiving governmental services.

Beginning in the 1970s, there has been a gradual reconstruction of the concepts of citizenship connected to both the theory and practice of public administration. In *The Spirit of Public Administration*, we set out those concepts, arguing that the linkages between professional public servants—teachers, police, regulators, and so on—and the citizens they serve constitute an entirely authentic and legitimate form of citizenship. This is the modern-day equivalent of the observations that Tocqueville made in 1835. In this modern public administration we find professional, expert public servants with sophisticated concepts of the public and of citizenship interacting routinely and productively with individuals as citizens, or organized as groups of citizens formed in private for-profit, nonprofit, voluntary, quasi-governmental, and governmental organizations. Citizens are increasingly participating directly in governance through this pattern of interaction. We find it in "neighborhood watch" groups and community policing, in parent-teacher schooling, in policy issue forums, in focus groups, and in many other forms. This citizenship is more than just governmental—it is public. As a form of citizenship, it is as fully authentic and legitimate as voting or campaigning for office.

Ethics

The Spirit of Public Administration closes with three chapters dealing with ethics. One could argue that the entire book is about an ethical perspective in public administration. Certainly the definitions of the public in public administration and the connection between citizenship and public administration in the early chapters of the book set the stage for a social equity ethic. Indeed, Terry Cooper (1991) makes the direct link between ethics, citizenship, and the theory and practice of public administration.

In Chapters Seven through Eleven, we examine ethical perspectives in terms of ethical models as well as the link between knowledge (particularly research-based knowledge) and ethics. Chapter Nine offers a short synthesis of ethics and an application of ethical concepts to the treatment of Jews in Europe in World War II. This discussion links *The Spirit of Public Administration* to an ethic of patriotism and benevolence. Without such a noble ethic, the spirit of public administration is diminished.

Public administration is a big subject involving many academic disciplines, many theories and philosophies, and the whole range of policy issues. *The Spirit of Public Administration* takes a big approach to the field. Public administration is grounded in values and beliefs, and the notion of spirit is well suited to describing those values and beliefs. In public administration, management—*how* we do things—is important, but much more important is *what* we do and *why* we do it. The purpose of this book is to set out the values and beliefs of contemporary public administration and to suggest that our commitment to these values and beliefs explains what public administrators should do and why we practice in the field.

Part One

Governance, Politics, and the Public

Chapter One

Finding the Public in Public Administration

*Government is an instrument of the public for acting
collectively. The government is the property of the public.
Public and government are quite different in that political
relations in the public are lateral (people to people),
whereas in the government they are usually vertical
(from authorities to subordinates).*
DAVID MATHEWS, *POLITICS FOR PEOPLE*, P. 202

Public administration is both a profession and a field of study. We
assume that the term *public administration* is descriptive of the concepts and theories that make up our field of practice and the decisions and actions that constitute our craft. Should we not,
therefore, also assume that *both* words in the term public administration be fully defined and generally understood? The word *administration* is the subject of extended study, analysis, and discourse.
Theories of administration abound, and approaches to improving
it are everywhere.

The word *public* is, however, another matter. There are few developed definitions of the public, nor are there many descriptions
of how the public should connect with our field and our work.
Some surrogates for the word public are in common usage and are
the subject of some study and theorizing, such as *citizenship, the public interest, the common good,* and *the common will.* Our primary approach to understanding the public is to conveniently assume that
government and *the public* are similar concepts, yet we know that not
only are they different things—they are in fact starkly different.

Government, of course, is the platform upon which political science rests and about which we have fully developed theories and extensive experiences and practice.

In public administration, we ordinarily use government as the surrogate for public, yet we continue to use the phrase public administration as the primary descriptor of thought and practice in our field, rather than the phrases *government administration* or *government management.* But we have virtually no elaboration of the word public in public administration.

If we persist in using the term public administration, and if we believe it to be a fair descriptor of both thought and practice, would it not be important to more fully describe and define the public and begin to develop perspectives or concepts of the public in public administration?

This chapter explores the meaning of public in public administration.

The Meaning of Public

The classic meaning of public derives from two sources. The first is the Greek word *pubes,* or "maturity," which in the Greek sense means both physical and emotional or intellectual maturity and emphasizes moving from selfish concerns or personal self-interest to seeing beyond one's self to understand the interest of others. It implies an ability to understand the consequences of one's individual actions on other people. The derivative *public* means moving to an adult state, understanding the relationship between oneself and other individuals, and being able to see the connections (Palmer, 1981, p. 18; Mathews, 1994).

The second root of public is the Greek word *koinon,* from which the English word *common* is derived. *Koinon,* in turn, derives from another Greek word, *kom-ois,* meaning *to care with.* The terms common and to care with both imply the importance of relationships.

The concepts of maturity and seeing beyond oneself seem to indicate that the word public can be both a *thing,* as in the case of a public decision, and a *capacity,* as in the ability to function publicly, to relate to others, and to understand the connection between one's actions and the effects of those actions on others (Mathews, 1984). Adding the terms common and to care with to maturity makes an even stronger case that public means not only working with others but also looking out for others.

David Mathews (1984) reminds us that "the Greeks had two words for private. One word described an individual who was able to understand only his or her own perspective. The Greek word for that kind of private person has become our word 'idiot.' The other term for 'private,' though, is not at all negative, but quite the contrary. The second word derives from the Greek 'oikos,' for family or household. There is nothing wrong in attending to one's own household, nor does it preclude attending to public matters" (pp. 122–123).

It appears that the origin of the English word *private* likely means to be deprived of a public life. As Parker Palmer (1981) pointedly reminds us, "The private status that we so value in our day, the life on which we lavish such energy and attention, was once regarded as a state of deprivation" (p. 18).

The Greeks conceived of the public as a political community—the *polis*—in which all citizens (that is, adult males and nonslaves) participated. The political community was to establish prevailing standards and practices and to support, promulgate, and enforce those standards. The standards were for the greater good. Loyalty from the citizen to the city-state was significant, as was the city-state's responsibility to protect and "care with" the citizen.

The modern English usage of the word public has both retained and lost some of its original meaning. We refer to *the public* to mean all the people in a society, without distinguishing between them. A public school, for example, is open to all and is thought of as a place where the common knowledge of the people is passed along. The public press is available to everyone, too, as is the public library. The English pub (short for public house) has always been a gathering place for the whole community. And we use the term public figure to describe a person whose responsibilities, and therefore life, are visible to all.

But much of the original meaning of public has been lost. Public has come to be synonymous with *politics* or *government*. We study and practice politics and government but seem unable, as Mathews (1984) puts it, to deal with the concept of the public "as an independent idea" (pp. 122–123). The word public is often regarded as so vague or ambiguous as to be useless. Public implies to some a challenge to individualism, to others opposition to private business, and to still others an inclination to collectivism. It gets even worse, because to many people the word public means the trivial, the ordinary, the vulgar, and the masses (Mathews, 1984, pp. 122–123). And when public is tied to other phrases, such as *the public good* or *the public interest,* it is often seen as so idealistic or romantic as to be impractical or useless.

What happened? The philosophy of the utilitarians has replaced the Greek perspective on the public and has dominated political thinking and governmental practice for 150 years. Collective attempts to find and govern toward a greater good were replaced by individual calculations of pleasure or pain, personal utility, or costs and benefits. The purposes of government have been reduced to private well-being. We are to determine well-being, pleasure, or utility by consequences or results—preferably by bureaucratic, technological, or scientific means. There is no public, only the sum of atomistic individuals. And there is no public interest, except in summing up the aggregate of private interests (Leys, 1952, pp. 13–32).

Utilitarian philosophy has been compatible with the development of the market model in economics—to judge consequences or results by the technology of the market. The public choice perspective brought utilitarian logic and the technology of the market to public administration (Downs, 1967; Ostrom, 1973; Niskanen, 1971). The faith in science and technology to answer questions and solve problems is wholly compatible with utilitarian philosophy and with much of the early theory of public administration. Positivism in law, which argues that law is the command of the sovereign rather than a codification of the public will or the greater good, is utilitarian. Finally, attempts to apply "decision theoretic" analysis to achieve efficiency and economy to public agencies are utilitarian (March and Simon, 1958).

While utilitarian philosophy has contributed to significant improvement in public administration because of its emphasis on efficiency, economy, bureaucracy, and technology, it also contributed to the loss of an ennobling concept of the public. Certainly, the present usage of public has moved away from the classic meanings of the word; however, both the classic and contemporary meanings are filled with implications for the theory and practice of public administration.

Contrasting Philosophical Perspectives on the Public

Although there has never been a focus on the definition or meaning of the word public in public administration, in twentieth-century philosophy the concept of the public has received extensive treatment. Those who have studied the public in this century have generally agreed, as John Dewey (1954) puts it, that "the public seems to be lost; it is certainly bewildered. The government, officials and their activities, are plainly with us. Legislatures make laws with luxurious abandon; subordinate officials engage in a losing struggle to enforce some of them; judges on the bench deal as best they can with the steady mounting pile of disputes before them. But where is the public which these officials are supposed to represent?" (pp. 116–117).

Often in philosophical discussion, the issue turns on the distinction between those things that are private and those that are public. The most common difference, of course, is human action that affects only one person as opposed to many, or the distinction between self-regarding and other-regarding action. According to John Dewey (1954), when the action of some people affects the welfare of others, then the act "acquires a public capacity" (p. 13). To Dewey, the public is not fixed but is created and re-created, depending on actions and interactions between people. The public is lost because people seemed unable or unwilling to organize themselves into a political community for the general protection of common interests. The public is lost because it cannot *act* as a public.

Walter Lippmann (1955), however, indicates that the public is lost because there is an absence of a public *philosophy*. To him, the assertion of individual rights has resulted in a loss of a sense of public responsibility for the effects of individual decisions. In the absence of a public philosophy, according to Lippmann, the consequences of most human actions are strictly private, without anyone taking responsibility for public acts.

Richard Sennett, in *The Fall of Public Man* (1977), agrees with both of the earlier views, and he states boldly that no recognizable public realm remains. Preoccupation with our private selves causes us to understand everything that occurs outside of the self as a reflection of that self rather than distinct from it. Therefore, all actions are defined in terms of effects on each individual. In such a perspective, according to Sennett, there can be no public as distinct from the aggregation of individuals. Under such circumstances, how can an individual or an aggregate of individuals share responsibility for collective action?

It is puzzling that the word public has come to have such a narrow meaning in our time. We think of public as pertaining to government and voting and the conduct of elected officials. We do, of course, associate it with those policies made by a representative government that are binding on all. Parker Palmer (1981) asks, "Why has this word—which should evoke a common bond in a diverse people—taken on such a narrow political meaning? I suspect the answer lies in an assumption which pervades the political thought of our society, the assumption that only through the processes of government can a public be created, and only through legislative enactment can the many become one" (p. 47).

Political theory, having been heavily influenced by utilitarian philosophy, seems primarily concerned with self-interest. That being the case, the public emerges primarily as a means to umpire and control the diversity of self-interest. According to Palmer (1981), "The task of government is to provide a framework of rules and penalties within which a community can be constructed out of the convergence of self-interest, with those interests which do not fit being deflected or simply denied. In this stream of political theory, the public has been reduced to an arena in which individuals compete for the most they can get, with the government as the referee" (p. 47). Palmer argues that this image of the public holds no promise for an authentic public life. It provides no vision or unity and does not lead toward community.

The agreement that there is a loss of the public seems not to be associated with either liberalism or conservatism. Indeed, both liberal and conservative philosophers seem to agree on this point, perhaps for the wrong reasons. The liberal philosopher William Sullivan, in his treatise *Reconstructing Public Philosophy* (1982), suggests that the modern premises of liberalism coming to us from Hobbes, Locke, Adam Smith, and John Stewart Mill

> foster excessive individualism, anti-public spirit, competition among warring self-interest groups: they militate against a sense of the common good. . . . Conceiving human beings as exclusively

self-regarding, liberal philosophies use human association as a kind of necessary evil, and politics as an arena in which the clashes of individual and group interests can be more or less civilly accommodated. As a philosophy of government and social life, liberalism exalts both the supremacy of private self-interest and the development of institutional means for pursuing those interests. In its extreme form, this philosophy denies meaning and value to even the notion of common purpose, or politics in its classic sense [p. 14].

The well-known conservative George Will (1983) has a similar critique. He suggests that politics has been reduced from a concern for civic virtue to an emphasis on power and order. He is especially concerned with the social contract, because it locates "the origins of government in an agreement between the rational, self-interested but pre-civic persons. They are motivated to associate neither by neighborliness (affection) nor political allegiance (shared political philosophy), but only by anxiety about their physical safety and the security of their property" (p. 109).

These views are strong but not altogether correct. The so-called liberal origins of the concept of public, while fostering self-interest and individualism, also have resulted in significant social gains in justice and freedom (Murchland, 1984, p. 15). Justice now calls for civil rights for many groups according to their sex, age, race, ethnicity, sexual orientation, able-bodiedness, and so forth. Procedural due process for those with such rights is broadly applied in the pursuit of those rights (Glendon, 1991). This emphasis on justice as rights has had many positive results, particularly in areas such as voting rights. Freedoms are also deeply established as a part of our constitutional and legal systems. The communitarian argument is that we have made much more progress in establishing individual justice and freedom than we have made in collective systems of determining and implementing the general or common good (Etzioni, 1991). In other words, our individual capacities to achieve our rights have been greater than our collective capacities to achieve public purposes.

David Mathews (1984) suggests that when we distinguish between the public as practice and the public as an idea, we find that the unavailability of the former is due to the unavailability of the latter (pp. 122–123). Because we are unable to practice or exercise the concept of public as action or capacity, we therefore find it impossible to develop a very compelling idea of the public—let alone a theory.

Modern political scientists, particularly the so-called behavioralists or logical positivists, have studied the public interest. From their perspective, the public manifests itself through groups and other complex aggregations. Whichever way the public acts or behaves is assumed to be the public interest. If there is a popular will, it is the sum of the interaction of the interest groups legitimized through governmental and political processes (Schubert, 1960).

Another version of the same theme is found in the contemporary "civic capital" literature. Daniel Kemmis (1990), Robert Putnam, Robert Leonardi, and Raffaella Nanetti (1993), Francis Fukuyama (1995), David Mathews (1994), Ben Barber (1986), and others argue that the decline in public trust, in public discourse, and in agreed-upon collective action constitutes a generally diminished civic capital. The need to reinvest in civic capital is understood by these intellectual and opinion leaders to mean an increased emphasis on citizenship and civics courses in schools; an engaged citizenry, particularly at the local level, that is involved in policy deliberation; and a general retaking of political responsibility by individuals and groups.

The civic capital argument is long on diagnosis and short on prescription, in part because it is easier to see problems than to effect solutions. One solution is the "less government" model that emphasizes governance—the subject of Chapter Four. Another solution is to deemphasize the federal government and national solutions and move toward local and state action (Kemmis, 1990; Mathews, 1994). And yet another solution is to rebuild the political culture through a reformed "public" journalism, through civic education, and through policy forums and focus groups (Mathews, 1994).

Despite the negative views of philosophers, empiricists, and opinion leaders, the fact that the United States is a functioning society certainly means that a public spirit is at work. Many forms of public life exist to channel individual and collective energies to a common or public set of purposes. To be sure, self-interest, individualism, greed, and consumerism flourish everywhere, but the polity does function. The question for those who study and practice public administration, is how to focus on public administration rather than just government administration.

Framing the Public in Public Administration

Ordinarily, public administrators are thought of as government employees. It should be no surprise, then, that our theory and practice revolves around the functioning of the city, the county, the state, and the nation. Should we assume that these entities or jurisdictions will set the intellectual agenda for public administration? Is there a role for public administration beyond or in addition to the functioning of particular governments? What are our responsibilities to the general public that we ultimately serve?

The characteristics of modern society militate against the effectiveness of modern public administration. Orion White (1981) reminds us that there has been a sharp decline in the ability of public agencies or of the public at large to act authoritatively. He suggests that "it is the American bias against authority that has led us to accept a reified image of the human being as merely a satisfaction-seeking organism. We now virtually have what we say we have wanted: a society without authority, where each of us is marching to his own drummer, held together as a society mostly by our technical infrastructure" (p. 216).

No wonder, then, that it is not easy to run a government these days. White suggests a solution: to transcend the traditional concept of citizenship that allows us to talk mostly about what we need so that we may feel good—and find a format for communicating about our mutual realization and development. Such a point of orientation will allow us to be more open to the establishment of authoritative social institutions, according to White. When the use of authority is seen as being aimed toward people's positive maturation and development rather than as a way to referee the competition for the resources required for the gratification of needs, it is considered more acceptable (p. 218).

It is not just the culture that militates against the development of a fuller conception of the public; public administration itself is part of the problem. One of the dominant themes in contemporary public administration theory is the so-called public choice perspective derived primarily from utilitarian logic. Public choice theorists and practitioners favor the lowest common denominator of governmental agencies and the design of governmental agencies for the purpose of setting the rules by which people compete for costs and benefits. Such a perspective holds the marvelous convenience of calculation and is a haven for the methodologist. The analyst with a personal computer and the right software and data can calculate the best possible distribution of resources. This reduces the role of public administration to decision making—a calculation of the distribution of individual costs and benefits following minimal levels of political acceptance. Such a public administration is bereft of a purpose beyond the ordinary day-to-day application of our job descriptions (which, incidentally, we do very well!).

Another common theme in modern public administration is the difference between it and so-called private administration. The drastic narrowing of both the idea and practice of public administration has resulted in a concomitant growth of what is currently defined as private and/or business administration. How things have changed. Originally, of course, the corporation was a public enterprise chartered by a governmental agency to engage in commerce, but for the common good. As Robert Bellah and colleagues (1985) remind us:

> Reasserting the idea that incorporation is a concession of public
> authority to a private group *in return* for service to the public good,
> with effective public accountability would change what is now
> called the "social responsibility of the corporation" from its present
> status, where it is often a kind of public relations whipped cream
> decorating the corporate pudding, to a constructive social element
> in the corporation itself. This, in turn, would involve a fundamental
> alteration in the role and training of the manager. Management
> would become a profession in the older sense of the word, involving not merely standards of technical competence, but standards of
> public obligation that could at moments of conflict override obligations to the corporate employer [p. 290].

Following this concept of corporate responsibility, one could plausibly argue that both government employees *and* corporate employees are public administrators (Bozeman, 1987). On the one hand, public employees are directly engaged in managing governmental functions such as police and fire protection or the conduct of national defense—the so-called indivisible public goods. On the other hand, corporate employees engage in providing goods or services for sale to the public. To what extent, then, can the public assert that it has as much say about the manner in which goods and services are prepared and presented for sale to the public as it has in the organization and delivery of governmental services?

There can be little doubt that the old and simple distinctions between public and private no longer pertain. For example, the Department of Defense and the National Aeronautics and Space Administration (NASA) contract with major defense and aerospace contractors. Which is more directly related to the public service: the contracting officer at NASA or the individuals responsible for delivering safe, reliable, and fairly priced defense and space equipment? Are they not both responsible to and for the public?

We have so narrowed the definition of public and the public interest as to leave the public with what appears to be great individual freedom and a laissez-faire business environment. And we have broadened the definition of private so greatly as to leave people without an effective and authoritative way to express their common interests above and beyond, say, buying a Ford instead of a Chevrolet (or voting for either a Dole or a Clinton). Narrowing the definition of public has resulted in approaches to teaching business administration that are under heavy criticism for being shortsighted, noncompetitive, and preoccupied with the appearance of progress through merger rather than with real growth and development.

The critique of public administration thought and practice is probably not much better. We pursue efficiency, economy, order, and predictability. Like good utilitarians, we tend toward a high regard for moral ambiguity. We stress operating efficiency and procedural due process, protecting the boundaries and longevity of each bureau and agency, and reducing all big issues to questions of means and short-run benefits. We avoid policy discussions that tend to focus on purposeful long-range ends. Louis Gawthrop (1984b) refers to this as an "ethic of civility" in which we function under the rule of law, based on written codes and standards, rather than of people. We seek to do good by not doing evil. Because we cannot define what is good, it is simply easier to find what is wrong and try to fix it. We assume that through the detailed specification of what is wrong, public officials can be counted on to do what is right. Gawthrop argues that this results in a static, dry, and barren desert of mediocrity and unresponsiveness. Civility, he suggests, will be failed reform (pp. 138–145).

Gawthrop suggests a creative ethic, drawn from Dewey's philosophy, designed for a dynamic rather than a static world. Because the world is dynamic in this view, sociopolitical reality cannot be found in objectivity; it can be found only in relating. "The objective situation must always be replaced by the evolving situation, which depends extensively on the cumulative development of progressive experience" (Gawthrop, 1984b, p. 146). Reality, according to Gawthrop, "is in the relating, in the activity between the subject and the object in any behavioral interaction. Yet reality emerges from the endless evolving of these relatings, and indeed relating emergent component situations, which also might be called the evolving situation" (p. 146).

What Gawthrop is describing is the public both as an idea and as a capacity. The capacity here is the structured pattern of interaction between public administrators, interest groups, elected officials, and citizens to find the evolving and changing public will. In this pattern, there is no escape from responsibility nor is there a collective responsibility. Only individual responsibility will do. We cannot be absolved because we work for government, and we should not be absolved because we work for corporations. All of us are, to some degree, public officials.

With this concept of public administration, we include not only our obligations as public employees to carry out the laws efficiently and effectively, but also our responsibility to constantly exercise an ethic of concern for our neighbors and fellow citizens.

Having reviewed several philosophical, empirical, and conceptual perspectives on the public in public administration, we turn now to five formal models of the public taken primarily from the social sciences. We will use these primary models to make a simple evaluation and comparison. At a minimum, this should help to describe the shifting ground on which public administration stands. Following discussion of the primary social science perspectives on the public in public administration, we will attempt to outline a general theory of the public for public administration.

The five perspectives are

1. The public as interest groups (the pluralist perspective)
2. The public as rational chooser (the public choice perspective)
3. The public as represented (the legislative perspective)
4. The public as customer (the service-providing perspective)
5. The public as citizen

The Public as Interest Groups: The Pluralist Perspective

The pluralist perspective on the public is well developed in American political science. Pluralism describes the natural development of interest groups—of bringing together individuals with similar concerns. Interest groups interact and compete in the governmental setting, seeking the advantages and preferences of the individuals they constitute. Interest groups certainly further the right of the citizen to organize to advance their interests in the governmental marketplace. In the mid-1950s, two distinguished political scientists, David B. Truman (1957) and Robert Dahl (1956), detailed the interest group perspective on democratic government, and pluralism became the commanding perspective on the public for the following two decades.

The pluralist perspective was particularly useful because it enabled analysts to define and describe particular interest groups, their strategies, their use of power, and their effectiveness. Political scientists could both define the natural processes of group interaction and assert that these processes constitute democratic practices. Pluralism also had the advantage of supporting notions of individualism, private ownership, and capitalism. The public is certainly manifest in the processes of group interaction. It can also be argued that the net result of group interaction constitutes a definition of the "public interest" (Flathman, 1966; Schubert, 1960).

There is considerable evidence that pluralism has adherents in the practice of public administration. Specialization is a key tenet of public administration, and governmental agencies are designed around specialties. Effective interest groups will find allies in particular specialized governmental agencies. Thus, it should be no surprise that road-building companies and suppliers of asphalt, sand, and gravel all come together in their interests and are able to work closely with state highway departments. Similarly, modern computer hardware and software companies have close associations with federal, state, and local agencies that handle large amounts of data. Compatible interest groups and governmental agencies often find friendly committees in the legislature and form so-called iron triangles. In the traditions of American public administration, this form of pluralism has been widely practiced with considerable effectiveness.

Some critics believe that many of our current governmental problems can be traced to pluralism. Burns (1963) argues that the elaborate system of checks and balances has resulted in "inter-locked gears of government that requires consensus of many groups and leaders before the nation can act; and it is the system that exacts the heavy price of delay and devitalization" (p. 6). Lowi (1969) believes that our fragmented society stems from our spe-cial-interest state and endangers our entire governmental system. Lowi also suggests that individuals are not truly represented by a system limited to special-interest groups.

The political scientist Benjamin Barber (1986) is perhaps the most critical. According to Barber, pluralist democracy is deficient because it relies on "the fictions of the free market and a putative freedom and equality of bargaining agents; because it cannot gen-erate public thinking or public ends of any kind; because it is in-nocent about the real world of power . . . because it uses the representative principle [and because of] the illusions of the free market and of the invisible hand and of simplistic utilitarianism . . . by which the pursuit of private interest is miraculously made to yield the public good" (p. 144).

In addition to these criticisms is the claim that interest group theory is fundamentally inimical to the efficiencies and economies that are associated with effective public administration. Yates (1982) sets out the contrasting values of pluralist democracy on one hand and administrative efficiency on the other. In his view, pluralists favor dispersed and divided power, while administrators do not. While Yates's observation about pluralists is accurate, many administrators, due to their interest in specialization and exper-tise, tend also to favor dispersed power. According to Yates, plu-ralists favor decentralization while administrative efficiency calls for centralization. This characterization of the public administra-tor is incorrect because decentralization is a dominant theme in both the theory and the practice of public administration.

Yates also claims that pluralists tend to be suspicious of execu-tive power or any concentration of power. Power, to pluralists, should be in the hands of citizens, interest groups, and politicians. Administrators, by contrast, tend to favor centralized power with elected executives or civil servants. It is correct that public admin-istrators feel the need for sufficient power to carry out public policy, but the differences in pluralist and administrative perspectives are not as great as Yates contends.

Finally, pluralists favor political bargaining and accommodation, while administrators favor keeping politics out of administration. Because the politics-administration dichotomy was dismissed decades ago, Yates's view of public administration no longer holds true.

Important differences exist between the strict notion and practice of interest group pluralism and public administration conceptions of the public. These differences do not, however, focus on arguments of centralization versus decentralization, on power concentration or dispersal, or on political bargaining as opposed to administrative expertise. Yates himself reconciles these perspectives. The significant differences have to do with contrasting views of the potential for a general public interest being greater than the sum of individual private interests. Modern public administration theorists tend to assume a generalized public interest, and practitioners are inclined to pursue that interest.

Is pluralism or interest group theory an adequate representation of the public? The answer is no. In addition to the foregoing criticisms, it is increasingly clear that the preferences, attitudes, and needs of many citizens are not adequately expressed through interest groups. This is especially true of the economically and socially deprived, whose preferences are seldom expressed effectively. Conversely, the well-established and economically favored have an exaggerated ability to appear to represent the public's interests.

Evidence is mounting that as a general rule, an issue that is not economically or politically beneficial to a particular group has difficulty making itself heard. There are some exceptions. We see, for example, the significant concern in the American public about drunk driving and the resultant organization of interest groups pursuing the matter (Gusfield, 1986). Although it has neither a natural administrative constituency nor an obvious political home, drunk driving does appear to be an enduring public concern. Many generalized public concerns, such as poverty, are not well represented through the interest group process. Although the drunk-driving example lends credence to the pluralist perspective, many equally serious social problems do not stimulate an effective interest group dedicated to their solution.

The Public as Rational Chooser: The Public Choice Perspective

The pluralist perspective on the public has a very close cousin in the public choice perspective. Individualism is what ties pluralism and the public choice perspective together. Bentham ([1789] 1948) says it best: "The community is a fictitious body, composed of the individual persons who are considered, as it were, its members. The interest in the community then is what?—the sum of the interests of the individual members who compose it" (p. 3). This view, commonly known as the utilitarian perspective, pursues individual interest, pleasure, and happiness without particular concern for community values and notions such as ethics, a "greater good," or the possibility of a public interest. Altruism, according to the utilitarian perspective, while desirable, is not often found. Therefore, the dominant perspective must be individualistic.

The self-interest assumption provides a view of the public as if it were a consumer functioning in the marketplace. In short, this assumption applies market economics to the public sector.

The primary methodological assumption of economists is that public action must be understood as the action of motivated individuals whose interests typically differ. Each individual is a rational calculator pursuing his or her own interests. Government and social order simply provide a stable environment in which free individual choice may be exercised. Each individual's efficiency is the equation by which utility is calculated. Buchanan and Tullock (1962) apply the economics of the market model and the individualistic postulate to the functioning of the American political system. Their primary concern is how to organize a democratic government to provide for the pursuit of self-interest as a fundamental requisite.

This approach was followed by Downs (1967), who brought market economics to bureaucracy and public administration. Downs applies economic theory to the bureau as if it were an individual engaging in the rational calculation of personal preferences. Similarly, the bureau has "bureau ideologies." In Downs's theory, the governmental agency

1. Emphasizes the positive benefits of the bureau's activities and deemphasizes the costs.

2. Indicates that further expansion of the bureau's services would be desirable and any curtailment thereof would be undesirable.
3. Emphasizes the benefits that the bureau provides for the society as a whole rather than its service to a particular "special interest."
4. Stresses the current high level of the bureau's efficiency.
5. Emphasizes its achievement and capabilities and ignores or minimizes its failures and inabilities.

Bureau ideologies become part of the bureaucracy's culture because, as Downs (1967) puts it, "all officials exhibit relatively strong loyalty to the organization controlling their job security and promotion" (p. 276); therefore, administrative specialization and bureaucratic socialization color the perspectives of the public servant. As a consequence, teachers, police officers, military personnel, and social workers all regard their functions as most crucial to the future welfare of society. The tendency, then, is for these individuals to see themselves more as, say, educators or police officers and less as public servants or public officials.

Downs's perspective was followed by Ostrom's *The Intellectual Crisis in American Public Administration* (1973), which applies a mixture of political philosophy and the public choice perspective to public administration. Ostrom claims that public administration got off on the wrong foot by blindly accepting Woodrow Wilson's arguments about the separation of politics and administration and by accepting the Weberian model of centralized bureaucracy. Ostrom advocates a public choice version of public administration that emphasizes decentralized small jurisdictions that function like "commons" in which rational individuals pursue their political interests.

The problems with this perspective are many. While a number of scholars have increasingly come to view the public process as a group struggle, this concept is not wholly accurate as a description because it does not present the whole picture; it leaves out, for example, the large number of individual officeholders, interest groups, and civil servants seeking to maximize what they regard as the public interest. As Fleishman (1981) points out, "Even worse than their incompleteness, however, is the extent to which these models appear to have crossed the boundary from partial description to implied, even if unintended, prescription. They tend to imply that because some interests expressly use politics to maximize their respective interests, all groups and individuals should do likewise. Indeed, to the extent that they don't do so, their behavior is irrational and cannot be comprehended by the model" (pp. 56–57).

A second weakness in the public choice perspective is the profound cynicism it engenders about the intentions of public officials. As Downs (1967) puts it, public officials "act solely in order to attain the income, prestige and power which come from being in office, thus politicians in our model never seek offices as means of carrying out policies; their only goal is to reap the rewards of holding office per se. They treat policies purely as a means to the attainment of their private ends, which they can reach only by being elected" (p. 28).

We see in this argument the justification for the uninhibited pursuit of self-interest. This portrait of the public and of the political process is not appealing. It sanctions a range of motives and practices that history—as well as most of the present-day public—regards as debased, if not unethical. As Fleishman (1981) writes, "If deliberate sacrifice of self-interest for the good of the whole constitutes the most admirable and most ethical kind of politics, the greedy, blind, ambitious politician is the antithesis of our image of the statesman of integrity" (p. 57).

Both the pluralist and public choice perspectives on the public, whether simply description or normative theory, may be an important cause of unethical behavior by public officials. By glorifying and legitimizing the motive of self-interest, these perspectives encourage self-interested behavior—from the individual citizen to the appointed public administrator to the candidate running for office. As Fleishman points out, "Self-interest does not exactly require encouragement for it to express itself" (p. 57).

Like the pluralist view, the public choice perspective tends to hold little regard for the less privileged in society. One can function in the marketplace if one has the resources to buy and sell. Without these resources, the marketplace is left to the more privileged. Indeed, some applications of the public choice perspective are avowedly elitist: If one has the resources, one can make a "public choice" to move to the suburbs, thereby avoiding high crime and enjoying good schools and social and economic homogeneity. But if one does not have the resources, no such choice is available.

The concept of vouchers in place of public education is a popular public choice theme. With vouchers, citizens can "buy" education for their children at a public or private institution of their choice. This has the decided effect of weakening the public schools and therefore limiting their services to those who either cannot afford or cannot manage to enroll their children in private schools.

Is the public choice perspective an adequate and fair representation of the public in public administration? The answer is no.

The institutions of democratic government depend for their survival on the support of the governed. What the people believe about the motives and actions of those who govern them greatly influences popular support for the government and popular willingness to abide by its laws and actions. According to Fleishman (1981), "Nothing—not errors of judgment, not waste, not efficiency, not high taxes, not overregulation, not even the loss of a war—so shakes representative government at its root as does a belief by the public that the officials who govern act chiefly out of a concern for their private self-interest rather than for the public interest of those who elected (appointed) them. When such a belief becomes pervasive among the electorate and persists over a long enough period, the public tends to lose faith not only in the officials who govern, but also in the institution of government itself" (p. 58).

The issue here is faith. The public will not cooperate in carrying out difficult decisions—particularly if those decisions require any sacrifice during times of crisis or shortage—if it does not have faith in the institutions of government and in appointed and elected officials. If public servants are the trustees of the public in carrying out its will, then self-serving behavior violates the public trust and results in a loss of public faith in government.

The Public as Represented: The Legislative Perspective

For the most part, modern democratic government in practice has been representative rather than direct. The public entrusts to Congress, to the state legislature, to the county commission, to the city council, and to the school board the authority to act for and in its behalf. Because elected officials directly represent the public, they have the most legitimate claim for a public perspective on public administration, and public administrators are expected to operate the agencies that legislators establish and to obey and enforce the laws that legislators pass.

In the practice of government, public administrators are given wide latitude in carrying out enabling legislation. But statutes are often vague, ambiguous, incomplete, or contradictory, and court interpretations are typically slow in coming. Elected executives often expect public servants to follow the executives' policy preferences, despite either existing statutes or legislative intent. Still, the public's elected representatives are the clearest single manifestation of a public perspective.

Yet representation occurs in other ways. Redford (1981) reminds us that "the attainment of the democratic ideal in the world of administration depends much less on majority votes than on the inclusiveness of the representation of interests in the interaction process among decision makers" (p. 44). Therefore the public is represented both through the votes of legislatures and by the activities of interest groups.

Long (1952), Krislov (1974), and Meier (1985) have all demonstrated that the public service, in a demographic sense, is more representative of the public than are elected officials. Add to that the expertise embodied in public service, and mix in the effects of equal employment opportunity and affirmative action programs, and there is every possibility that public service generally mirrors the public.

Do problems exist with the representational perspective on the public in public administration? Yes. An old adage says that in a representative government the voters are free only on the day they cast their ballots. If the public exercises its franchise in a limited way—and if that public, aside from exercising its franchise, is generally inactive in public affairs—are we not left with a government that only minimally reflects its public? The most forceful critic of representation is Barber (1986), who stated:

> The representative principal steals from individuals the ultimate responsibility for their values, beliefs, and actions. . . . Representation is incompatible with freedom because it delegates and thus alienates political will at the cost of genuine self-government and autonomy . . . freedom and citizenship are correlates; each sustains and gives life to the other. Men and women who are not directly responsible

through common deliberation, common decision and common action for the policies that determine their common lives are not really free at all, however much they enjoy security, private rights and freedom from interference [pp. 145–146].

Those who are too reliant on the representative perspective of the public in public administration soon learn that individuals and groups of citizens often regard themselves as not being effectively represented by those they elect. Their concerns and grievances are as often laid at the doorstep of the public servant as on the legislative table.

Is the representational perspective on the public in public administration adequate? While it is necessary, it is not sufficient.

The Public as Customer: The Service-Providing Perspective

One of the most interesting perspectives on the public is that of the customer. Here we define *customers* as the individuals and groups served by so-called street-level bureaucrats. So schoolchildren, for example, are the customers of teachers, counselors, principals, superintendents, and school boards; victims of crime (as well as those who commit the crimes) are the customers of the police; and those who are ill or handicapped, either physically or emotionally, are customers of the wide range of medical professionals in public health agencies. All citizens are at one time or another customers of government. Certainly, we are all customers of the Internal Revenue Service.

Does the individual's status as customer constitute a perspective on the public? To some extent it does. To the millions of public employees who serve them, customers surely constitute a public. While this public is fragmented, disconnected, and inchoate, it probably more nearly represents the general public than do interest groups. However, because they are organized and generally better off financially, interest groups wield much more power than do customers.

Lipsky (1981), the best-known analyst of street-level bureaucracies and their customers, pointed out, "To deliver street-level policy through bureaucracy is to embrace a contradiction. On the one hand, service is delivered by people, to people, invoking a model of human interaction, caring, and responsibility. On the other hand, service is delivered through a bureaucracy, invoking a model of detachment and equal treatment under conditions of resource limitations and constraint, making care and responsibility conditional" (p. 69).

Street-level bureaucrats are expected to be advocates for their customers, using their skills, education, and knowledge to secure for their customers the best treatment or position. The education or training of teachers, police, social workers, lawyers, doctors, and others explicitly calls for an altruistic dedication to placing primary importance on customers' needs. Social agencies, however, rarely have sufficient resources to enable street-level bureaucrats to approximate their altruistic commitments. Caseloads are so large that qualitative individual counseling is generally precluded. Classrooms are too large; prison, probation, and parole systems are seriously overloaded. Under these conditions, any real advocacy for the customers' interests by public servants is unlikely. The organizations in which street-level bureaucrats function tend to be bound by rules and procedures (often as a result of political intervention) and to be controlling in style. Bureaucrats look for loopholes and discretionary provisions in an attempt to meet customer needs.

Street-level work tends to result in alienation. Public service workers are alienated from their customers—the products of their work—because they tend to do only a segment of the work. They cannot control the outcome of their work, they do not control the raw materials of their work, and they cannot control the pace of their work (Lipsky, 1981, p. 74).

How do public workers respond? As Lipsky pointed out, "Public service workers have increased their share of national wealth through higher pay and benefit levels, increased their collective bargaining power, and acquiesced in and often encouraged developments such as specialization, computerization, and fragmentation of responsibilities for customers. Street-level bureaucrats have enhanced their position in the political system to the neglect of aspects of service constituents with more humanistic models of customer involvement, or at the expense of taking positions on customers' behalf" (p. 79).

If Lipsky is right, the evidence is clear: the customer perspective on the public in public administration is weak. While there are exceptions, customers seem unable to function as a public. In fact, street-level bureaucrats have organized as interest groups, pressed their interests through the political process, and achieved significant benefits—in some cases at the expense of their customers. Thus, as in the pluralist model, self-interest prevails, and it prevails not necessarily for the public but for those who are supposed to serve the public.

The Public as Citizen

The concept of citizenship is closely tied to the origins of the modern field of public administration. The era of reform—calling for an educated and merit-selected public service—also required an informed citizenry that was generally active in public affairs and knowledgeable of the Constitution. This notion of citizenship would have the public pursue not only its individual self-interest but the public interest as well. In early concepts of public administration, citizens were the public (Frederickson and Chandler, 1984). This notion predates the rapid growth of government, the development of interest groups, and theories such as pluralism and public choice.

In the 1930s, public administration began to drift away from its emphasis on citizenship and move almost entirely toward administrative issues. The late 1960s saw the beginning of a drift back to concern for the public in public administration; but by then pluralism and public choice theories were the dominant notions of the public, and citizenship seemed less interesting, particularly to established scholars in prestigious American universities.

The real resurgence in citizenship was occurring in U.S. cities. In the inner city, models for citizen participation in policymaking were supported by the federal government. Some governmental services were experimenting with forms of citizen control. By the mid-1980s, it could be concluded that citizen participation had modified the usual methods of decision making in a host of policy areas and had taken its place as a major feature of democratic administration. While those people in positions of power yielded grudgingly to citizen groups, it is unlikely that the gains made during that time will be lost; if anything, the near future seems to hold promise of greater direct involvement of citizens (Ventriss, 1984; National Performance Review, 1993).

In public administration, there has been renewed interest in the concept of citizenship. As was the case in the field's early years, that interest seeks an informed, active, and strong citizenry participating in the policy process with administrators, legislators, and interest groups. Generally, the modern development of the citizenship perspective in public administration assumes that a vigorous citizenry is compatible with an effective public administration. Indeed, citizenship theorists argue that an informed and active citizenry is essential to effective government administration (Frederickson and Chandler, 1984).

The notion of citizenship can, however, go much further. Benjamin Barber, in *Strong Democracy: Participatory Politics for a New Age* (1986), indicates that representative forms of democracy, merit-based civil service, pluralism, and public choice all diminish the ability of the public to govern itself (see also Marone, 1990): "Strong democracy requires unmediated self-government by an engaged citizenry. It requires institutions that would involve individuals at both the neighborhood and the national level in common talk, common decisionmaking and political judgment, and common action" (p. 261).

Barber recognizes that his recommendations are utopian. Therefore, he suggests more moderate steps that "place strong democracy in an institutional framework where its realistic potential as a practice can be assessed" (p. 262). He specifically suggests the following activities to enhance direct citizen involvement in government (pp. 262–311):

1. Neighborhood assemblies
2. Television town meetings and a civic communications cooperative
3. Civic education and equal access to information: a civic education postal act and a civic video text service
4. Supplementary institutions, including representative town meetings, office holding by lot, decriminalization, and lay justice
5. A national initiative and referendum process
6. Electronic balloting
7. Election by lot: sortition and rotation
8. Vouchers and the market approach to public choice

9. National citizenship and common action: universal citizen service and related volunteer programs and training and employment opportunities
10. Neighborhood citizenship and common action: extensive volunteerism and sweat-equity
11. Democracy in the workplace

While some of Barber's suggestions seem impractical, many of them are relatively accepted parts of the modern citizenship perspective.

Does the citizenship approach hold real promise for defining the public in public administration? Yes and no. Its strength derives from its potential for an enhanced and ennobled public motivated by a shared concern for the common good. Its weakness is in its failure to recognize the complexity of public issues, the critical need for expertise and leadership, and the problems of motivating the public to participate.

Requisites for a General Theory of the Public in Public Administration

The five perspectives on the public in public administration that we have outlined here illustrate the importance of both social science and philosophical influences. Political scientists are generally more concerned with interest groups, representation, and citizenship, while economists place more importance on markets, customers, and rationality. Traditional public administration theory would suggest support for professionalism, expertise, and strong executive government; by contrast, contemporary public administration would favor smaller government, more direct citizen involvement, contracting out and privatizing, and marketlike incentives.

Having reviewed these perspectives we close with a consideration of what *ought* to constitute the requisites of a theory of public in public administration. We attempt to determine which of these perspectives is in the spirit of public administration. A fully developed theory of the public requires more attention than can be given here. Our purpose, then, will be to outline such a theory and to set out some requisites for it.

A general theory of the public in public administration must be unique—designed not just for the purpose of theory development but also to guide those in public service. Because it is to be used by those who must make government work, such a theory must be practical. It should also be empirically based—and, of course, it must further the interests of the public both specifically and generally.

Each of the five perspectives we reviewed contribute in some way to a general theory of the public. None is complete, though, and when taken together they still suffer from significant omissions.

The Constitution

The first requisite for a general theory of the public in public administration is that it be based on the Constitution. The principles of popular sovereignty, representative government, the rights of citizens contained in the Bill of Rights, procedural due process, the balance of powers, and other aspects of both federal and state constitutions are the foundation of such a theory, and that foundation must be firmly and fastidiously adhered to.

In *To Run a Constitution,* John Rohr (1986) demonstrates that the modern administrative state is not only compatible with the Constitution but is necessary for the realization of the Constitution's vision. To Rohr, the public administrator under the Constitution must be both technically competent and morally obligated to the Constitution, and that moral obligation must transcend the technical requirements of administrative performance. The primary purpose of American government, according to Rohr, is to guarantee the nation's founding values to all citizens, making democracy instrumental to that end rather than an end in itself.

In Rohr's view, then, government is legitimized through the original act of accepting the Constitution rather than only through democratic election. Thus, the actions, intentions, and acceptances of the founding constitute the wellspring of legitimacy. Obviously, each generation of citizens must return to that original debate to confirm the Constitution's legitimacy (Dewey, 1954). Because the Constitution is a mere piece of paper, its legitimacy derives from the act of the sovereign people breathing life into it. All government officials, elected as well as appointed, are legitimized by and representative of all people. These officials are controlled by a higher principle than that of majority decisions: the constitutional order. The primary moral obligation of public administrators is to be the guardian and guarantor of the founding values to every citizen.

The constitutional requisite is especially compatible with the representative and citizenship perspectives on the public.

The Virtuous Citizen

The second requisite for a general theory of the public must be based on an enhanced notion of citizenship; elsewhere this has been called the theory of the "virtuous citizen." It is said that a government can be no better than the people it represents. It is appropriate that an enhanced concept of citizenship should be a public administration commitment.

Hart (1984) suggests four aspects of the virtuous citizen. First, the citizen understands the nation's founding documents and is able to "do moral philosophy"—engaging in judgment of policies that further both specific and general citizen interests and are compatible with the Constitution. The citizen should have a civic life of which making philosophical judgments is a significant part.

Belief is the second aspect of the virtuous citizen concept. The citizen must believe that the values of the American regime are true and correct and not just ideas that are psychologically gratifying or accepted by the majority. Philosophers have referred to these values as "natural rights." As Hart puts it, "If we do not believe in the regime values, why should we accept the necessary sacrifices they entail? How can we set any priorities? If everything is ratified by majority opinion, and the majority desires that which is iniquitous (racial or sexual discrimination for instance), can we only acquiesce? The American regime values must not only be understood, but must be believed and accepted as nonnegotiable" (p. 114).

The third characteristic of the virtuous citizen is taking individual moral responsibility. Whenever any situation compromises regime values, the virtuous citizen is required to act in defense of those values. Thus, when one encounters racism, sexism, invasion of privacy, or violation of due process, one must oppose it. This moves citizens well beyond a concern for graft and corruption in government: it moves all of us toward an individual moral responsibility for each other's natural or fundamental rights.

Finally, Hart requires civility as a distinguishing feature of the virtuous citizen. The first aspect of civility is forbearance—that is, an understanding that public rules cannot compel virtue, that rules and requirements should be kept to a minimum so as not to impair liberty, and that people cannot expect too much from human institutions. Tolerance is the second aspect of civility. In tolerance, we understand that ideas are the coin of the civic marketplace, and through moral discourse the expression of ideas cannot be suppressed. Action is, however, another matter; any action that could interfere with nonnegotiable regime values must be stopped.

It is a responsibility of the public servant to nurture the development of a virtuous citizenry, and such a citizenry will respect and revere a caring and committed public service.

Responsiveness to Collective and Noncollective Publics

The third requisite of a general theory of the public is the development and maintenance of systems and procedures for hearing and responding to the interests of both the collective and inchoate public. Generally speaking, the collective public—the interest groups—are able to find mechanisms for the expression and pursuit of their views. However, in its concern for efficiency, timeliness, and order, public administration tends to avoid mechanisms for the expression of interests. Exactly the reverse should be true. Hearings, deliberations, grievance procedures, ombudsmen, sunshine laws, and the like are all friendly to a general theory of the public in public administration.

The more difficult task, of course, is accounting for the well being and interests of the inchoate public. Within the framework of the Constitution and a commitment to its principles, and within the context of the virtuous citizen theory, the public administrator should account for the inchoate public. Under the Constitution each citizen is, after all, entitled to enjoy the equal protection of the law. This doubtless means that the public administrator must be an advocate for the equitable treatment of citizens. Glaring inequities in the distribution of public services or in access to employment cannot be tolerated. As has been stated elsewhere, public administration must be committed not only to efficiency and economy, but to social equity as well (Frederickson, 1980).

Benevolence and Love

The fourth requisite for a general theory of the public must be based on benevolence and love. Benevolence, or the love of others, is the key. Smith (1982) states that

> the love of our country seems, in ordinary cases, to involve in it two different principles; first, a certain respect and reverence for the Constitution or form of government which is actually established; and secondly, an earnest desire to render the condition of our fellow citizens as safe, respectable and happy as we can. He is not a citizen who is not disposed to respect the laws and obey the civil magistrate; and he is certainly not a good citizen who does not wish to promote, by every means in his power, the welfare of the whole society of his fellow-citizens [p. 231].

The purpose of government is to extend the protection of regime values to all citizens. It should be the purpose of public administration to have a concept of the public that is based on benevolence. Embodied in the notion of benevolence is the sense of service, which has long been associated with public administration. Similar, too, is the belief in a commitment to the greater good and the dedication of one's professional life to that end. It is no wonder that there has been a loss of public regard toward public service; such regard can be reclaimed only by a public administration that esteems the public through benevolence.

Conclusions

In our culture, thinking has never been as important as doing. Experience has always been more important than theory as a guide to action. Bernard Murchland (1984) puts it well: "Experience rather than theory generates the controlling metaphors of public life: process, plurality, experiment, growth. That is why the native philosophy of this country is the radical empiricism of the pragmatist. . . . The point is not that ideas are not important; but rather that if they are not realized in experience, they're not deemed much good" (p. 14).

The great danger in this pragmatism, this learning by doing and by experience, is that it may result in anti-intellectualism and thoughtless action that can cripple the public's ability to function. Murchland (1984) points out that "to feel the truth before we know it is to run the risk that we may only feel it and never know it. . . . [T]he fact is, practice soon becomes inchoate without theory, and the pragmatists themselves are always out of balance between the respective claims of each" (p. 14). It is for this reason that theory is often as important as action. Theory holds the promise of grounding practice in legitimizing concepts, metaphors, visions, and ideas. As Murchland puts it, "Public in the strong sense means knowing as well as doing; above all it means knowing in common what we can never know alone" (p. 14).

One of the unfortunate effects of narrowing the practice and idea of the public to the functioning of government has to do with careerism. If, in our education for and practice of public administration, we define ourselves only as government employees, we prepare the seedbed for careerism and individualism. When public administration is defined more broadly to include the effective operation of governmental agencies and nonprofit organizations coupled with a structured pattern of interaction with the public to improve the common good, it heightens the potential that people will choose a life in public administration for reasons other than pure ambition.

To many in public administration, the public seems too large and abstract for the individual to identify with and respond to. Indeed, utilitarianism was partially a response to urbanization and industrialization, the argument being that things were too large and complex to operate like the Greek city-state. For this reason we have been slow to develop a cogent theory of the public. There may be an emergent theory; if so, it would likely include four concepts: first, the company of strangers; second, solutions to problems of space and public relations; third, the validity of impersonal relations, and fourth, the development of a contemporary public of interdependence.

The Company of Strangers

Can there be an authentic public life in the company of strangers? Parker Palmer (1981) notes that "the vision and reality of community come when people have direct experience of each other, experience of mutuality, interdependence, unmediated by governmental sanctions and codes. The vision and reality of community come when people have a rich array of opportunities to interact in public, interactions which draw out and encourage the human impulse toward life together" (p. 49). We find this interaction most commonly in public streets, where strangers in pursuit of private interests meet. Public life can be the encounter of strangers occupying the same territory—the same human community—impressed with the need to acknowledge that fact and the impulse to get along. Parks, squares, cafés, museums, and galleries are all settings for public life, where strangers can meet, spend time in each other's presence, and share common interests. These interactions are multiplied by activities such as rallies, forums, hearings, and debates, in which more formal interaction among strangers can occur (Brown, 1995). The neighborhood is an important setting for public life. Increasingly, voluntary associations provide settings in which strangers can come together.

A healthy public life, in other words, involves continual interaction with other individuals moving in and out of one another's lives in an endless panorama of meeting, interacting, leaving, and meeting again. This public life is as authentic and valid a form of human experience and is as able to authenticate common and shared beliefs as are other more intimate forms of human interaction. It is the public as both an idea and a capacity (Lasch, 1990, 1995).

The Problem of Public Space

The nature of public life can be determined by the quality of space in which human interactions can occur. When neighborhoods are separated from commercial areas, and when both are separated from parks or public squares, it is more difficult to see the structured interaction of strangers. The need for strangers to leave their neighborhoods of row after row of homes and the long hallways of offices to find the modern equivalent of the town square or other public place is clear.

Our present arrangements of space do not enhance the public life. However, two developments hold some hope: (1) the rising importance of the architecture of public places, and (2) contemporary television and communications. We see in the works of

Charles Goodsell (1988) the significance of public meeting places' architecture. The purposeful design of public places to do more than facilitate commerce and to enable meeting in forums, councils, assemblies, and schools and other public activities is critical to a reemergence of an effective public.

Systems of televising public meetings help, too—especially if they include audio feedback for questions and comments from the "distant" public. The preoccupation with automobiles and the tendency of people to move from work to suburban homes and back again via this mode of transportation lessens the opportunity for strangers to meet. Modern computer data communications systems, and the increasing popularity of the Internet and online services, wonderfully illustrate the importance of the company of strangers as an approach to an authentic public life. They are also good examples of using technology to overcome factors such as architectural limitations, commuting, and suburban life that work against the development of an effective public life.

The Validity of Impersonal Relations

Public life is also partly determined by the psychology and mindset of our time. Richard Sennett (1977) makes an important point about the reigning belief today: that closeness between individuals is a moral good. The dominant aspiration today is to develop individual personality through experiences of closeness with and warmth for others. The reigning myth today is that the evils of society can all be understood as the evils of impersonality, alienation, and coldness. The sum of these three is an ideology of intimacy: that social relationships of all kinds are real, believable, and authentic the closer they approach the inner psychological concerns of each person. This ideology transmutes political categories into psychological categories, and it defines the humanitarian spirit of a society without gods; warmth is our god (Sennett, 1977).

The problem with this ideology comes from its impression that all meaningful relationships must have closeness and warmth. These qualities are critical to one's private life, but as Palmer (1981) puts it, "the problem arises when we impose the norm of intimacy on public life. In the public realm, where most relations are necessarily distant and impersonal, the demand for closeness and warmth distorts and eventually destroys the potential for public experience" (p. 47). We become preoccupied with the characteristics, style, and appearance of others. The personal characteristics of those in public life—rather than their intellect, views on issues, or capacity to affect the general good—become the dominant interest. In addition, when we personalize public life, we begin to fear that if we were to enter public ranks, our own private lives would become subject to scrutiny and criticism (Lasch, 1978). This causes us to withdraw. As Parker Palmer (1981) points out: "Historically, Americans have worried about the incursion of public powers in the private realm. But now we see that there is also a problem when the psychology of private relations is forced upon the public sphere. . . . We must learn to accept and appreciate the fact that public life is fundamentally impersonal. . . . To receive full benefit from public life, one must realize that impersonal relations have a validity of their own" (p. 47).

The Contemporary Public of Interdependence

The world is too complex to attempt to reconstruct the Greek city-state, but it is possible to rebuild the public through an understanding of human interdependence. The realities of the atomic age—air and water pollution throughout the world, famine, and the increasingly international nature of the economy—all indicate our global interdependence. Homelessness, drug addiction, poor schools, and highway gridlock inform us of our local interdependence. Through technology, we now know directly the horrors of war and famine.

We may be building the public because of an increasingly strong sense of interdependence. The company of strangers can now be had both locally and globally. We experience the circumstances of unknown others and join them, usually in brief or sporadic ways, in an endless sequence of public encounters. If in these encounters there is a general sense of the public good, at least in terms of our collective responsibility to each other in basic humanity—nutrition, shelter, education, work, protection—we may find the beginnings of the emerging global village. Interdependence may drive us into each other's arms.

We see here the beginnings of a concept of the public that is in the spirit of public administration. Such a concept would include recognition that the term public is not the same as government—

that it is indeed very much more than government. The public lives independently of government, and government is only one of its manifestations.

We also know of the public as an idea and as a capacity. By reducing the term public to mean government, we limit the capacity of people to be public. As an idea, the public means all people coming together for public purposes rather than for personal or family reasons. The public as capacity implies an informed, active ability to work together for the general good. In many cases such action will occur through government—but not always. Voluntary associations, nonprofit organizations, and corporations are all manifestations of the public.

It follows then that public accountability and responsibility lies in enabling citizens to set agreed-upon community standards and goals and in working in the public's behalf to achieve those goals. Public responsibility and accountability is expected of both public and corporate administrators. One cannot hide behind labels of "private" or "business" to escape responsibility to the public. Nor can one hide behind an organization, a government, or a business. Public responsibility is not collective but is individual.

Within the framework of the Constitution and American regime values, public administrators have a responsibility to structure relations between organizations and the public so as to foster development of an evolving concept—on the part of both organizations and the public—of the common good. Elections, legislative decisions, executive policy implementations, court decisions, and the continual pattern of interaction between public officials and the public are all expressions of public preferences. We must nurture and protect these forms of interaction to come as close as possible to an evolving creation of the public, an evolving definition of the public will, and an evolving spirit of public administration.

Chapter Two

The Political Context of Public Administration

If they are to be understood, political theories must be construed in relation to their material environment and ideological framework. The political theories of American public administration are not exceptions. For, despite occasional claims that public administration is a science with principles of universal validity, American public administration has evolved political theories unmistakably related to unique economic, social, governmental, and ideological facts.

DWIGHT WALDO, *THE ADMINISTRATIVE STATE*, P. 7

The first and most important context of public administration is political. To understand and nurture the spirit of public administration, it is essential to know politics, appreciate politics, and see the limits of politics. Consider the following bits of history.

After the riot, when asked why it happened, the prison warden replied, "Politics. The citizens wanted stricter law enforcement and longer prison sentences. The police and the judges responded, filling the prison to overflowing. Yet the budget of the Department of Corrections has not kept pace with inflation. The inmate crowding got worse; so did the food, the educational and counseling services, and the quality of the staff. A riot was certain to happen, and it did. The reason was politics." Shortly after making these comments, the warden was replaced, and the governor appointed a task force to study the possibility of contracting out prison services.

Presidents Jimmy Carter, Ronald Reagan, George Bush, and Bill Clinton all favored the deregulation of business, including airlines.

The responsibilities of the Federal Aviation Administration (FAA) for schedules, fares, and service regulations were discontinued, and the airlines were left to compete with each other. As a result of airline mergers caused by deregulation, less than half of the major airlines that were in service in 1977 now survive. Some major airports, such as those in St. Louis and Minneapolis–St. Paul, are now served primarily by only one carrier. Passengers flying from one urban center to another now have lower airfares and more available flights, but those flying to or from smaller locations face diminished service and higher fares. Traffic delays at large urban airports are routine. Since the firing of the air traffic controllers in early 1980, the air traffic control system has not returned to earlier levels of staffing, although air traffic has increased.

A new competitive group of airlines emerged in the 1980s and 1990s, luring customers on high-volume routes with cut-rate fares. Lower ticket prices were made possible by buying and refurbishing old airplanes, contracting for maintenance and other services, and paying lower salaries to pilots and other employees. Then in May 1996, a ValuJet airplane with 111 people on board crashed in the Florida Everglades; there were no survivors. The disaster was evidently caused when oxygen canisters in the cargo bay exploded. Full oxygen canisters are not supposed to be shipped in passenger airplanes (it appears that an airplane refurbishing company on contract to ValuJet shipped these particular canisters). Although the secretary of transportation and FAA leaders immediately stated that air travel in the United States was safe, many leading political leaders called for some reregulation and for investigations.

In 1977, the U.S. Food and Drug Administration (FDA) announced a ban on saccharin because research indicated that it may cause cancer. After a protracted political battle, Congress delayed the ban for eighteen months (to mid-1979), and it has been delayed in consecutive two-year periods to this day.

What accounts for all of these situations? Politics. The prison warden, the secretary of transportation, and the FDA were all experiencing this single most consistent and significant phenomenon in American public administration. Indeed, public administration is embedded in politics. It follows, therefore, that a public administrator's effectiveness is predicated on an understanding of politics and the political process as well as on an ability to manage public agencies in a political context.

Understanding Politics and Public Administration

At its best, politics is a noble expression of the human capacity to co-operate in anything collective, be it a business, a village, or a nation. It is through politics that the particular interests of diverse individuals are brought together to fashion a common or general view.

At its worst, however, politics means using power to advance the interests of some at the expense of others. Therefore, politics is the perfect venue for the person who wishes to receive extraordinary attention, or to exercise unjust dominion over others.

As *Webster's Third New International Dictionary* tells us, politics good and bad is the art and science of government. It is the context in which public administration works. Politics takes many forms, each of which affects public administration in different ways. There are partisan politics, interest-group politics, bureaucratic politics, media politics, corporate politics, and boardroom politics, to name just a few. In the United States, all forms of politics are carried on according to the political agreements of the founders in the federal and state constitutions.

The U.S. Constitution

To understand the relationship between politics and public administration, one must begin with the U.S. Constitution. To know the Constitution does not, however, reconcile the differing perspectives on public administration in American democratic government that flow from differing views on the Constitution. Donald F. Kettl (1993b) characterizes these differences as follows:

> Different approaches to the study of administration usually come from one of two conflicting traditions in American politics—and each tradition leads to a very different perspective on the role of administration in American democracy. Some students of administration come to the subject with a fundamentally Hamiltonian bent. Like Alexander Hamilton, they seek a vigorous state vested with a strong administrative apparatus. They see the task of administration as carrying out publicly defined goals effectively; they see an energetic government doing good. Other students of administration, however, are fundamentally Madisonians. Like James Madison, they are wary about too much governmental action, and they

are cautious about the concentration of governmental—especially administrative—power. Like Madison, they see in a delicate balance of power the best protection against tyranny. The competition of political interests, in their view, lessens the risk that bureaucracy can abuse individual liberty [p. 408].

So the original basis of the public administration field was tied to an earlier argument about the role of the state in American democracy.

The U.S. Constitution and state constitutions established democratic governments based on popular sovereignty; that is, they established government by the consent of the governed. Sovereignty, though, does not mean that we as citizens are self-governing. Ordinarily, this sovereignty is expressed through the selection of representatives—senators, members of Congress, state senators and representatives, county commissioners, and city council members. Based on the appropriate constitutions, these representatives set up laws, establish rates of taxation, and provide for public services. In almost all cases, representatives are selected by a majority of voters, as is the passage of most legislation.

In American representative government, majority rule is the basis of the concept of popular sovereignty, but the sovereign majority cannot legislate away the constitutionally protected rights of individuals. The Bill of Rights guarantees freedom of the press, of assembly, and of religion. It also guarantees privacy and protects the individual against government in a general sense; in particular, it protects minorities from the tyranny of the elected majority.

Because of long experience with despotic governments in Europe, the framers of the U.S. Constitution designed a system of limited government, so that all governmental power was not to be placed in the hands of one person or even one group. The first principle of this limited government is the separation of powers. Legislators pass laws and control the budget, elected executives carry out the laws, and courts protect individuals and review the actions of the other government branches.

The second principle of limited government is that the three branches are to be balanced so that possible excesses in one branch can be checked by the two other branches. Justice Louis D. Brandeis once noted that "the doctrine of separation of powers was adopted not to promote efficiency but to preclude the exercise of arbitrary power" (Seidman and Gilmour, 1986, p. 280).

The third principle of limited government is federalism, a decentralized form of government that remains close to the people. Under federalism, all powers not expressly given to the national government are reserved to the states. The states follow suit by providing for the creation of counties, cities, and other local jurisdictions to carry out governmental services. All of these features of our federal and state constitutions are decidedly Madisonian.

The constitutions also provide for the rights of citizens to organize to advance their individual and shared interests. By guaranteeing such rights, the constitutions essentially codify what has come to be known as pluralism.

Over the years, the U.S. Constitution has been amended, and many state constitutions have been completely revised. For example, sovereignty—which has generally been manifested through the right to vote—has, over the years and as a result of protracted political struggles, been extended to women and minorities. As far as public administration is concerned, the most critical change in the U.S. Constitution was the Fourteenth Amendment and its "equal protection of the laws" clause, which extended equal rights to minorities. (It is important to note here that many state constitutions have been revised in the last two decades to strengthen the power and authority of governors.)

No mention is made in the U.S. Constitution of political parties, interest groups, or administration—and yet all three obviously have become significant parts of contemporary American government. Because administration is not mentioned in the national constitution (it is mentioned in most state constitutions), one should not assume that public administration does not have a legitimate role in government (Rohr, 1986). Governmental power can be legitimized either through state and national constitutions or directly through the political process. It is by way of the political process that public administration has developed and become a legitimate part of American government (Goodsell, 1995). Indeed, not only has public administration effectively managed the daily affairs of government, it has made "a significant contribution to the process of self-government in the United States by providing opportunities for groups of citizens to be more intimately involved in government decision making than the traditional election system permits" (Rourke, 1987, p. 230).

In a thorough and persuasive assessment of the role of public administration in the constitutional order, John Rohr (1986) describes public administration's legitimate place, correcting a defect in the U.S. Constitution. The founding document, writes Rohr, "does not make adequate provision for public participation in government decision making. The role of bureaucracy in government opens an opportunity for many people to become actively involved in the work of government. They may do so as civil servants, as citizens attending public hearings, or by taking advantage of other opportunities to participate in the many activities of administrative agencies" (p. 230). Obviously, these champions of modern public administration are distinctly Hamiltonian in perspective.

Legislative Politics

In the practice of politics in the constitutional order, legislators pass enabling statutes and delegate to administrative agencies the authority to operate federal, state, and local programs. Once an agency is established and staffed—ordinarily through a personnel system applying standards of merit for initial appointment and promotion—the agency is funded through an annual budget passed by the legislature. The legislature also engages in routine oversight of agency functioning. The professional staff, then, is left to operate the agency on a day-to-day basis.

In the classic theory of public administration, this practice is described conceptually as the *politics-administration dichotomy*. In this concept, elected representatives decide politically which programs the government will operate, and administrators then carry out those programs. Once an agency's mission is defined and its budget established through legislative means, the political process stops and the administrative process begins. Partisan political interests are not expected to meddle in routine administrative affairs, nor are administrators expected to participate in partisan politics (Wilson, W., 1887).

The politics-administration dichotomy is an "ideal type"—a theoretical construct or an abstraction used to differentiate between those governmental processes that are primarily political and those that are largely administrative. But, as in any abstraction used for purposes of description and prescription, there is often a considerable difference between theory and practice. In its initial usage, the politics-administration dichotomy was a convenient tool for separating administrative practices based presumably on expertise, professionalism, and merit-selected civil service appointments from those practices based on compromise and even corruption. It was in this initial sense that those who practiced public administration could claim to be neutral, at least in the partisan-political sense. This was the ultimate in Hamiltonian thinking.

Public administration came to be associated with the executive features of American constitutionalism. It was simply assumed that the president (or governor or mayor) sat at the top of the hierarchy. Therefore, the politics-administration dichotomy began to resemble the separation of powers into legislative politics and executive administration. By the 1950s, Dwight Waldo (1949) was arguing that the values of administration, such as efficiency and economy, are at their base political values. Soon thereafter, John Gaus (1950) wrote the now-famous line, "A theory of public administration means in our time a theory of politics also" (p. 168). Thus began the unraveling of the dichotomy as the primary conceptual basis for the field of public administration. The field was left with this question: If political neutrality, professionalism, and the principles of scientific management are not the bases of public administration, what is?

There have been many contenders. In the Madisonian tradition, Graham Allison's work (1971) accounts for the place of pluralism in administration and suggests that the field should be based on concepts of bureaucratic politics. Vincent Ostrom (1973), Anthony Downs (1967), William Niskanen (1971), and many others developed public-choice theory, or the application of market logic to public administration. Public choice is a Madisonian concept. From the policy-studies specialists came theories of implementation—also a Madisonian argument (Pressman and Wildavsky, 1984). The most direct challenge to the field could be described as bureaucratic control theory. It is highly Madisonian and would be characterized by Lowi (1969) in his call for a bureaucracy essentially without latitude of discretion in the context of a robust democracy in which elected officials would resolve even the smallest matter of application.

Within each of these four perspectives lie substantial bodies of research and theory, and each perspective is treated at greater length in later chapters of this book.

The Spirit of Public Administration is more Hamiltonian than Madisonian in viewpoint. It is drawn from the traditions of public administration scholarship and practice. It is linked to the modern "new public management theory," as well as to concepts of leadership now common in the field. *The Spirit of Public Administration* both describes and advocates a form of public administration and policy implementation that provides considerable latitude and wide discretion in carrying out the daily affairs of public organizations.

Why is this so?

In practice, legislative statutes are often vague. Usually, governmental programs are statutorily described in overreaching ways. The experience has been that public administrators must exercise a good bit of discretion in trying to bring definition and specificity to unspecific and sometimes contradictory legislative language (Seidman and Gilmour, 1986).

In practice, budgets are seldom adequate to carry out legislative expectations. One significant task for public administrators is to align reasonable expectations with both budget realities and the overambitious rhetoric of statutes.

In practice, when governmental agencies are unable to meet the expectations of the legislature or of citizens' sometimes exaggerated expectations resulting from political promises, legislators often find it convenient to practice the politics of blame—pointing a finger at the amorphous bureaucracy or hinting at fraud or waste.

In practice, the national and state legislatures, as well as larger city councils and county commissions, follow a division of labor based on committees and subcommittees organized around particular governmental functions, such as national defense at the federal level or law enforcement at the state and local levels. These committees and subcommittees often match in a general way the organizational structure set up to administer these laws. In legislative politics, there is often a close working relationship between legislators in a particular committee or subcommittee and top-level officials in the functionally connected administrative agency. Some of these connections are legendary, as in the case of state highway departments and of highway committees in state legislatures, or the agricultural committees in Congress and the U.S. Department of Agriculture (Kelman, 1987).

In legislative politics, higher-level legislatures ordinarily follow the policy preference of lesser levels. If a legislative subcommittee adopts a particular position, it is usually supported by its parent committee and by the full legislature. This is the reason that committee and subcommittee chairpersons are especially powerful. They are ordinarily chosen on the basis of seniority and by the party in power. Legislators do a great amount of jockeying for power to get committee assignments suitable to their particular regions of the country.

Because legislators are chosen by state, or by counties within a state, they encounter not only regional preoccupations and tensions but also the tendency to distribute governmental services or programs on a regional basis. A notable example is the annual funding of pork-barrel projects for rivers and harbors to be carried out by the U.S. Army Corps of Engineers. The Department of Defense and the Corps of Engineers participate directly in the development of these projects, testify favorably before their counterpart legislative committees in the budgeting process, and support the politics of regional distribution. By sponsoring such local projects, of course, incumbent legislators can show the public that they have caused the government to effectively serve local interests.

In the past, national and state legislatures were not well staffed, either in numbers or in expertise. Now, however, virtually all national legislative committees and subcommittees, as well as most state and major-city legislatures, have relatively large and often expert staffs. Legislators no longer must rely entirely on public administration professionals or specialists for expertise (Seidman and Gilmour, 1986).

Finally, one of the most significant factors affecting legislative politics and public administration is the *iron triangle*. An example of an iron triangle is the legislative committees on highways working with the administrative bureau of highways, and the two being supported by the highway interest groups or lobbyists representing road-construction companies, trucking companies, the Teamsters Union, and sand, gravel, and asphalt interests. Such triangles can be found in most major areas of American public policy.

The iron-triangle metaphor as a way to describe legislative–executive–interest-group politics may be changing. In many highly technical policy fields, such as monetary policy and arms control, the triangle has given way to issue networks, in which highly sophisticated knowledge and expertise becomes more important than the distribution of economic benefits (Heclo, 1978). In certain social service areas in which the courts have been particularly active, such as entitlements of rights to governmental assistance for the elderly or physically handicapped, the triangle is being replaced by a quadrilateral as the courts join legislative committees, administrative agencies, and interest groups in influencing policy and policy implementation (Shapiro, 1981).

Laurence E. Lynn (1996) goes so far as to suggest that any understanding of modern public administration must assume a network of interest groups, legislative groups, and administrative agencies.

Executive Politics

Elected executives—presidents, governors, mayors—have, in the last twenty years reacted sharply to the growth in government spending. Presidents Nixon, Carter, Reagan, and Clinton, as well as many state governors and large-city mayors, have campaigned on platforms of reducing the size of government, cutting out waste and fraud, and trimming the budget. This political style has been highly successful, most notably in the case of Ronald Reagan. Similarly, President Clinton campaigned on a promise to cut the size of civil service, to cut regulations, and to reinvent government (Osborn and Gaebler, 1992; National Performance Review, 1993).

Once executives are elected, they discover that they have very little command authority over public administration. They soon learn that most agencies are not beholden to the chief executive for their political survival and that executive leadership is a product more of political persuasion than of authority (Neustadt, 1960; Nathan, 1983). As Harry S. Truman was leaving office he remarked that his successor, Dwight D. Eisenhower, would "say, Do this! Do that! *And nothing will happen.* Poor Ike—it won't be a bit like the Army. He'll find it very frustrating" (Neustadt, 1960, p. 9).

It is usually the case that a chief executive has the high ground with respect to initiatives in formulating public policy. Executives can often effectively set the agenda for discussing new policy directives (Kingdon, 1995). Individual administrative agencies, though, are usually specialized, and they are staffed with persons who have narrow sets of interests and who are often resistant to change. Agency or departmental interests are usually buttressed by legislative and interest-group support and are, therefore, sometimes not responsive to executive directives.

Chief executives also quickly learn that budgets ordinarily have very little flexibility. Increasing percentages of both national and state budgets are made up of entitlements such as social security, veterans' benefits, aid to farmers, welfare, and the like, which are not easily reduced. Newly elected chief executives, feeling that they have a mandate for the policies they espoused in the election campaign, are often frustrated in attempting to bring about those policies.

The political problem for elected executives is *not* primarily the bureaucracy. One problem is the separation of powers; another problem is the long chain of legislative policy commitments backed by significant political support—which is exceedingly difficult to change. Still, it is more convenient for elected executives to "see" the bureaucracy as the source of resistance to their policies, rather than to directly face political resistance coming from elected legislators.

Recent years have seen marked and significant changes in the world of executive politics. Because of the rapid growth of the administrative parts of government beginning in the 1930s and stretching into the 1960s, elected executives have not only campaigned against "bureaucracy"—they have developed their own administrative capabilities. It was once the case that all but the very top-level positions in governmental administrative agencies consisted of people in the merit-appointed civil service. At the national level, cabinet members and immediate subcabinet members were appointed by the president, as were a few individuals such as confidential secretaries and drivers. Each cabinet member had a few appointments.

This is no longer the case. There are now thousands of political appointments throughout the administrative apparatus of the national government, and increasingly the same situation is occurring in state and local government. As Laurence E. Lynn (1987) indicates: "The Reagan administration appeared from the outset to embrace the notion that faithful supporters in key executive positions could be a potent tool for administrative leadership. The primary

qualification for appointment—overshadowing managerial competence and experience or familiarity with issues—appeared to be the
extent to which an appointee shared the president's values" (p. 340).

It was once the case that presidents, governors, and mayors
were plagued by office seekers (usually seeking lower-level jobs)
and were politically successful on the basis of their effectiveness
with the spoils system. The massive political reforms between 1880
and 1940 largely eliminated the spoils system and implemented
merit-appointed civil service in most governments. But now we see
a return to the politicizing of the administrative apparatus of government. Indeed, Chester A. Newland (1987, p. 55) refers to the
modern era as one of "high-level spoils." He argues that

> experience since the late 1960s suggests that concerns for govern-
> mental excellence in the contemporary presidency are matched by
> a concern for political loyalty and the prizes of high-level spoils. In
> contrast with spoils practices of the earlier era, today's appointees
> generally lack long-standing ties to Congress (which formerly en-
> hanced shared powers); they owe their loyalties and access to the
> special interests which comprise the president's sources of support
> and funding. Playing this new form of spoils may be required of a
> president to sustain support in this era of weak political parties,
> powerful but fluid interest groups, and image projection through
> mass media [p. 50].

In an analysis titled *The Administrative Presidency,* Richard P.
Nathan (1983) indicates that all of the thousands of appointments
made in the Reagan administration had to be approved by the
White House primarily on the basis of their loyalty to the president's perspective. Indeed, Nathan quotes Reagan as having said,
"Crucial to my strategy for spending control will be the appointment to top government positions of men and women who share
my economic philosophy. We will have an administration in which
the word from the top isn't lost or hidden in the bureaucracy. . . .
[We will bring about] a new structuring of the presidential cabinet
that will make cabinet officers the managers of the national administration—not captives of the bureaucracy or special interests
they are supposed to direct" (p. 72).

In addition to much stronger political control of administrative agencies, most chief executives have also considerably in-

creased their immediate staff. While they give lip service to "cabinet government," many elected executives rely less and less on their cabinet secretaries (and the secretaries' staffs) and more and more on their immediate staffs. The classic examples of this, of course, are Haldeman and Ehrlichman and their staffs in the Nixon administration; Meese, Baker, Deaver, and others in the Reagan administration; and Panetta in the Clinton administration. Where the chief executives have used these strategies, the result has been a marked decline in the administrative effectiveness of the agencies of the national and the state governments. However, it is likely that the ideological preferences of the chief executive have been somewhat furthered by these increased levels of elected executive political involvement in administrative matters.

But there has been a much more significant price to pay. In the Nixon administration, the price was Watergate; Nixon lost his presidency as a result of activities associated with the White House staff. In the Reagan administration, White House involvement in the Iran-Contra arms sales affair crippled the president's effectiveness. And, of course, the Iran-Contra and Watergate scandals, the Housing and Urban Development (HUD) scandal, the Ill-Winds scandal, and the savings and loan scandal all indicate that there has been a sharp increase in incompetence, graft, economic advantage-taking, and lawlessness throughout the politically appointed levels of the national government (Pasztor, 1995; Welfeld, 1992; Light, 1993b).

The paradox is this: many recently elected executives have campaigned against waste, fraud, and corruption, yet there has been a marked increase in waste, fraud, and corruption in government (*Time*, 1987). It is clear that waste, fraud, and corruption are not primarily connected with the civil service or with public administration, but they are directly connected to the political appointments of elected executives.

In the separation of powers, public administration is almost always identified with executive politics. The bureaucracy is still seen as an executive hierarchy. But the era of presidential government has given way to modern forms of congressional government, in which the administrative agencies of government are co-managed (Gilmour and Halley, 1994). Obviously, co-management is a serious challenge to the logic of executive-based concepts of public administration. Chapter Three treats this challenge in detail.

Interest-Group Politics

In the discussion of iron-triangle and network metaphors in Chapter One, interest groups were described as being associated with particular committees or subcommittees of legislatures and their counterpart agencies in the executive branch. Interest groups are probably as old as government, and they certainly have played a significant part in the practices of American government from its beginning. In our time, the strongest warning against iron triangles was Dwight Eisenhower's speech about the military-industrial complex—a network that continues to be politically powerful. At one time, the two senators from the State of Washington, Henry Jackson and Warren Magnuson, were referred to as "the senators from Boeing." There are similar "complexes" associated with highways, tobacco, liquor, farms, and health care, to name a few, and all exercise significant influence in federal and state politics.

At the beginning of this chapter is a brief description of the U.S. Food and Drug Administration's inability to put into effect a ban on saccharin, although the agency's expert researchers have determined that the chemical has cancer-causing properties. The food-production interest groups who use sugar substitutes in the production of low-calorie products such as diet soft drinks have worked through the legislative process to "delay" the saccharin ban for many years. An administrative agency is significantly aided in the political process if it has an interest group or two as a strong ally. Just as the prison warden described at the beginning of this chapter lacked an interest group that was supportive of prison employees or prisoners, the primary political support for prisons in recent years has come from the courts and their enforcement of the constitutional prohibitions against cruel and unusual punishment. Without a natural clientele or an interest group for support, there must occur a crisis, such as a riot or a scandal, or outside intervention from the courts, for an agency to improve its effectiveness (Hargrove and Glidewell, 1990).

In recent years, there has been new and significant development in the field of interest-group politics. While interest groups have always provided some financial support for political candidates, we now see the development of powerful and well-financed political action committees (PACs), which have grown from 608 in

1974 to more than 6,000 in 1995. Approximately 75 percent of all PAC contributions go to incumbents. PAC officials—primarily fundraising specialists working with interest groups—sometimes receive political-level appointments in the new president's or governor's administration. Indeed, this is a new kind of spoils system that both provides big funding to assist in the election or reelection of executives (and legislators) and secures jobs in the administration in the bargain (Newland, 1987).

Media Politics

American government has always included a special politics of the media; indeed, the adoption of the Constitution depended in part on the Federalists' effective pamphleteering. Some early politicians, most notably Benjamin Franklin, came from the media, which at the time consisted primarily of newspapers, magazines, pamphlets, and books. But the media are probably more influential in politics now than they were in the past. Many television newscasters and anchors have held public office, including former mayor Charles Royer of Seattle, Senator Jesse Helms of North Carolina—and, of course, Ronald Reagan, who gained his initial name recognition as a film star.

In the modern politics of the media, the principal issues have to do with the power of television and the relative ineffectiveness of that medium when it deals in-depth with the complexity of public issues. This is compounded by the remarkable effectiveness that television has when it portrays personalities. As a consequence, we are in an era of high-level personality politics, accompanied by the waning of the political parties and the lessening of our capacity to "process" the complexity of public problems and to develop policies to deal with these problems. Media politics is a double-edged sword that exaggerates the importance of the personalities and private lives of politicians, corporate executives, athletes, film and television stars, and others while punishing them for personal indiscretions or failings.

The new era of media politics involves a great deal of money, particularly to pay for television spots. It should not be surprising that a close connection exists between the expenses of media politics and the emergence of PACs. High-profile media personalities who can command significant PAC resources are able to dominate television coverage.

The effective use of the media has long been a hallmark of good politics. In the administrative arena, J. Edgar Hoover's use of films, magazines, and early television to promote the interests of the FBI is legendary. John F. Kennedy's personal skills with reporters during his term in the Senate sharply increased his effectiveness as a presidential candidate. Ronald Reagan's acting skills were exceptional. Conversely, television did not effectively capture Lyndon Johnson's prodigious political skills. Bill Clinton skirted the centralized Washington, D.C., media establishment and cleverly used grass-roots media in cities all across America. He also used the talk-show format to get "softer" coverage than he would receive from television news reporters. Rush Limbaugh and other conservative talk-show hosts have similarly used the media to undercut Clinton's message as president.

Washington, D.C., virtually every state capital, and most larger American cities are centers of governmental public relations. Public-relations firms advise candidates on how to improve the effectiveness of their presentations. They conduct political polls to determine the interests of the public and to determine how to "package" their clients. Public-relations firms also work closely with administrative agencies to improve the agencies' public image, and of course, interest groups make effective use of these firms. Business corporations not only use public-relations firms to advertise their products—they increasingly hire these firms to make effective public presentations so as to enhance their potential for government grants and contracts or to exercise influence on particular policy issues.

In contemporary American politics, there is a three-way intersection involving (1) the politics of the media, and the expenses associated therewith; (2) interest-group politics and the ability of PACs to raise large sums of money; and (3) electoral politics of both legislators and executives. It is Chester Newland's contention (1987) that these three forces have left "American national government—both the presidency and congress generally—largely mechanisms through which special interests operate in a process of exchange. By contrast, the historical leaders termed great by James MacGregor Burns (1963) engaged in transformational leadership for 'the

achievement of real change in the direction of higher values'"
(Newland, 1987, p. 49).

In all of this, according to Newland, we find a significant
diminution in the administrative effectiveness or capacity of government, particularly at the national and state levels.

The Politics of Government by Proxy

In the past twenty-five years, a new and powerful form of politics
has emerged. It is generally understood that government has
grown dramatically. During this twenty-five-year period, there has
been a sevenfold increase in the size of the federal budget and an
equally dramatic growth in state and local spending. In addition,
the extension of governmental regulation into such fields as environmental protection, equal employment, energy, health care, education, product safety, and economic development has been
described and understood. What has received far less attention,
however, has been an equally fundamental change—one that does
not involve the scope of governmental action but the *form* of that
action (Salamon, 1989). This new form of politics is known vari-
ously as *government by proxy, third-party government,* or *privatization.*

Government by proxy takes a variety of forms. The primary
categories are (Kettl, 1993a):

1. The federal, state, and local governments, which contract with
   the private sector (profit-making corporations and businesses,
   such as Boeing Aircraft; nonprofit organizations, such as mental-health clinics; and not-for-profit organizations, such as the
   Rand Corporation) for goods and services. In 1990, contracts
   amounted to 21 percent of all federal spending, the Defense
   Department being the largest federal contractor. Contracting
   out by government has grown significantly in recent years.
2. Grants and contracts to state and local government, which now
   amount to approximately 11 percent of federal spending. The
   national government provides grants in fields such as interstate
   highways, management of welfare, and construction of sewage
   treatment facilities. States contract out road construction,
   counties contract out mental-health services, and so on.

3. The federal and state tax codes, which have elaborate systems of preferences, breaks, loopholes, and the like. This taxing system enables, in effect, each individual to adjust his or her economic behavior to realize favorable tax circumstances. Even with the Tax Reform Bill of 1986, tax expenditures are still a significant form of privatization. For example, would the housing industry continue to flourish if deductions for interest on both primary and vacation-home mortgages and property taxes were not allowed? By allowing tax deductions for interest on home mortgages and providing low-cost home-ownership loans, the federal government underwrites the housing industry.

4. The lending capacity of the national government, which makes loans for everything from houses to education. More than $1 trillion in loans is now outstanding to the national government. Through these lending programs, the government makes credit available to the individual at lower interest rates than the private sector could provide.

5. The participation of all levels of government in the regulation of both business and personal activity. The costs of regulating private-sector goods and services—such as insuring the safety of drugs and food or licensing businesses—constitute a significant expense. The costs of regulation to government as well as to businesses and citizens who are regulated is unknown and probably immeasurable; however, it is no doubt very large.

During the Reagan administration, the growth of government by proxy was significant. In 1982, President Reagan appointed what came to be known as the Grace Commission, which was headed by the industrialist J. Peter Grace. The commission claimed to find billions of dollars of "savings" that would occur if the national government would either contract out more or privatize the Tennessee Valley Authority, the Bonneville Power Administration, and even the National Parks System. In fact, the Grace Commission, largely because of exaggerated claims and politically unacceptable reform proposals, is now seen as an example of the wrong way to attempt to bring about either policy or management reform in the national government (Downs and Larkey, 1986).

It should not be surprising that this particular perspective on public affairs would tend to be favored by interest groups—and particularly by big business. As a consequence, all of the forms of proxy public administration, shadow bureaucracies, and privatization described above have enjoyed significant political support. For example, the prison-riot scenario at the opening of this chapter is not entirely fictional: contracting out services to a profit-making "prison" company is now a serious alternative, and such companies are presently experiencing rapid growth in the value of their stock.

An additional reason that this perspective has been influential is the closely associated belief that governmental agencies are inefficient—that public employees tend to be primarily concerned with enhancing their own job security and with increasing their agencies' budgets and scope of authority (Buchanan and Tullock, 1962; Downs, 1967). Although this is a widely held view among business leaders, the evidence indicates that government employees are more often motivated by civic duty and the desire to serve others than are persons employed by businesses (Goodsell, 1995).

One important reason for the growth of government by proxy is the influence of the so-called public-choice economists on both the theory and practice of public administration. The public-choice theorists follow the simple assumption that human beings are rational and will favor things that are important to them. According to Schultze (1976), self-interest and individual rationality are seen as desirable, and the public-choice theorists would hold that "the desirable mode of carrying out economic and social activities is through a network of private and voluntary arrangements—called, for short, 'the private market.' The theory of social intervention is thus concerned with defining the conditions under which that presumption is indeed rebuttable. We think of the public sector as intervening in the private sector and not vice versa" (p. 13).

In this concept of public affairs, the government is to serve as the arena for the exchange of private interests or preferences. In other words, the government becomes a market. James M. Buchanan, one of the principal proponents of public-choice theory, won the 1986 Nobel Prize in economics for his initial descriptions of the theory. The public sector would provide fewer services directly and would rely more on the private sector for achieving government's goals. Put another way, the idea is to *provide services* without *producing services*. Following the theory, privatization would transfer the actual provision of services to the private sector—where, economic theorists believe, the pressures of competition would improve efficiency.

Donald F. Kettl (1993a, 1993b) reviewed several federal forms of government by proxy. His analysis includes the Defense Department contracts for building the Sergeant York tank, the growth of federal grants to state and local government, the 1986 tax reform, the federal student-aid program, the farm-loan crisis, and the deregulation of airlines. He concludes that the values of government on the one hand and proxies on the other are usually different: more graft and corruption probably occur under government by proxy than in more traditional forms of public administration, and there are deeply serious problems of accountability when things go wrong.

Managing Public Agencies in a Political Context

Career professional public administrators understand that they must function in a political context. Ordinarily, however, they come to this understanding with some conception of the politics-administration dichotomy, assuming that politics and administration are distinct and should be distinct.

As we have learned, administrative values are not the same as the values of elected executives or elected legislators. Administrative values include partisan neutrality; selection and promotion on the basis of merit, specialization, and expertise; the use of information for analyzing public-policy issues; record-keeping for purposes of continuity; application of the work ethic; and the justification of decisions based on efficiency (achieving the most productivity for the money available) or economy (achieving a given level of productivity for as little money as possible) or both. To put these values into effect, administrators think in terms of "principles and practices," such as strategic planning, matching responsibility with authority, using hierarchy and its companions, spanning control and chain of command, and requiring specialization and expertise.

Following these principles and practices, administrators assume rationality in decision making. Rationality through the use of cost-benefit analyses would determine the most efficient and effective policies possible, and the administrator would then proceed to implement those policies.

In American politics, power tends to be dispersed, divided, and decentralized. Effective administration finds the concentration of power useful. In the political world, power belongs to politicians, interest groups, and the citizenry, whereas for purposes of administrative efficiency it is important that power be given to experts and professionals. In the world of elected officials, bargaining and accommodation are part of the democratic process, while in administrative efficiency there is a desire to keep politics out of the processes. In the political world, the individuals' and politicians' preferences or interests are paramount, while in administrative practice efficiency—technical or scientific rationality determined on the basis of detached analysis—is the means by which to decide interests (Yates, 1982).

Given these contrasting values, it should not be surprising that a fragmented government operating on broadly democratic principles is Madisonian—that is, often inefficient and uneconomical. Douglas Yates suggests that these values can be reconciled by a "combination of centralized planning and goal-setting and decentralized implementation and service delivery" (1982, p. 200).

A pattern of administrative politics and power can be discerned that is fundamental to the operations of government. Indeed, Harold Seidman and Robert Gilmour (1986) suggest that "economy and efficiency are demonstratively *not* the prime purpose of public administration. . . . [The basic issue of] organization and administration relate to power: who shall control it and to what ends?" (p. 28). And there is little doubt that an adequate theory of public administration must also be a theory of politics (Waldo, 1990).

The Spirit of Public Administration, which is also a theory of politics in the Hamiltonian tradition, has the following features:

• First, in most legislatures there is a lack of cohesive and continuing policy majorities able to form clear-cut mandates for administrators to follow. Administrators must, therefore, take responsibility for bringing some definition to the fuzziness and ambiguity of the programmatic intent of statutes. The wise public administrator will attempt to fashion a mandate by carefully seeking support and understanding from critical elements in the legislature and in the staff of the elected executive; he or she will also try to find as much support as possible with interest groups and among the public. There is little doubt that effective administration requires the administrator to practice this kind of politics. In modern public administration, this is called *entrepreneurial leadership* (Bryson and Crosby, 1992).

• Second, legislation often calls for sweeping mandates. As Lerner and Wanat (1983) point out, "Legislators, not being technical experts, frequently write laws embodying goals that are exemplary but which lack details. Skeletal legislation, as it is frequently called, is phrased in occasionally grand and, therefore, fuzzy terms. The implementing agency is told by the legislature [in national, state, or local government] to provide a *safe* environment for workers to see that school children are served meals with *adequate* nutritional content . . . to *assist* the *visually impaired,* to maintain *adequate* income levels, and so on" (p. 500).

Not only is enabling legislation fuzzy, but the steps to be taken to implement that legislation are rarely clear-cut. It is, therefore, the effective administrator's responsibility to design those steps and to make them as practical and politically feasible as possible. The administrator must "clear" them with key elements in the legislature, with the chief executive, and with relevant interest groups.

• Third, expertise and specialization are fundamental to effective administrative politics. The basis of bureaucratic power consists of (1) full-time attention by experts to a problem or subject area, giving rise to both demand and opportunity for professionalism in public service; (2) specialization in the subject; (3) a monopoly on information in the subject area, which if successfully maintained by one's own staff experts makes them indispensable in any decision making involving "their own" subject; (4) a pattern of increasing reliance on bureaucratic experts for technical advice; and (5) increasing control by experts of bureaucratic discretion (Rourke, 1984). Public administration no longer has the level of domination over expertise that it once had. Expertise is now shared with the staffs of legislative committees as well as with some experts on the immediate staff of the chief executive. The effective program manager will, therefore, serve in a bridging or transactional role and attempt to keep all of the experts informed and working in the same policy direction.

• Fourth, in the politics of government by proxy, Kettl (1993a) and Salamon (1989) suggest that there should be much greater attention given, on the part of both elected officials and public administrators, to the "co-alignment" of goals. Because the values of governmental agencies and proxies are different, they suggest a mechanism for reviewing goals and for using a system of feedback to co-align goals, so that government and the proxies doing governmental business are more nearly synchronized. Tucker further suggests a new role of leadership for program administrators: their job is to serve a diagnostic function, to provide feedback, and to "define the situation authoritatively for the group" (1983, pp. 19–20).

Elected and appointed government officials alike should give much greater concern to the questions of accountability and performance in the tangled web of proxy government. Government officials now have responsibility for programs that they do not really control. In Kettl's view (1993a), "as government by proxy has grown, the success of government programs has come to depend more on all Americans and their sense of citizenship. All of those responsible for the performance of government—whether part of government or not—must recognize their broader responsibility to the public for their behavior. Accountability thus has to extend beyond creating government mechanisms to detect and cure problems. Whether filling out an income tax form, taking out a government loan, following a federal regulation or working for a government contractor, each citizen plays an important role in making programs work" (p. 161). Kettl's view closely parallels the conception of the public in public administration set out in Chapter One.

Modern government by proxy presents a significant new challenge to public administration theory and to administrative practice. Our classical theory is generally hostile to the phenomenon of third-party government because it poses a threat to accountability. In the classical theory, political power is to be centralized in the hands of elected executives who exercise control over professional public administrators, who in turn are held accountable for what their agencies do. Third-party government violates these principles because (1) it fragments power, (2) it obscures who is doing what, and (3) it severs lines of control (Salamon, 1989).

Effective public management, then, cannot rely on control through the hierarchy, the use of budgeting and personnel techniques, or other management theories that emphasize internal bureaucratic controls. Public management has spilled beyond the borders of the governmental agency. The effective public manager

will understand the manipulation of "a complex network of play-
ers and institutions over which the public manager has only imperfect control, yet on which he or she must depend to operate an
agency's programs" (Salamon, 1989, p. 20).

• Fifth, partisan neutrality is part of the professional public administrator's concept of governmental work. The effective program
administrator will not, however, be expected to be neutral about the
mission of the agency with which he or she is associated. Governmental agencies, like all organizations, expect employees to be both
professionally qualified and dedicated to their responsibilities—
and the citizens who pay the bills deserve to be served by dedicated
professionals.

One characteristic of qualified and dedicated professionals is
the tendency to advocate their specialization (see Chapter Three).
The best social workers, schoolteachers, FBI agents, and soldiers
all believe in their work and expect to have sufficient resources and
support to do their jobs properly. One of the biggest challenges to
public servants is doing the best they can with the resources available, especially when they know that additional funding would
make them more effective.

In the competition for public funding, is it unreasonable to expect the U.S. Department of Agriculture, for example, to be neutral? The department's leaders will actively seek the funding they
believe is necessary to accomplish their responsibilities, as will the
leaders of other departments. One should not mistake the commitment to partisan neutrality to mean that public administrators
will be neutral in the competition for funding. In fact, the effective administrator will make the best possible case for his or her
agency—will seek support, but will recognize the point at which
advocacy oversteps partisan neutrality and becomes politics that
can affect elections. This can require a careful balancing of advocacy and neutrality—and once the budget is passed, the effective
administrator will provide the best or the most services possible for
the dollars available.

• Sixth, public administrators are often at a point in the governmental system at which the public may need their constitutional
guarantees. Effective public administration requires a solid grounding in the Constitution and in court interpretations of the Constitution. In fact, administrators—and especially attorneys in the

administrative branch—often find it necessary to advise (that is, warn) elected executives and legislators of the limits of majority rule in light of the rights of the individual.

• Seventh, public administrators are the lubrication that makes the federal system work. Most governmental functions now involve all three levels of government. The public administrator must, therefore, understand the role that each level of government plays in his or her particular function. As Derthick (1987) puts it, effective administrators know that "bargaining and negotiation, not command and obedience, appear to characterize the practice of intergovernmental programs now, as in the past" (p. 69). This is especially critical as the responsibility for public programs is being developed from the national level to state and local levels.

In summary, technical expertise is expected of good public administrators, but effective political skills are what make the spirit of public administration possible. This is especially the case with higher-level or leadership positions in public agencies. Working with elected officials, within the constitutional order, and with good political skills, public administration leaders are essential to democratic government. And when this is done well, the politics of public administration becomes a noble calling and an expression of the human capacity to govern for the general good.

Chapter Three

Public Administration as Governance

The greatest mistake citizens can make when they complain of "the bureaucracy" is to suppose that their frustrations arise simply out of management problems; they do not—they arise out of governance problems.
JAMES Q. WILSON, *BUREAUCRACY*, P. 376

Not only is this an antibureaucratic era, it is also an antigovernment era, an antitax era, and an anti-institution era. The symbols and rhetoric of contemporary politics reflect, amplify, and exaggerate the "anti" characteristics of the present era (Edelman, 1977). Consequently, these are very difficult times for a public administration that tends to be governmental, organizational, and expensive. Despite such circumstances, public administration has demonstrated considerable adaptability and creativity. Part of these qualities are substantive, involving new managerial and organizational theories and techniques. An equally important response to the antigovernment and antibureaucratic mood is conceptual. This chapter describes one of the primary modern concepts of public administration.

In contemporary public administration, the concept of choice is governance. *Governance* is a word and concept that performs a kind of rhetorical distancing of public administration from politics, government, and bureaucracy. In their popularized and influential book *Reinventing Government* (1992), David Osborne and Ted Gaebler write that "this is a book about governance, not politics" (p. 247). As we shall learn, there are many other generous examples of the use of governance as public administration. The following section of this chapter covers the *description* of public administration as governance. Following the consideration of description, we attempt to *define* public administration as governance. Once governance is defined, we sketch out the implications of that definition.

Public Administration as Governance: Some Descriptions

Many leading contemporary scholars of public administration use the word *governance* as either a companion to the term *public administration* or a surrogate for it (Kettl, 1993a; Salamon, 1989; Garvey, 1993; Peters and Savoie, 1995; John, Kettl, Dyer, and Lovan, 1994; Lan and Rosenbloom, 1992). These scholars compare traditional public administration with a "new theory" that is sometimes clearly labeled governance and sometimes not. Garvey (1993) describes an old theory emerging from the Progressive Era—one based on expertise, specialization, a merit-selected civil service, institution building, a science of administration, and an assumption of a collective public interest. The new theory, by comparison, is based on a premise that "humans are strongly rational and they are dominantly driven by self-interest" (p. 3). Using market logic, privatization, contracting out, the logic of transaction costs, and issue networks, Garvey states:

> The New Theory also helps us understand the origin of that fundamental structure of modern governance, the issue network (Heclo, 1978). Whenever decision makers become aware of a buildup of avoidable transaction costs in their relationships with one another, they are likely to respond by organizing an informal issue network. Public officials and private decision makers, noting the need for constant coordination and exchanges of information, develop informal but continuing and cooperative relationships. Networking can be viewed as a perfectly natural response to problems, especially the problem of coordination across the public-private interface, that are inherent in modern governance [p. 7].

Lester Salamon (1989), while not using the word governance, presents a comparison of traditional public administration that is essentially the same as Garvey's.

Traditional public administration, with its focus on the management
and control of governmental agencies, has only limited relevance
to the operation of many of these newer forms of public action.
Where traditional public administration emphasizes the internal
dynamics of public agencies, the newer forms of action often involve elaborate partnership arrangements with nongovernmental
actors. Where traditional public administration stresses hierarchical
lines of authority and the mechanisms of command and control,
the newer forms of action utilize decentralized modes of operation
and the techniques of bargaining and persuasion" [p. 255].

In Donald F. Kettl's splendid treatment (1993a) of federal government contracting, he labels one chapter "Managing Versus Governing" (pp. 199–212) and uses distinctions similar to those of
Garvey and Salamon. In treating the specific topic of contracting
out, Kettl makes these distinctions:

Government's role has changed. Government is less the producer of
goods and services, and more the supervisor of proxies who do the
actual work. In more traditional programs, where government itself
produces goods or services, top managers give orders, which they
expect agency employees to follow. . . . What matters is the presence
of a hierarchical chain that links, whether well or poorly, those who
shape policy with those on the front lines of service delivery.

In public-private partnerships, contracts replace hierarchy. Instead
of a chain of authority from policy to product, there is a negotiated
document that separates policymaker from policy output. Top officials cannot give orders to contractors. They can threaten, cajole,
or persuade, but in the end, they can only shape the incentives
to which the contractors respond. There is a gap in the chain of
authority, which the contract fills.

The argument here is not that the contractual relationship, which
lies at the core of the competition prescription, is prone to breakdown, but that it entails a *different kind* of public management
[pp. 21–22].

As we reviewed in Chapter Two, there is a more sweeping set
of distinctions (Kettl, 1993a). Much of what is characterized here
as traditional or old theory could be categorized as Hamiltonian—
that is, as Kettl puts it, "associated with a vigorous state with a

strong administrative apparatus. . . [seeing] the task of administration as carrying out publicly defined goals effectively [and seeing] an energetic government doing good" (p. 407). Many, although not all, of the features of the new theory—the public-administration-as-governance approach—are Madisonian: "wary about too much government action . . . cautious about the concentration of governmental—especially administrative—power" (p. 407). It should be no surprise, then, that public administration as governance, in the extent to which it is Madisonian, is popular politics in the present antigovernment era.

B. Guy Peters concludes a recent collection of studies of public administration in several countries with a chapter titled "Governance in a Changing Environment" (Peters and Savoie, 1995). Peters makes distinctions similar to those of Garvey, Salamon, and Kettl. He writes that there has been a

> decline of the assumption of hierarchical and rule-based management within the public service, and the authority of civil servants to implement and enforce regulations outside the public service. The neat Weberian model of management does not apply within public organizations to the extent that it once did, and in its place we encounter a variety of alternative sources of organizational power and authority. As one example, the market may be an increasingly significant standard against which to compare the structure and performance of governmental organizations. While the inherent differences between the public and private sectors are crucial to understanding governance . . . even governments on the political left have implemented a number of market-based reforms in their structures and procedures [p. 289].

By far the most sophisticated treatment of the concept of governance is by James G. March and Johan P. Olsen in *Democratic Governance* (1995). They describe two perspectives on governance. One is the exchange perspective, which essentially mirrors the description of governance used by the authors cited earlier who equate modern public administration with governance. In the exchange perspective, March and Olsen find rational (bounded) actor assumptions, competition, markets, bargains, the crafting of winning coalitions, and utilitarian concepts of Pareto-improving criteria by which changed policies leave at least one person better off and no person worse off. But the purpose of March and Olsen's argument is to challenge the exchange concept of governance with an institutional or new institutionalism concept of governance in which rules, rights, a collective instinct toward the common good, and identifiable roles are associated with actors in the governance process. March and Olsen essentially confirm the contemporary primary conception of governance as exchange. They agree that governance is the appropriate metaphor, but they strongly argue that governance should be defined institutionally rather than as exchange.

Although they also do not use the word governance to describe modern public administration, Lan and Rosenbloom (1992) present essentially the same distinctions. In what they call "marketized" public administration, there are diverse competitive service centers, flat hierarchies, entrepreneurial leaders, contracting out, competition, empowered citizens making choices, hollowed-out career service, and a generalized market orientation. Lan and Rosenbloom add legal perspectives to marketized public administration involving alternative dispute resolution, contract negotiations, and individual responsibility and liability.

In the prestigious National Academy of Public Administration (NAPA), governance is an especially broadly used word and concept. A recent summary of NAPA's work with the U.S. Department of Agriculture's Rural Development Initiative describes a "new governance" and states that "President Clinton is a member of the movement for a new governance" (John, Kettl, Dyer, and Lovan, 1994, p. 170). This new governance is approximately the same as each of the preceding descriptions of governance in public administration, and it is also essentially the same as the "reinventing government" argument. The NAPA report suggests that this movement is reaching "critical mass" (p. 175).

Finally, in *Reinventing Government* (1992), Osborne and Gaebler set out the now well-known dichotomies that distinguish entrepreneurial and bureaucratic approaches to public administration. Because they use the word governance extensively, it would seem fair to regard the entrepreneurial approach and governance as essentially the same thing. If these words were interchangeable, the dichotomies would read:

Governance	*Bureaucracy*
Steering	Rowing
Empowering	Service
Competition	Monopoly
Mission-driven	Role-driven
Funding outcomes	Budgeting inputs
Customer-driven	Bureaucracy-driven
Earning	Spending
Preventing	Curing
Teamwork/participation	Hierarchy
Market	Organization

The single most interesting facet of the Osborne and Gaebler perspective is its essential similarity to the governance perspective that is now broadly influential in the "new public management" described and advocated by many leading public administration scholars.

Governance: The Search for Definition

Webster's Third New International Dictionary notwithstanding, in public administration we appear to define governance as it suits us.[1] To paraphrase Lewis Carroll ([1871] 1960), "When we use governance, it means just what we choose it to mean, neither more nor less." Many in the field regard this as an entirely useful and acceptable practice—a kind of public administration construction of a preferred reality through the development and use of symbols and metaphors. Others argue that this unique use of the word governance violates

---

1. *Webster's Third New International Dictionary* (1986) defines *governance* first as "the act or process of governing," or "government." Governance may also mean "the office, power, or function of governing," "the state of being governed," "the manner or method of governing" as in "the conduct of office," or "a system of governing."

The pivotal word, then, is governing, which is a verbal noun.

To govern means "to exercise arbitrarily or by established rules continuous sovereign authority over," or especially "to control and direct the making and administration of policy in." *Governing* means controlling or directing influence or the manner or method of conduct of office.

the traditions of shared meanings out of which public administration arose.

Before we engage this debate, we will set out what appear to be the contemporary definitions of public administration as governance. This is necessary because the term governance often is used without definition, without presenting a logical underpinning for the word, and without conceptual rigor. It is likely that some who use the word in their speech or writing know what *they* mean by governance, but choose not to define it because they assume that readers or listeners know the intended meaning. Others who use the word governance to mean public administration may appreciate the emotive power of the word but may not have given serious consideration to its fundamental meaning.

The first and most evident meaning of governance as public administration is that it describes a wide range of types of organizations and institutions that are linked together and engaged in public activities. For example, the phrases *public management* and *public administration* are weak descriptors of a metropolitan-area transportation system, while governance is an excellent descriptor of such a system.

The splendid research on redundancy in the San Francisco Bay Area's transportation system describes several modes of transport provided by governmental, nongovernmental, nonprofit, and mixed entities (Landau, 1991). Such a system is not managed or administered, at least not in the classic meaning of those words. But the network of organizations and leaders in such a transportation system collectively engages in governance. Although it might put too fine a point on the distinction, the chief executive of BART (the Bay Area Rapid Transit, an autonomous public special district operating a subway and surface rail system) would practice public administration in the internal management of BART and would practice governance through interjurisdictional coordination with cities and counties, as well as through coordination with other transportation providers. Some people would call these *networks* (Lynn, 1996).

Some have always defined public administration or public management very broadly to include what is defined here as governance. Still, the word governance is probably the best and most generally accepted metaphor for describing the patterns of inter-action of multiple-organizational systems or networks.

In international affairs, the stark contrast between governance and government, and the definition of governance as the management of multiple organizational systems, is clearly evident. This approach is especially informative because it is at the level of the nation-state that sovereignty is assumed, and the government is assumed to be the symbol of authority. No longer. Rosenau and Czempiel recently edited a book with the telling title *Governance Without Government: Order and Change in World Politics* (1992). In his homage to Fred W. Riggs, Lucien W. Pye (1992) describes the "myth of the state" and "the reality of authority."All of this international-relations literature describes a governance that transcends national borders—a governance of open systems of information, international corporations, and regional alliances. There are forms of order and authority in this governance, and there are managers and bureaucrats managing this governance. All of this is "public," but only some of it is governmental.

The March and Olsen concept (1995) of loosely coupled systems is another form of governance. Such systems are an alternative to both centralization and hierarchy and are, therefore, especially popular in the modern world of governance. Loose coupling in an organization describes high levels of delegation and decentralization mixed with fuzzy boundaries between subelements of the organization, its clients or customers, and other organizations.

This definition of public administration as governance assumes to reconcile the difference between things public and things governmental described in Chapter One. In governance, the network of action involves the full range of public organizations—governmental, nongovernmental, for-profit, nonprofit, state, and parastatel. Thus, the domain of public administration is considerably enlarged. In this larger domain, the distinctions between things political and things administrative is also blurred. So public administration as governance presumes to reconcile the old politics-administration dichotomy as well; and as we reviewed in Chapter Two, the dichotomy has been reinforced by the separation of powers. It should come as no surprise, then, that public administration as governance presumes to bridge the separation of powers for the purpose of making public organizations more effective. We will take up these issues again later in this chapter.

A close cousin of the first definition of governance is the use of that word to comprehend contemporary pluralism and hyper-pluralism, which was described in Chapters One and Two. In this case, however, governance includes all of the so-called stakehold-ers: political parties, legislative bodies and their subdivisions, in-terest groups, intermediaries, organizations, clients, the media, vendors, and so forth. Thus, governance is a useful descriptor of high complexity, both in making and implementing policy. Years ago, Harlan Cleveland (1972), in his usual prescient way, described public administration as "interlaced webs of tension in which con-trol is loose, power diffused, and centers of decision plural" (p. 13). Now, in the mid-1990s, this part of public administration would most likely be described as governance.

In Chapter Two, we described the pluralistic context of modern public administration. In hyperpluralism, it is, in fact, the public-administration-as-governance argument that presumes to provide the glue holding the stakeholders together in some semblance of order. The interesting twist here is that public administrators, not elected politicians, are doing the governance.

The third meaning of governance is associated with modern trends in the literature of public management and is often associated with management specialists in public policy schools (Garvey, 1993; Behn, 1991; Doig, 1983; DiIulio, 1994). Governance accounts for the multi-institutional-organizational setting in which contemporary lead-ers and policy entrepreneurs carry out policy implementation. Their work in a governance setting is more freewheeling, more political, more inclined to taking risks, and more creative and empowered; and less organizational, hierarchical, rule-bound, and managerial than is the work of traditional public administrators.

To some extent, this distinction turns on defining governance as working in and among both horizontal and vertical networks of organizations to achieve some public purpose, in contrast with managing the inside, day-to-day affairs of a single institution. Of course, one can fairly argue that public administration has always included what is presently described as governance. Nevertheless, governance is a powerful and legitimizing descriptor for this very important aspect of public administration.

The fourth meaning of governance is seldom explicit but almost always implied. Governance implies importance. Governance implies legitimacy. Governance implies a dignified, positive contribution to the achievement of public purposes. While government and bureaucracy may be despised, governance is considered acceptable, legitimate, and perhaps even good. Traditional public administration is viewed as hierarchical, slow, and lacking in imagination, while governance is seen as creative and responsive.

When taken together, these four definitions of governance constitute a concept, or a set of concepts, that is in many ways useful to public administration both as a professional field of practice and as an academic discipline. It can be argued that this concept of governance carries with it a considerable empirical warrant. In the real world of practice there is actual and observable governance in the existential sense, and it is surely a scientific and theoretically describable phenomenon. When governance is studied and described, it ordinarily includes at least some of the characteristics set out in the four definitions of the term.

These definitions of governance are not inconsistent, contrasting, or competitive. Together they move from a list of definitions to a relatively cohesive concept or set of concepts.

In an antigovernment, anti-institution, and bureaucrat-bashing era, a word and concept such as governance is a helpful antidote. If some political leaders, journalists, and scholars use the word bureaucracy as a powerful rhetorical sword against public administration, merit-based civil service, and bureaucracy, then it seems altogether appropriate for modern public administration to co-opt the word governance and use it in a positive way to describe and define what is good in both the study and practice of public administration.

The Strengths and Limitations of Public Administration as Governance

Any serious student of the field will recognize that the use of the word and concept governance to describe public administration is laden with problems—both of practice or application and of conceptual rigor.

The first practical problem is one of emphasis. Governance emphasizes interinstitutional coordination, entrepreneurial creativity, experimentation, and risk taking. It does not emphasize those features of management of agencies and organizations that often are highly prized—order, predictability, stability, responsibility, and equity. Governance emphasizes the choice, competition, and decision-cost perspectives. Despite claims to the contrary, such emphases are favorable to those who are in a position to make sensible choices and who can compete. Governance does not emphasize fairness and equity when it is understood that fairness and equity are almost always primary decision criteria in a democratic polity (Hochschield, 1981; Rae and Associates, 1981; Frederickson, 1990). Governance emphasizes the top of the pyramid and what goes on there; it does not emphasize the line or the points in public administration at which bureaucrat encounters citizen or customer. This is rowing.

The problems of alienation (Lipsky, 1980) and power (Long, 1949) at the line are not emphasized except to suggest that customers should have choices. In the freewheeling entrepreneurial spirit of governance, there is little emphasis on responsibility and accountability, both of which are fundamental concepts in representative government (Romzek and Dubnick, 1987; Denhardt, 1988; Thompson, 1987). Finally, and most important in practice, the governance emphasis is on policymaking by nonelected public officials. We will return to this issue in the last part of this chapter.

The second practical problem with public administration as governance has two parts. The governance perspective is presented as a reform—a better way to do public administration. Proposals for reform often are oversold and hyperbolic (Downs and Larkey, 1986). In this case, it is argued that, as the National Performance Review (1993) puts it, reforms associated with the governance perspective will result in a "government that works better and costs less." To deliver on that promise, the "savings" mentioned in the National Performance Review are being taken up front, with a goal of eliminating 250,000 federal positions.

The extent to which the federal government "works better"— and for whom it works better—will take time to determine. In one view, the sharp reduction in the federal workforce will hollow out the government, reducing its capacity to be effective and diminishing the institutional memory (Milward, Provan, and Else, 1993). In another view, the hollowing out of government will make it more effective precisely *because* of downsizing, outsourcing, and contracting. Rather than staffing an agency and its services, the government will comprise contract officers, with services provided by contractors. The record of the national government as a contractor is less than sterling, however, so positive expectations from the expansion of contracting out require a considerable leap of faith (Kettl, 1993a).

In the recent assessment of the five years of reform using a governance perspective under the leadership of Lawton Chiles, the current two-term governor of Florida, Berry, Chackerian, and Weschler (1995) reach the following conclusions:

> The lessons of Florida's administrative reform effort are complex—they reflect the real difficulties encountered in reinventing government. Lawton Chiles and Buddy MacKay promised that they would fundamentally change government and governmental operations. Underlying their approach was the assumption that these reforms would benefit all of the affected stakeholders—citizens, state government managers, and public employees. Not surprisingly, the stakeholders had very different interests, and these personal, organizational, and political interests produced considerable resistance to virtually every element of the reform package. As a consequence, Florida's reforms have gone slowly and have had an uneven impact. The reformers themselves were not without blame for these results. The administration overpromised what would come from their efforts, emphasized symbolic over substantive change, lost interest at critical moments, and adopted popular nostrums that were often contradictory or inapplicable to Florida's situations. Nonetheless, some important changes have occurred, and current efforts to deregulate government and to link budgeting to measurable outcomes show considerable promise. As we said earlier in the paper, five years into the reinvention effort we can identify important lessons; however, the final story of Florida's reforms will be told in the future [p. 28].

One practical feature of public administration as governance is clear: it makes for resoundingly popular politics for elected executives and those who would be elected executives. In the 1990s, virtually every candidate for mayor or governor in the United States has promised to reinvent government more or less along the lines of the governance perspective. The rhetoric of governance rather than government—and government that works better and costs less—is just as useful to mayors and governors as it is to public administrators. Of course, it is especially interesting that while he was governor of Arkansas, Bill Clinton used the ideas associated with governance and learned both their managerial utility and their political usefulness. So with the coincidental publication of Osborne and Gaebler's *Reinventing Government* in 1992 and the Clinton-Gore campaign, we saw formalized at the national level a new fusion of public administration, governance, and politics. As Dwight Waldo (1949) always taught us, public administration is a form of politics.

The conceptual and philosophical problems with the use of governance as a surrogate term for public administration go to the core of our field.

The word and concept governance is a form of rhetorical reconciliation of the politics-administration or policy-administration dichotomy. Because there is no politics-administration dichotomy in the modern view, it is unnecessary to ask whether a particular activity in the governance process is correctly regarded as either politics or administration. In the received wisdom there are elements of politics in administration, and of administration in politics, so governance seems a perfectly good way to describe public administration. The received wisdom also teaches us, however, that some domains of democratic government or the democratic polity are (or ought to be) the political representation of the people, while other domains should be based primarily on expertise, administration, or management. When public administration becomes governance, the importance of the proper distinctions between these domains is diminished.

At one level, it is exciting, even exhilarating, for a public administration to be made bold, legitimate, and engaged as a form of governance across the full range of governmental processes. At another level, however, it is risky—even dangerous. Could public administration be unwittingly shifting from the model of professional, politically neutral managers carrying out the daily affairs of government—the law in action—to public administration as merely another form of politics or another political idea? The widespread contemporary use of the word governance to describe public administration suggests that this question needs to be addressed by both theorists and practitioners.

The word and concept governance substitutes managerial words and ideas for political and policy issues. Some believe that by governance or "reinvention" it will be possible to manage our way through policy issues. Downs and Larkey (1986) identify this feature of reform movements as "the wrong problems problem," in which policy issues are defined as managerial problems and are approached as issues of efficiency, cost savings, and incentives. By using wrong-problems techniques, policymakers can avoid making tough choices. In public administration as governance, we can have all of our policy choices because we are downsizing and managing better. In public administration as governance, there is more than a little evidence of the wrong-problems problem.

The leadership features of governance are also problematic. After years of downsizing, rightsizing, and load shedding, it comes as no surprise that our public institutions suffer from diminished capacity. Our institutions are weak. And because they are weakened, we more clearly see the need for strong leaders. Somehow we imagine that confident, entrepreneurial types will transform our weak institutions, but will it be possible for even the most heroic leaders to significantly improve the functioning of under-staffed institutions?

In the logic of public administration as governance, we imagine lean and flexible public institutions with muscular entrepreneurial leaders and empowered workers. In addition, more of the work would be privatized and contracted out. Put this way, it indicates that those who presently do public work are probably ineffective. Public administration can be improved only if fewer workers are involved and if we contract out, because private organizations and nonprofits can do it better and more economically; however, there is little evidence that business can take on public tasks more effectively or cheaply than can governments (Kettl, 1993b).

There is every possibility that the results of such a public administration will not be the joy of reinvention that managers imagine. Rather, it may produce a demoralized public workforce with a reduced commitment to public service—in part because public organizations have a reduced commitment to the workforce. In the end, there may be dim prospects for a more efficient or equitable public administration.

Public administration as governance is a distinctly political description and definition of the field. Although Osborne and Gaebler (1992) argue that governance is not politics, everyone else understands it to be just that—and it is especially useful politics for elected executives.

Conclusions

In 1950, John Gaus used this sentence to close an essay on trends in public administration: "A theory of public administration means in our time a theory of politics also" (p. 168). Dwight Waldo used that sentence as the title to a 1990 critique of the field.

To Waldo (1990), all theories of management and organization are political, at least in the sense that they favor or put into effect certain values such as efficiency or equity. As he demonstrated, all states either are administrative states or they are not states. If all public administration is, at a fundamental level, political, then what can be said of public administration as governance? Donald Kettl (1993a) offers an answer in his prescient observation that "no theory of politics is complete without a theory of administration" (p. 408). It is likely that governance is the preferred modern theory that attempts to marry politics to administration.

We suggest these conclusions:

- First, governance is a positive symbol at a time when positive symbols are sorely needed in public administration.
- Second, governance is a remarkable fusion of popular literature on government reform, popular executive politics, serious empirical scholarship, and modern public administration theory.
- Third, in public administration as governance—as in all reforms—the windup is better than the pitch.
- Fourth, the use of governance as a surrogate for public administration masks the fundamental issue of what ought to be the role of nonelected public officials in a democratic polity.

Governance represents a swashbuckling, muscular, and yet thinner (that is, downsized) approach to public administration—a sharp contrast to the earlier notion of public administrators trained with "a passion for anonymity" (Appleby, 1945). For decades, people in public administration have attempted to emphasize neutrality and to distance the field, at least rhetorically, from politics. Although it is seldom forthright about it, governance *is* political. I recall Henry Reining, when he was dean of the School of Public Administration at the University of Southern California, making a statement that is apropos: "Good city management is the practice of the arts and sciences of politics, but always in the language of management."

The dangers inherent in public administration as governance are many. Because it is so closely connected to particular elected executives, it is at political risk. The marketized model deemphasizes the role, and possibly the strength, of government. Serious issues of equity may plague governance approaches to public administration. The approach may also raise questions of legitimacy regarding the proper range of policymaking power and the exercise of authority by civil servants and nonelected public officials.

We close with an observation about lost opportunities and future prospects. Public administration has always been about governance, not merely management. The great scholars of our field, as well as our leading role models from practice, have always emphasized the broader issues of governance—the Constitution, the interplay of democratic institutions, the well-being of the community, the public interest, and the morality of administrative actions. As described by Evans and Wamsley (1995), these scholars and role models have

> recognized that the coherence and sense of stability provided by institutions of governance cannot be reduced to management technique. . . . Governance inescapably involves . . . "accepting responsibility for the whole life of the institution . . . it has the care of a community or quasi-community" (Selznick, 1957, p. 290). Governance is both an inherently political and an inherently moral enterprise—something outside the capacity of the . . . "well-ordered world of expertise and rationality, of deference and limited commitment"—public management—where ends are taken as given and instrumental means are the sole focus of concern. Governance, thus, is more about the evocation of a relationship between citizens and their government than it is about steering toward some sort of collective goal [p. 13].

Public administration as governance is here, is fashionable, and is in many ways helpful. But the descriptions and definitions of public administration as governance are, as March and Olsen (1995) tell us, essentially a public administration of exchange. That public administration suffers from the weaknesses described above; but more important, it lacks the strengths of a definition of public administration as governance that is not only associated with exchange but is deeply associated with institutions. Governance, properly understood, requires strong political institutions and equally strong administrative institutions. Both are critically important for the effective management of exchange, and they are equally important for the crucial management of redistribution when market or nonmarket failures occur. Strong political and administrative institutions are essential to developing a shared political culture and in building and maintaining the general framework by which citizens and their leaders practice democratic self-government (March and Olsen, 1995).

In public administration as governance, it is essential that we do not diminish our institutions to such an extent that we lose our capacity to support the development of sound public policy, as well as our ability to effectively implement that policy. If public administration as governance is to succeed, we must have at our disposal the dynamics of exchange, the order of institutions, and the moral grounding of democratic legitimacy.

Part Two

Issues of Fairness

Chapter Four

The Question of
Administrative Discretion

*To demonstrate that American students of administration
have elaborated theories of "Who should rule?" is
unnecessary labor. The assertion that there is a field of
expertise which has, or should have, a place in and claim
upon the exercise of modern government functions—this is
a fundamental postulate of the public administration
movement.*

DWIGHT WALDO, *THE ADMINISTRATIVE STATE*, PP. 90–91

The introduction and first three chapters of *The Spirit of Public Administration* treated the public and political context of the field. We turn now to a key element of the book: fairness and equity. Chapters Four and Five describe the development and application of the concept of social equity. In Chapter Seven, we specifically discuss the challenging issue of intergenerational equity.

Introduction

In American public administration, efficiency and economy have long been the twin pillars of theory. Efficiency—to achieve as much public good as possible for the available dollars—is a compelling rationale for administrative practices. Economy—to accomplish a public goal for the fewest possible tax dollars—is an equally beguiling objective. Much of contemporary public administration, and especially the public choice and policy analysis perspectives on public administration, uses efficiency and economy as the correct measures by which to evaluate policy or assess its implementation.

Evidence shows that concern for equity in public administration did not begin with the advocates of new public administration. Woodrow Wilson provides such evidence in a speech to his followers on election night in 1912: "I summon you for the rest of your lives to work to set this government forward by processes of justice, equity, and fairness. I myself have no feeling of triumph tonight. I have a feeling of solemn responsibility" (cited by Link, 1971).

In the early twentieth century, when corruption threatened to overcome the purposes and methods of government, reformers rallied support for efficiency and economy, the more familiar pillars of public administration. While the reformers sought public values that went beyond economy and efficiency, no other values came to be associated with public administration at that time. This was consistent with the view that policymaking and administration were separate functions. The antidote for incompetent and corrupt government was an administrative government concerned with economy and efficiency.

Efficiency and economy were necessary but not sufficient as guides for public administration (Frederickson, 1971, pp. 309–332, 1980). A third pillar of theory, social equity, had to be added to make the field responsive to the needs of the citizens. A governmental program could be very efficient for some citizens yet inefficient for others. And a public program could be economical for some citizens but expensive for others. Without considering the distributive effects of policy implementation, and following a concept of social equity, public administration could neglect the legitimate interests of all citizens.

Although there have been many critiques and evaluations of the argument for social equity as the third pillar of public administration, we shall focus on only one of them. The sharpest criticism holds that public administrators should not have the discretion to use social equity as a guide for policy implementation. To do so would "steal the popular sovereignty" from elected officials who make the law (V. A. Thompson, 1975). In this chapter, we demonstrate why administrative discretion is a fact of governmental and nonprofit organizational life, and why social equity should stand with efficiency and economy as guides in the exercise of that discretion.

The Philosophical Beginnings of the Equity-and-Administrative-Discretion Debate

From the Western tradition, we inherit two general philosophical perspectives on the nature of public administration: administering society's public decisions and allocating its public resources. The two perspectives differ as to how public decisions shall be applied in practice by administrators. One approach argues that no problem of administrative discretion exists—that administrators can neutrally and successfully apply the law—and that they actually make no decisions regarding public resource allocation. The other approach recognizes the ambiguity of administrative discretion and the fact that administrators depend on substantive norms (values) to guide their interpretation of law and their allocation of resources. This tradition proposes that *equity* be the value that guides officials in their decisions. Plato has been associated with the first approach, Aristotle with the second.

The debate in the Western tradition over the role of public officials revolves around application of the law, and it dates to a disagreement between Plato and Aristotle over the role of judges. In the Platonic approach, courts can simply and clearly apply laws (Plato, 1970 trans.). The Aristotelian approach argues that this is impossible in principle, because every application of a law involves further elaboration of that law, and elaboration of law (allocation of public resources) without reference to equity results in injustice (Aristotle, 1962 trans.).

The Platonic-Aristotelian debate over the nature of legal interpretation can clarify the issues facing modern public administration. We argue, as Aristotle did, that to administer laws without reference to social equity results in injustice; equity must therefore be recognized as fundamental to the practice of public administration. This means that developments in the Aristotelian-Platonic dialogue may be applied fruitfully to discussions of public administration's role in society. We survey these developments here.

Attempts to define precisely and limit severely the role of public administrators fall within the Platonic tradition of legal theory. Plato created a dichotomy between integrity to the general law on one hand and the application of justice in the particular case on the other. He maintained that using "justice" as a criterion for interpreting the law in particular cases required absolute wisdom and knowledge on the part of the judge. Since absolute wisdom about the nature and application of justice is, of course, an impossible quality in mortal judges, Plato sacrificed justice in these particular cases for adherence to law in its general form. Plato defined the issue in terms of a choice between perfect, abstract justice and imperfect but stable human law. Since most people recognize that perfection is impossible, we naturally agree with Plato if we accept his definition of the issue.

Aristotle did not accept Plato's definition. He argued that people choose not between perfection and stability but rather between various *possible* ways of approximating justice in society. In administering any general law, officials will necessarily encounter some questions that legislators simply could not anticipate. Public officials (judges, in Aristotle's framework) are, in principle, always faced with discretionary decisions about how to proceed. Aristotle argued that public officials must continually choose between various possible ways of reaching justice in the particular administrative decisions they confront. The issue for Aristotle is practical rather than ideal and theoretical: How can officials reach the most practically just decisions?

To simply follow the law, as Plato suggests, is not an adequate answer when an unexpected case arises. Aristotle argued that what the law demands should be interpreted in light of the more general goal of justice, which the law was meant to approximate. Thus justice, Aristotle argued, is of two kinds: legal justice and equity justice. Legal justice results from applying a law that is clearly and undoubtedly interpretable in its requirements. Equity justice characterizes cases in which the application of a law depends on substantive principles (the "spirit of the law") to resolve ambiguity. It also characterizes cases in which legal justice would result in substantial injustice.

Aristotle therefore argued that the equitable is superior to the just; to apply the law without regard for equity results in injustice, *not* in the best approximation of justice, as Plato claimed.

A further implication of Aristotle's argument is that, contrary to Plato's assumptions, administrators can never neutrally apply the law for two reasons. First, legal justice is not neutral in cases calling for equity justice, in which strict adherence to the written law is decidedly unjust. Second, in many cases what the law requires in all its details is not so completely clear that only one interpretation is possible. Officials always use some interpretation of the law rather than following it to the letter, because its ambiguity forces them to do so. However, in Aristotle's approach officials should be criticized if their interpretations of the law are not based on reference to the principles of justice lying behind the law.

What are the implications of these arguments for public administrators? Plato would prefer that public officials simply apply the law as it is written. But if Aristotle is right, what is "simple" about applying the law? Aristotle would have officials interpret the law with regard to its spirit as well as to equity. But if Plato is right, by what shared standards can officials' interpretations be limited once they have crossed the line from application to interpretation?

These questions are precisely those facing public administrators in the modern state, who are charged with fulfilling particular mandates that vary with their position. Administrators may be charged with administering a public school system or a city budget or a snow removal system. In each position, the administrator's mandate is defined by an enabling statute, a city code, or some other authoritative statement. The Platonic argument is that public officials should simply follow the statute or other authorization to fulfill their mandate. The only additional guidelines that administrators need, this tradition argues, are the principles of efficiency and economy—which, in turn, are merely the rational corollaries of any authoritative mandate and do not really add any demands beyond the mandate. Efficiency and economy simply guide the administrator toward the *best* means of fulfilling the mandate.

In the Aristotelian argument, on the other hand, the mandate of the public official can be understood only in light of its spirit. The mandate—the actual, written words directing the administrator—never so clearly defines what the task is that the administrator can act as a machine, efficiently and economically doing the job. This argument suggests that officials must have an understanding of the spirit of the mandate to guide them as they make the inevitable discretionary decisions. This understanding of the spirit of the mandate, according to the Aristotelian tradition, should incorporate the principle of equity, which is a concern for justice that varies appropriately by situation.

We now can clarify several issues that need resolution. First, which tradition—the Platonic or Aristotelian—is more appropriate as a guide for modern public administrators? We argue that the Aristotelian approach is more appropriate, and we will defend that choice. Second, do administrators acting under the Aristotelian framework illegitimately usurp power from democratically elected officials? They do not. Third, what does equity within the Aristotelian tradition really mean? How can we give determinacy to the general notion of equity? Does equity mean the same thing for all administrators in all positions? Is it a process or an outcome value? To help answer these questions, we look to recent developments in philosophical analysis, in social-psychological theory, and in the American political tradition itself.

Dworkin and the Necessity of Principle in Law

Ronald Dworkin distinguishes between the "rule-book" and "rights" conceptions of law (1985, pp. 11–15), a distinction that parallels the disagreement between the Platonic and Aristotelian traditions on the role of equity for public officials. While Dworkin's discussion applies most directly to judges, it is relevant to our discussion of equity in public administration. Most important, the rule-book concept of law is exactly the one held by theorists in the Platonic tradition, and Dworkin shows clearly why that concept is wrong. We differ with him on the issue of exactly which theory should replace the rule-book concept because we are developing a theory for public administrators not judges.

The rule-book concept of law holds that the requirements of law are spelled out somewhere in written statutes or case law, and that those requirements, at least in principle, could be brought together in one clearly stated book of rules. Thus, legal requirements are those—and only those—that appear in the rule book; if some supposed requirement or right is not listed in the stated rules, it does not exist. The rule-book concept has an affinity with democratic rule, because under this conception only elected legislatures have the authority to add new rules to the rule book or to take others out—a strict application of the policy-administration dichotomy.

The problems with the rule-book conception of law arise, Dworkin argues, most sharply in "hard cases," in which a dispute occurs over what the correct decision should be. Hard cases arise not because there are no rules that relate to the case—in modern law, rules relate to almost any situation—but rather because the rules that relate to the case at hand either are ambiguous or present several possible interpretations in the concrete situation. Hard cases in law are analogous to a public administrator's practical everyday questions about fulfilling his or her mandate, which is never so completely clear that he or she can simply act mechanically. The administrator always needs some guidelines for fulfilling the mandate; economy and efficiency are the traditional ones.

The rule-book conception of law proposes several suggestions for judges to use in deciding hard cases; these suggestions attempt either to make the decision as mechanical as possible or, when that is impossible, to allow the judge to use personal policy preferences to resolve the issue. These rule-book solutions parallel the standard public administration reliance on efficiency as a guide to interpreting the administrator's mandate. The rule-book solutions beg crucial questions, just as the efficiency argument begs the question "Efficient for whom?"

When the application of a law is unclear, the rule-book position is that judges should use the *intent* of the legislature to decide the issue. Dworkin points out, however, that apart from the practical difficulty of determining that intent, there is a significant problem in principle with the idea of intent. Intent can never give an unambiguous solution to an ambiguous hard case, because the majority that passes a law is always composed of a number of factions, each with its own intent. In addition, each faction (or even each individual) has several layers of intent, from vote seeking to public policy preferences. An appeal to legislative intent to determine the application of a law is always ambiguous and always involves interpretation.

The rule-book approach to law acknowledges that in rare cases no clear answer will be found and that the judge must then make an independent decision based on his or her policy preferences. This approach provides two polar alternatives for judges: either they mechanically apply the law as it is written or, when this is impossible, they are free to act on their own personal preferences.

Dworkin provides a third alternative between the option of neutral application and the democratically questionable option of personal preferences. He argues that judges should make judicial decisions based on their understanding of the spirit behind the letter of the law. Under Dworkin's alternative, judges should interpret based on their relatively coherent overall understanding of what *principles* the legal tradition as a whole embodies. The interpretation is limited by the community's shared concepts of these principles and by the historical tradition of the community. Such principles provide coherent guidelines for judges when they must decide how to interpret law in a unique case; that is, judges *do* have guidelines for defining justice in particular cases, and they *do* have guidelines for defining equity in cases in which "legal justice" would produce substantial injustice. In Dworkin's view, then, application of the law is inherently political but not personally preferential.

There are obvious difficulties in applying Dworkin's argument directly to public administrators. While Dworkin's devastating critique of the rule-book concept of law applies directly and usefully to the standard Platonic concept of the public administrator's mandate, Dworkin's suggestions for how judges *should* decide cases are inappropriate for public administrators. Public administrators are not judges, and the discretionary situations they face are not cases. The Aristotelian tradition, however, provides an alternative concept that avoids the pitfalls of the rule-book notion of the administrator's mandate.

To avoid the muddles of both neutral application and unbridled personal preference, Dworkin proposes that judges base their legal interpretations on their understanding of the spirit of the law. Public administrators, on the other hand, can avoid the two unacceptable options by recognizing the principle of equity and by engaging the citizens they serve in a dialogue about the appropriateness of their mandate.

Lowi, Gruber, and Modern Platonic Public Administration

Both Aristotle and Dworkin recognize the problematic nature of administrative discretion and propose methods of tying discretionary decisions to the public interest. Theodore Lowi proposes a very different solution—a modern administrative Platonism (Lowi, 1969). Lowi attacks the institutional nexus between the administrative state and interest-group politics, and he notes that the expansion of the administrative state is connected to an expansion of administrative discretion. Unable or unwilling to make difficult and controversial policy decisions, Congress has delegated many of those decisions to administrative agencies. Congress has given vague and general authorizations of power to these agencies, which now govern in conjunction with interest groups. The broad discretion of administrative agencies, coupled with the influence of interest groups in the administrative process, violates the public interest and denies the rule of law.

Lowi's solution is to limit administrative discretion by "restoring the rule of law" (p. 297). To accomplish this, the Supreme Court should reject as unconstitutional all broad and vague authorizations of power by Congress to administrators. The result would be, Lowi hopes, a transfer of administrative decision making back to Congress and a diminution of administrative discretion. Like Plato, Lowi would attempt to prescribe for administrators exactly what they may do to fulfill their mandate.

But also like Plato, Lowi fails to recognize that proliferation of authoritative rules does little to harness administrative discretion; every rule itself requires interpretation. As John Dewey noted more than sixty years ago, the proliferation of laws reflects a breakdown of public spirit but does nothing to revitalize that spirit (Dewey, 1930, p. 73). Administrative discretion is harnessed to the public good not by more rules but by appreciation of the spirit of the law and its relation to the public good. Ways of revitalizing that spirit must be found, but they will not be found by passing more laws, no matter how clear. Modern arguments about the need to rebuild our civic capital (Putnam, Leonardi, and Nanetti, 1993) and the extreme applications of the law that are criticized in *The Death of Common Sense* (Howard, 1995) suggest that the answer does not lie in more laws or in a bureaucracy that can implement the law only in a strict and narrow sense.

Judith E. Gruber, noting the growth and power of public administration, shares Lowi's diagnosis but proposes a different cure (Gruber, 1987). Instead of making laws that are more precise, and creating a "juridical democracy," the discretion of public administrators should be controlled by the theory of exchange. "In an exchange model, control results not from political actions telling bureaucrats what to do but from constructing conditions in which bureaucratic behavior is constrained in exchange for resources that bureaucrats seek" (p. 211). Gruber then refers to stringent budgetary controls to "strip recalcitrant administrators of their funding and, in some cases, of their jobs."

Under certain circumstances and at certain times, Gruber's cure works. It does not, however, cure the use of administrative discretion. It uses a false argument about bureaucracy and administrative discretion to cure ailments that have to do with policy disagreements and the exercise of political power. For example, both the Reagan and Bush administrations preferred the dismantling of many federally funded domestic programs that were carrying out what Congress had authorized and funded. Were those programs "out of control" or exercising unwarranted administrative discretion? Probably not. It was simply easier and more politically effective to use rhetoric about bureaucratic bumbling, waste, and red tape than to address the policy issues more directly. Many of the domestic programs formerly administered or funded by the federal government are now operated by state and local government—by public administrators who must exercise discretion in carrying out policy. Exchange theory can certainly explain how budgeting control can diminish or even eliminate a particular public program. But it cannot explain why the bureaucracy or the exercise of administrative discretion is defined as the problem when, clearly, the problem is a debate over what should be done in American government, at what level in the federal structure, and by which agencies.

Equity as Process

The means of revitalizing the public spirit for administrators can be developed by consulting Aristotle and Dworkin. Plato argued that judges should simply "apply the law" because to do more—to interpret the law based on a standard such as equity—seems to cross the line separating neutral expertise from political bias. Dworkin and others argue persuasively, however, that even (or especially) neutral expertise is subject to political bias, which is all the more egregious because it is not open to public evaluation. Dworkin suggests that we choose not between neutral application and political interpretation, but between hidden and publicly open political interpretations. Thus, he suggests that judges should carefully, coherently, and publicly elaborate their political theory in their decisions and opinions.

But public administrators need a different method of making their decisions open before the public. As noted earlier, administrators are not judges; they do not make autonomous decisions and then present the formal reasons for those decisions. Aristotle dealt with this problem as well; he, too, was concerned about making official decisions nonarbitrary, even when those decisions are not directed completely by the written law.

Aristotle suggested that equitable decisions develop most fully from public dialogue among friends and equals. For Aristotle, friends are those engaged in the same social practice and who, as a result, know the ins and outs and the risks and benefits of that social practice. Equals are those who have the same rights and responsibilities for decision making and participation in a political community. Aristotle argued that only friends and equals are in a position to understand the issues related to equitable public decision making; friends and equals, through dialogue, can decide what is equitable for different members of their community. He denied the possibility of defining in objective, neutral, universal terms what equity would mean across a variety of issues. Equity, following Aristotle, can be determined only through political dialogue within a political community. This position is remarkably similar to contemporary concepts of networks and governance.

Public dialogue between friends and equals is a high standard if applied to the process of administering government and its programs. But if the process of administration is political, as thinkers from Aristotle to Dworkin have argued, then some means must be found to make administration nonarbitrary from the standpoint of the public.

One approach attempts to remain faithful to the Aristotelian tradition of dialogue between friends and equals. This approach suggests that those citizens affected by public administration decisions should be included in public dialogue about the nature of those decisions. This is the *participatory-process* or *citizen-participation* approach (Frederickson, 1982), which suggests that public administration decisions will be equitable if the process used to reach them is fair. The process is fair if all affected citizens are given a real voice in the development of the decision. The participatory-process approach also stresses that the equitable outcome of administrative decisions is not the only benefit of such a process. Fair participatory processes are thought to cultivate educated, active, and virtuous citizens. This approach, like Aristotle's, emphasizes that by our methods of governing and administering we create not only our public policies but ourselves.

The participatory-process approach has obvious virtues; it has several weaknesses as well. Some administrative decisions involve such technical and complex issues that only with great difficulty and much time could the affected citizens understand, much less participate in, the decision-making process. Furthermore, this technical complexity is part of the nature of some issues and is not merely part of some plot to keep citizens uninvolved. To make that charge is naive and distinctly unhelpful. To respond equitably within a technically complex context requires principled thought and responsible action. John Rawls's *A Theory of Justice* (1971) can provide guidance here.

Although Rawls intends to provide a theory of justice for all societies, his approach is particularly applicable for a large, complex society like our own. Rawls argues that social structures and social policies should be so constructed that whatever inequalities they allow favor the most disadvantaged group. He reaches this conclusion by suggesting that if any of us were placed in an "original position" without knowledge of our particular place in society (among other things), we would choose such a principle to guide the construction of social structures and policies. We would choose such a principle because if we were to end up in the least advantaged group, we would want the society so constructed. Rawls's argument uses our own rational self-interest to encourage us to take the position of disadvantaged groups and sympathize with them.

The significance of Rawls's approach for our purposes is that it provides a structure for discussing the demands of an equity principle in those situations in which technical complexity precludes an actual dialogue between public administrators and the citizens they serve. This approach encourages public administrators to notice particularly the effects of their actions on disadvantaged groups in society and also to take the position of those disadvantaged groups in official dialogue over the development of administrative decisions.

The insight of both Aristotle and Rawls—that equity and justice have a participatory and dialogical nature—has been recognized for some time by those associated with the so-called new public administration, whose advocates have argued that equity in the practice of public administration can be determined only through the participation of affected citizens. Administrators, in this view, must work to include disadvantaged groups in the dialogue on administration and must at times take their position (Marini, 1971; Frederickson, 1980; Frederickson, 1990).

Equity and U.S. Public Administration

Dwight Waldo (1990) points out that we have called upon government to assume more and more societal functions. Waldo writes that the "core" state—serving military, legal, and economic functions—has been greatly expanded. Furthermore, he writes, it is now possible to "speak meaningfully of the Service State, the Promotional State, the Regulatory State, and the Welfare State" (p. 38). But recent trends have gone even further: "I raise now the question whether we are now trying to add another function, another layer, another state. This might be designated the Redistributive State or, better, the Equity State. My point is that recent years have seen an increase in programs that go beyond welfare as that has been traditionally conceived, programs that seek more directly to achieve intangibles indicated by words such as freedom, equality, and justice; and beyond these, such 'nonpolitical' words as dignity and fulfillment" (p. 39).

Increasingly, the courts are concerned with public organizations' observance of the legal and constitutional rights of their employees, clients, and charges. David Rosenbloom (1983) addresses these specific issues squarely, by examining the judicial response to the rise of the administrative state. He argues that the rights of individuals—employees, clients, and "captives" (prisoners and those confined to public mental health facilities)—have been greatly expanded by judicial action. The courts have imposed judicial and constitutional values upon areas where administrative values such as efficiency and economy formerly reigned supreme. Rosenbloom argues effectively that the courts have forced public administrators to add terms such as *due process, equal protection, right to treatment, right to habilitation,* and *constitutional standards* to their lexicon of administrative values. In

short, "judges have sought constitutionality, not efficiency or economy" (pp. 51–55). Court involvement in the financing of public
schools in many states and in public mental health facilities in Alabama and New York and in virtually all of the state prison systems
suggests that the courts are not merely making idle threats. What the
courts have imposed are not matters for ethical reflection but values
that must be incorporated into the way that public administrators
approach their jobs. These values cannot easily be swept away in the
name of economy or efficiency.

Equity is given second billing in public administration, often
being preceded by the phrase "efficiency or . . ." (Wilensky, 1981).
In the past, as Wilensky makes evident, the focus of equity considerations was on outcomes and distributional effects, while efficiency
matters were considered issues of process. Equity considerations
dealt with programs' goals of redistribution or with providing basic
services and outcomes in an equitable (that is, fair) way; equity-ef-
ficiency debates compared outcome and process values. Equity values emerging from constitutional developments and from trends
in political theory are now emphasizing process values in addition
to outcomes.

Equity as Social Glue

Social psychology contributes two insights to emphasizing the role
of equity in administering social rules. First, a shared conception
of equity is one element that enables groups to cohere—it defines
fairness for a group and thus provides a framework for resolving
disagreements over the allocation of value. Second, differences in
the power of various participants are an important factor in defining equity.

Social psychologists have not only a definition but an entire
theory of equity. Walster and Walster (1975) state their equity for-
mulation as follows: "In general terms, two people are in an equitable relationship when the ratio of one person's outcomes to
inputs is equal to the other person's outcome/input ratio. Inputs
are defined as 'what a person perceives as his contributions to the
exchange,' for which he expects a 'just return' . . . outcomes are
the individual's 'receipts' from a relationship" (p. 21).

Walster and Walster note that, depending on the situation, different societies at different times will consider different inputs to

be relevant to considerations of justice. They argue, however, that the same theoretical framework—equity theory—predicts "when persons will feel equitably or inequitably treated and how they will respond to their treatment" (p. 26).

The importance of social-psychological equity theory for public administration is made clear by Walster and Walster's summary (1975) of the theory's second proposition: "Groups can maximize collective rewards by evolving accepted systems for 'equitably' apportioning rewards and costs among members; thus, members will evolve such systems of equity and will attempt to induce members to accept and adhere to these systems" (p. 30).

Equity theorists argue that equity is the glue that holds groups together, that feelings of inequity engender distrust, and that the response to inequity predictably results in declining legitimacy of the regime.

Equity frameworks in social groups are not without a basis in power, however. Walster and Walster argue that those who wield power in a group are able to capture a disproportionate share of community goods and persuade others to acknowledge the equity of unbalanced allocation. Equity standards in social groups, according to this view, are partly the result of power struggles over the definition of values.

Conclusions

The Platonic ideal of the standards that govern public administration—neutrality, efficiency, and economy—is a myth. Thinkers from Aristotle through Dworkin and Rawls show the weaknesses and dangers of that ideal. The problem that public administrators face is how to formulate and put in practice a valid alternative ideal that emphasizes responsibility to the public but avoids the myth of neutrality. Such an ideal will recognize the political nature and political biases of any standard that public administrators might use to guide their decisions. It will therefore emphasize the value of a fair process for reaching administrative decisions.

Aristotle, Dworkin, and Rawls provide different conceptions of processual fairness, each suitable for different aspects of the administrator's job. Aristotle emphasized the importance of dialogue between friends and equals to derive equitable standards, while Dworkin emphasizes that decisions made by autonomous administrative processes must be as publicly open as possible, with full disclosure of the reasons behind the decisions. Rawls's theory suggests that issues too complex and technical for actual dialogue between citizens and administrators may still be resolved equitably by administrators who take the role of disadvantaged groups in the decision-making process. If the Platonic ideal of neutrality, efficiency, and economy is too often a mask for real political biases, as Aristotle maintained, then the philosophical and legal positions we have developed here are the primary responsible alternatives.

Because the concept of social equity is often associated with social liberalism, it is fair to say that concerns about equity have not been particularly salient in the past few years. The consistent opposition of the Reagan and Bush administrations to affirmative action efforts through the Justice Department stands as perhaps the clearest indication, but other examples can be found as well. The transformation of health policy considerations from concern about access to almost total preoccupation with cost containment furthers the point. The Clinton administration brought the access issue—which is essentially an equity issue—back to the policy table.

At the federal level, massive deficits have now forestalled even discussion of major social programs that address equity issues. State and local governments have been forced to scramble to make up for reductions in federal dollars, thus limiting their ability to maneuver. When governments suffer from fiscal scarcity, their tendency is to cut down to their core functions—to eliminate programs and aspects of programs that are not considered absolutely essential. The willingness of scholars in public administration to embrace cutback management, privatization, and third-party government indicates a lack of concern for those at the bottom of the economic ladder.

Clearly, the organizational and political environments are still not conducive to the flowering of social equity in practice. However, some theoretical and empirical progress has been made, and some programs have been established with the specific purpose of dealing with equity problems.

Aaron Wildavsky (1988) summarizes the present condition of public administration by describing the organizational environment as one of ubiquitous anomie. He then links the condition to ideological dissension in the political environment and concludes that public administrators are headed for difficult days. What better time to consolidate normative considerations into a single value? Social equity is the most frequently listed public administration value besides economy and efficiency. It is a residual value that stands for a cluster of considerations that must always be addressed.

Embracing equity as the third normative pillar of public administration requires public servants to seek out and work toward more just allocations of public goods and services, to represent those who do not otherwise have access to public policy processes, to seek the public interest or greater good, and to respect the dignity of individuals (public employees as well as other citizens) and tirelessly safeguard their rights.

Public administration should not be deterred by the complexity of the social equity concept. Economy and efficiency have not been without some theoretical confusion and yet have served us well as guides. The fact that pursuing equity requires more energy and reflection than pursuing economy or efficiency may simply come from our status as political descendants of Machiavelli. John Rohr wrote *Ethics for Bureaucrats* (1989) in response to his assessment of modern humankind's moral condition. In the book he states: "When Machiavelli told us to look at the way things are and not as they ought to be, he made us modern men; but in so doing he bequeathed us a sorry legacy of trained incapacity for sound moral argument" (p. 3).

Rohr proposes that, as a remedy for trained incapacity, a study be conducted of regime values, including equality, as found in Supreme Court decisions. His structured meditations on the values of equality represent an alternative to the proactive pursuit of a vague norm of social equity.

Perhaps more theory building—and a bit more practice in grappling with equity issues—will in time make the subject less formidable. It is time now to consolidate our understanding of the concept of social equity and shore up its place as a pillar of our field.

Chapter Five

Fairness and Social Equity in Public Administration

Equity is more important than efficiency in the management of many government agencies.
JAMES Q. WILSON, *BUREAUCRACY*, P. 132

In Chapter Four, we demonstrated that the full range of administrative discretion is philosophically and practically correct, and that administrative discretion is the essential presupposition to fixing social equity as a requisite element in the spirit of public administration. We turn now to the specifics of fairness and social equity in the theory and practice of public administration.

In the past twenty-five years, the term *social equity* has taken its place as a descriptor for variables in the analytic constructs of researchers in the field, as a concept in the philosophy of public administration, and as a guide for ethical behavior of public servants. This chapter begins, as it should, with philosophical and theoretical development, and follows with a consideration of some applied aspects of social equity in practice.

Philosophical and Theoretical Developments

As Dwight Waldo (1949) once put it, public administration is the marriage of the arts and sciences of government to the arts and sciences of management. Efficiency and economy are primarily theories of management, while social equity is primarily a theory of government. In the early years of modern American public administration, this marriage, particularly in the conceptions of Woodrow Wilson ([1887] 1941), was balanced. Theories of business efficiency were routinely mixed with theories of democratic government—the argument being that a government can and should be both efficient *and* fair. However, by the mid-1960s the marriage had become dominated by management theories and issues, having begged questions of equity and fairness. Even though the general opinion was (and still is) that public administration is part of the political process, there was little interest in developing specifics regarding the ends to which politics and public administration should be put.

Also, in the early years the conventional wisdom dictated that public administration was neutral and only marginally involved in policymaking. Following such wisdom, it was possible to ignore social equity. The current theology holds that public administration is a part or form of politics, that it often exercises leadership in the policy process, and that neutrality is next to impossible. If that is the case, then it is not logically possible to dismiss social equity as a suggested guide for administrative action that is equal to the values of economy and efficiency.

Initial attempts to return to the marriage of governmental and management questions of equity and fairness were simplistic and superficial. Willbern (1973), in his splendid review of the early literature on social equity, observed that we were "not very precise in defining the goals or values toward which administration and knowledge must be applied" (p. 376). He concluded that "those who wanted to challenge the 'system' and the 'establishment' on grounds of social equity have met with a good many rebuffs and even evidence of backlash. But it would probably be a great mistake to dismiss these essays as an expression of a passing mood, an articulation of the particular times in which they were written. On intellectual, analytical grounds, there is something of value and consequence here, a real addition to our faulty and inadequate understanding of human behavior in administrative situations" (p. 378).

So the task was clear: social equity needed flesh on its bones before it could be added to efficiency and economy as the third pillar of public administration.

The process started with a Symposium on Social Equity and Public Administration that appeared in the *Public Administration*

Review (Frederickson, 1974). In an especially important way, that symposium is illustrative of the theory-building process in public administration.

First, we parse the subject—in this case, into considerations of social equity (1) as the basis for a just democratic society, (2) as influencing the behavior of organizational man, (3) as the legal basis for distributing public services, (4) as the practical basis for distributing public services, (5) as understood in compound federalism, and (6) as a challenge for research and analysis (Frederickson, 1974).

Second, after taking the subject apart, good theory building suggests putting it back together. It is now clear that considerable progress has been made in thinking about, understanding, and applying various parts of the subject. But we have yet to put it back together.

Third, we begin the arduous task of definition. Here it is appropriate to turn to the theories of distributive justice for definition. The use of the terms *social equity* and *equality* have been essentially without definition in the field. As Douglas Rae and his associates (1981) said, "Equality is the simplest and most abstract of notions, yet the practices of the world are irremediably concrete and complex. How, imaginably, could the former govern the latter?" (p. 3). Yet social equity is to be the third pillar of public administration.

We turn then to a more descriptive theory, for both greater definition and a more likely applicability to the theories and practices of public administration, as well as to its spirit. Following Rae and his associates, we set out both a rudimentary language and a road map for the notion of equality with attendant definitions and examples. We presume to label this construct the *compound theory of social equity*. In this chapter, it will serve as the basis for later considerations of legal and research perspectives on social equity in the field.

The Compound Theory of Social Equity

The compound theory of social equity comprises types of equality and applications of those types.

Simple Individual Equalities

In individual equality there is one class of equals for which a single relationship of equality holds. The best example is the "one person, one vote" principle or the price mechanism of the market-driven economy that offers a Big Mac or a Whopper at a specific price to whomever wishes to buy. The Golden Rule and Immanuel Kant's Categorical Imperative are both formulas for individual equalities. In the practice of public administration, examples of simple individual equality are rare.

Segmented Equality

Any complex society with a division of labor tends to practice segmented equality. Farmers have a different system of taxation than do business owners, and both differ from wage earners. This concept assumes equality within the category (for instance, farmers) and inequality between the segments. All forms of hierarchy use the concept of segmented equality: all five-star generals with comparable seniority are equal to each other, as are all privates first class. Equal pay for equal work is also a form of segmented equality, which is, in fact, systematic or structured inequality. Segmented equality is critically important for public policy and administration because virtually every public service is delivered on a segmented basis—and always by segmented hierarchies. In segmented equality, people are equally unequal.

Block Equalities

Both simple individual and segmented equalities are in fact individual equalities. Block equalities, on the other hand, call for equality between groups or subclasses. In the 1896 *Plessy* v. *Ferguson* decision, railroad accommodations for blacks and whites could be separate, so long as they were equal. *Brown* v. *Topeka Board of Education* concluded in 1954 that separations by race were inherently unequal; it required that school services be based on simple individual equality rather than block equality (using race to define blocks). The claims for comparable worth systems of pay for women are, interestingly, an example of block egalitarianism mixed with equal pay for equal work, which is segmented equality.

The Domain of Equality

How do we decide what is to be distributed equally? The domain of equality marks off the goods, services, or benefits being distributed. If schools and fire protection are to be provided, then why not golf courses or other recreational facilities? Domains of equality can be narrowly or broadly defined and have to do with *allocations* based on a public agency's resources or *claims,* based on a claimant's demand for equality. Domains of equality constantly shift, aggregate, and break apart. Certain domains—jobs, wages, investments—are largely controlled by the market, while others are controlled primarily by government. Often the governmental domain seeks equality to correct inequalities resulting from the market or from previous governmental policies. Unemployment compensation, Aid to Families with Dependent Children, college tuition grants, and food stamps are all examples of government's practicing compensatory inequality to offset other inequalities outside its domain of allocation but within a broader domain of claims.

Domains can also be intergenerational—for example, should we or our children pay for the federal deficit? (Intergenerational equity is the subject of the next chapter.)

Equalities of Opportunity

Equalities of opportunity are divided into *prospect* and *means* opportunity. Under prospect opportunity, two individuals have an equal opportunity for a job if each has the same probability of getting the job. Under means opportunity, two people have an equal opportunity for a job if they both have the same talents or qualifications. Few examples of pure prospect equality of opportunity exist, but the draft lottery for the Vietnam War came close. In means equality of opportunity, equal rules—such as those for IQ tests, SAT scores, footraces, and so forth—define opportunity. "The purpose and effect of these equal means is not equal prospect of success, but legitimately unequal prospects of success" (Rae and Associates, 1981, p. 66). Aristotle's notion that equals should be treated equally would constitute an example of means-based equality of opportunity.

In any given society not all talent can be equally developed. According to John Scharr, "Every society has a set of values, and these are arranged in a more or less tidy hierarchy. . . . The equality of opportunity formula must be revised to read: equality of opportunity for all to develop those talents which are highly valued by a given people at a given time" (1967, p. 231; see also Scharr, 1964). How else, for example, can we explain the exalted status of rock musicians in popular culture?

The Value of Equality

The value of equality begins with the concept of lot equality, in which shares are identical (similar housing, one vote, and so on). The advantage of lot equality is that only the individual can judge what pleases or displeases him or her. Lots can also be easily measured and distributed, and they imply nothing about equal well-being. The problem, of course, is that lot equality is insensitive to significant variations in need. To remedy this, Rae and associates suggest a "person" equality in which a nonarbitrary rule-based distribution of shares is based on nonneutral judgments about each person's needs. For example, a threatened individual may require more police protection, if police officials so decide, merely to make that person equal to the person who has not been threatened. The same holds true for a child with a handicap compared with one who is able-bodied, or a mentally retarded person versus an individual of average intelligence. An equality that regards the person is often practiced in public administration to make the rules humane.

It is clear that any universal scope for equality is impossible as well as undesirable. Rather than a simple piece of rhetoric or a slogan, the *compound theory of social equity* is a complex construct of definitions and concepts. Equality, then, changes from one thing to many things, "equalities" (Rae and Associates, 1981). If public administration is to be inclined toward social equity, at least this level of explication of the subject is required.

In the policy process, any justification of policy choices claiming to enhance social equity would need to be analyzed in terms of questions such as these: Is this equality individual, segmented, or block? Is this equality direct, or is it means or prospect equal opportunity? What forms of social equity can be advanced so as to improve the lot of the least advantaged yet sustain democratic government and a viable market economy? The *compound theory of social equity* would serve as the framework for attempts both in theory and in practice to answer these questions.

Some Applications of the Compound Theory of Social Equity

From the history of the field of public administration comes this dictum: "Public administration is the law in action." Therefore, it should be no surprise that some of the most significant developments in social equity have their genesis in the law (McDowell, 1982). According to Haar and Fessler (1986), "Local, state and national legislators—and their counterparts in the executive branches—too often have ignored, abdicated or traded away their responsibilities. . . . By default, then, if for no other reason, the courts would often have the final say" (p. 18). The courts are the last resort for those claiming unequal treatment in either the protection of the law or the provision of service. Elected officials—both legislators and executives—are naturally inclined to the views and interests of the majority. Appointed officials—the public administrators—have until recent years been primarily concerned with efficiency and economy.

Employment

The most important legal influence on a more equitable government is in the field of employment, both public and private. The legal (not to mention administrative) questions here are, Who ought to be entitled to a job? What are the criteria and how do we apply them?

The Civil Rights Act of 1964 (as amended) and the Equal Employment Act of 1972 were designed to guarantee equal access to public and private employment. This was done by a combination of block equalities, whereby individuals in different racial categories could be compared. Any unequal treatment was tantamount to a violation of the law, and a means equality logic that fairly measured talent, skill, and ability could determine who got jobs. In the

1971 landmark case, *Griggs* v. *Duke Power,* the court held that job qualifications that were not relevant to the job to be done—and that on their face favored whites over blacks—were a violation of the law. In reaching its decision, the court clearly rejected the idea of prospect equality, but because it upheld the idea of equality by blocks (or, to use the language of law, "protected groups"), a strong signal was sent in favor of social equity. Race consciousness as a form of affirmative action was to be based on equality between blacks and whites both in the work cohort and between the work cohort and the labor market—a kind of double application of equality.

John Nalbandian (1989), in a thorough review of case law on affirmative action in employment, observed that cases subsequent to *Griggs* have systematically limited "affirmative action tightly within the scope of the problem it was supposed to solve" and have limited the negative effects, or unwanted inequality, from befalling nonminorities as a result of these programs (p. 39). The 1978 case of *University of California Regents* v. *Bakke* is the most celebrated example of judicial support for block equality to bring blacks up to an enrollment level equal to that of whites, while at the same time protecting a nonminority individual who would likely have qualified for admissions were he in a protected class.

The affirmative action laws, and the courts' interpretations of them, have had a significant effect on equalizing the employment opportunities between minority and nonminority racial and ethnic groups—and more recently by gender (Ingraham and Rosenbloom, 1989). Nalbandian does, however, predict that the values of social equity will decline in a shift toward a new balance in employment practices that puts greater emphasis on efficiency (1989, p. 44). By the mid-1990s, Nalbandian's prediction appears to be coming to pass. Both the courts and Congress, under the banner of "color-blind" policy, are rolling back affirmative action. Put in another way, segmented definitions of equality based on merit or status are again trumping block definitions of equality based on racial or ethnic origin.

Contracting

In the 1977 Public Works Employment Act, the federal government established a business enterprise set-aside for minorities. It required that 10 percent of all public works contracting be reserved for firms owned by members of minority groups. The 10 percent set-aside was tested and affirmed in *Fullilove* v. *Klutznik* (1980). Justice Thurgood Marshall, for the majority, wrote: "It is indisputable that Congress' articulated purpose for enacting the set-aside provision was to remedy the present effects of past racial discrimination. . . . Today, by upholding this race-conscious remedy, the Court accords Congress the authority to undertake the task of moving our society toward a state of meaningful equality of opportunity, not an abstract version of equality in which the effects of past discrimination would be forever frozen into our social fabric."

For the minority Justice Potter Stewart argued, "On its face, the minority business enterprise provision at issue in this case denies the equal protection of the law. . . . The Fourteenth Amendment was adopted to ensure . . . that the law would honor no preference based on lineage" (*Fullilove* v. *Klutznik*, 1980).

Clearly, justices Marshall and Stewart used different domains, and they diverged on the issue of what is to be equal. To Marshall, block equality was essential, while to Stewart, individual equality was required. Finally, Marshall would have contracting opportunities be based on prospect equality, while Stewart preferred that it be means based.

In a recent affirmation of the 10 percent set-aside provisions of the 1977 Public Works Employment Act, the Supreme Court struck down a 30 percent set-aside for minority-owned construction firms on contracts with the City of Richmond, Virginia—a significant setback for the affirmative action programs of thirty-three states and more than two hundred municipalities (*City of Richmond* v. *J. A. Croson Company*, 1989). The Richmond decision reasoned that the set-aside violated the Fourteenth Amendment because it denied whites equal protection of the law (*New York Times,* Jan. 24, 1989; pp. 1, 12). No doubt the set-aside provision has been enhancing social equity. It is clear, however, that the law uses inequality to achieve equality.

Governmental Service

In 1968, Andrew Hawkins, an African American handyman living in the Promised Land, an all-black neighborhood in Shaw, Mississippi, gathered significant data to show that municipal services such as paved streets, sewers, and gutters were unequally distributed. Because these services were available in the Caucasian section of the town, Hawkins charged that he and his class were deprived of the Fourteenth Amendment guarantee of equal protection of the law. The district court disagreed with Hawkins, saying that such a distribution had to do with issues of "municipal administration" that were "resolved at the ballot box" (*Hawkins* v. *Town of Shaw*, 1969). On appeal, the district court's decision was overturned by the court of appeals—in part on the basis of this amicus curiae brief from the Harvard-MIT Joint Center for Urban Studies:

> Invidious discrimination in the qualitative and quantitative rendition of basic governmental services violates an unyielding principle . . . that a trial court may not permit a defendant local government to rebut substantial statistical evidence of discrimination on the basis of race by entering a general disclaimer of illicit motive or by a loose and undocumented plea of administrative convenience. No such defense can be accepted as an adequate rebuttal of a prima facie case established by uncontroverted statistical evidence of an overwhelming disparity in the level and kind of public services rendered to citizens who differ neither in terms of desire nor need, but only in the color of their skin [Haar and Fessler, 1986, p. 14].

While the appellate court ruled in Hawkins's favor, it construed the issue of equal protection so narrowly as to all but preclude significant court intervention in service allocation decisions in which *intent* to discriminate cannot be demonstrated conclusively.

Desegregation of the public schools following *Brown* v. *Board of Education* resulted in varied and creative ways of defining and achieving equality. School busing, for example, achieves at least the appearance of block equality. However, busing has primarily taken place from the inner city out to the suburbs; magnet schools are an attempt to equalize the racial mix by busing in the other direction. Building schools at the margins of primarily white and primarily black (or Hispanic) areas preserves the concept of the neighborhood school while achieving integration.

The major problem has been one of jurisdiction—or, to use the language of equality, of *domain*. The typical pattern of the primarily nonwhite inner-city school districts surrounded by suburban primarily white districts significantly limits the possible equalizing effects of *Brown* v. *Board of Education.* This is especially the case when the wealth and tax base follow white movement to the suburbs. State courts have in many places interpreted the equality clauses of state constitutions to bring about greater equality. Beginning with California's *Serrano* v. *Priest* case in 1978, state equalization formulas for school funding have in many states required augmenting the funding of poor districts (*Serrano et al.* v. *Ivy Baker Priest*, 1978; Lehane, 1978). Ordinarily, this is done on a dollars-per-student basis. This procedure both broadens the domain of the issue to the state and achieves simple individual equality. It does, of course, bring about this equality through race-based inequality.

From the viewpoint of competing concepts of equality, the desegregation cases of the Kansas City, Missouri, School District may be the most interesting. After *Brown* v. *Board of Education* determined that separate but equal schooling was in fact unequal and unconstitutional, two questions remained: Was merely stopping segregation a sufficient goal of school districts and state departments of education? Or did they need to repair the damage done by a century of racially separate school systems?

In *U.S.* v. *Jefferson City Board of Education,* the circuit court declared that school officials "have an affirmative duty under the Fourteenth Amendment to bring about an integrated unitary school system in which there are no Negro schools and no white schools—just schools. . . . In fulfilling this duty it is not enough for school authorities to offer Negro children the opportunity to attend formerly all-white schools. The necessity of overcoming the effects of the dual school system in this circuit requires integration of faculties, facilities and activities as well as students (*Green* v. *School Board*, 1968)."

Later, in *Swann* v. *Charlotte-Mecklenburg Board of Education* (1971), the Supreme Court stated that "the objective today remains to eliminate from the public schools all vestiges of state-imposed segregation."

Two conditions pertained in Kansas City, Missouri. First, a two-tiered housing market had developed through interaction between private and governmental parties in the real-estate industry, resulting in racially segregated residential areas and schools that roughly mirrored the racial makeup of the neighborhoods. Originally segregated all-black schools were now attended and taught mostly by African American students and teachers. By contrast, the eleven suburban school districts surrounding Kansas City had almost all white students and teachers.

In *Jenkins* v. *State of Missouri* (1984), the trial court under Judge Russell G. Clark found the Kansas City, Missouri, School District and the State of Missouri liable for the unconstitutional segregation of the public schools. The problem, of course, was in the remedy the court chose. It is one thing to identify inequality, but it is quite another to achieve equality. The school district tried and failed to secure passage of tax levies and bond issues to comply with Judge Clark's order. Following the precedents set by the *Liddell* and *Griffin* cases, Judge Clark ordered both tax increases and bond issuances to cover the remedies sought in 1986 (*Liddell* v. *State of Missouri,* 1984). The court also held that 75 percent of the plan's cost was allocated to the State of Missouri for funding. The appellate court sustained all of Judge Clark's remedies, with the exception of a 1.5 percent surcharge on incomes earned in Kansas City by nonresidents; it also instructed the state and the school district to proceed with the remedies (*Missouri* v. *Jenkins,* 1995).

If most of the citizens had turned down bond issues and refused the higher taxation that the school district required to meet its desegregation objectives, how could the judge justify imposing those taxes as a matter of the law? Judge Clark stated that

> a majority has no right to deny others the constitutional guarantees to which they are entitled. This court, having found that vestiges of unconstitutional discrimination still exist in the KCMSD, is not so callous as to accept the proposition that it is helpless to enforce a remedy to correct the past violations. . . . The court must weigh the constitutional rights of the taxpayers against the constitutional rights of the plaintiff students in this case. The court is of the opinion that the balance is clearly in favor of the students who are helpless without the aid of this court [*Jenkins* v. *State of Missouri,* 672 F. Supp. 412].

From an equality viewpoint, there are several examples of competing definitions of fairness. First, in an individual definition of equality, each vote is equal to each other vote, and the majority wins in a representative democracy. The court here clearly stated that a majority cannot vote away the constitutional rights of a minority to equal schooling. A second example is the dimension of time, or *intergenerational equality*. A century or more of inequality for black children in schools was to be remedied by a period of inequality for nonminorities. A third example is the question of domain. To what extent should the issue be confined to one school district? Because schools are constitutionally established in the State of Missouri, Judge Clark concluded that the funding solutions for desegregation were ultimately the responsibility of the state.

Indeed, Arthur A. Bensen II, an attorney for the plaintiff, argued persuasively that it was fully within the authority of Judge Clark not only to impose either statewide or areawide financing to solve school desegregation, but also to reorganize the school districts to eliminate vestiges of prior discrimination. The judge chose not to go that far (Bensen, 1985).

(Bensen's argument was found counter to case law, based on *Milliken* v. *Bradley*, 1974, in which the U.S. Supreme Court found that jurisdictional boundaries are not barriers to effective desegregation, except under certain conditions. Bensen claims that the Kansas City case satisfied those conditions.)

In 1995, the Supreme Court revisited the Kansas City schools case and concluded that the remedy for past discrimination need not go on indefinitely. Indeed, the Court allowed the State of Missouri to begin reducing the special state allocation to the Kansas City schools.

There are many more examples of equality that can be traced to the courts, including equalizing funding for male and female student athletes in schools and colleges.

An especially interesting and relevant interpretation of the relationship between social equity and law as they pertain to public administration is provided by Charles Haar and Daniel Fessler (1986). They suggest that the basis for equality in the law is less likely to be found in the U.S. Constitution and federal statutes than in state constitutions and statutes. "Recognizing the growing practical difficulties in relying on the equal protection clause, we assert the existence—the convincing and determinative presence—of a common law doctrine, *the duty to serve*, as an avenue of appeal that predates the federal Constitution" (p. 43).

More than five hundred years before the U.S. Constitution was written, according to Haar and Fessler (1986), judge-made law in the England of Henry III held that "at a fundamental level of social organization, all persons similarly situated in terms of need have an enforceable claim of equal, adequate and nondiscriminatory access to essential services; in addition, this doctrine makes such legal access largely a governmental responsibility" (p. 21). In the common law, all monopolies—states, districts, utilities, and so forth—are clothed with a public interest and obligated to the doctrine of equal service. If Haar and Fessler are right, and if state-based cases for school-funding equalization are illustrative, then social equity will emerge at the grass roots rather than be imposed by the federal courts.

The notion that the duty to serve *implies* the duty to serve equitably is filled with implications for public administration. First, such a notion reinforces the place of social equity as one of the fundamental purposes of the field. Second, as the compound theory of social equity demonstrates, there are competing definitions of equity. It is one thing to elevate social equity to a fundamental principle of public administration; it is quite another to determine which definitions of equity are called for to achieve fairness in particular circumstances. In fact, other principles such as efficiency are also highly complex—and they have received much more conceptual and analytical attention than has the principle of social equity. Third, a fundamental duty to serve equitably puts the public administrator in an ethical dilemma whenever carrying out enabling statutes, budget appropriations, or management directives would result in greater inequality. This is a far bigger challenge to public administration than the ordinary problem of policy implementation that results in inefficiency or diseconomy. But it is easier for public managers to publicly mount defenses of economy and efficiency than it is to engage in an open commitment to equity. Still, as the next section of this chapter illustrates, support for social equity is widely practiced in public administration.

Social Equity, Analysis, and Research Findings

Consequent with the development of theories of distributive justice and the law of equality has been the emergence of policy analysis. Over the past twenty years, many of the nation's major universities have established schools of public policy that specialize in the interdisciplinary study of policy issues. In addition, many existing schools and departments of public administration have begun to emphasize the policy analysis perspective. Virtually every policy-related field—health care, transportation, law enforcement, fire protection, housing, education, natural resources, the environment, and national defense—is now the subject of regular review and analysis. Generalized scholarly journals as well as publications specializing in each policy field are now available, with virtually every issue containing articles dealing with some form of equity.

Both the ideological and methodological perspectives in policy analysis have been dominated by economics. Although governments are not markets, market model applications are widely used in policy analysis. The logic is simple. In economic theory, if both individuals and firms maximize their utility, then citizens and governmental bureaus do the same. This perspective has been especially compatible with popular contemporary governmental ideas such as deregulation, privatization, school vouchers, public-private partnerships, cutback management, and the minimalist or "night watchman" view of American government.

While the economic model has been a powerful influence on policy analysis, it has been tempered, especially in recent years, by the use of measures of both general and individual well-being that are more compatible with human instincts toward fairness expressed through government. Long-standing and powerful governmental concepts including justice, fairness, individual rights, and equality are now being measured and used in policy analysis; so, too, are broad collective measures—the so-called social indicators such as unemployment and homelessness. Measurements of variations in the distribution of public services by age, race, gender, income, and other factors are relatively routine. We use social equity concepts not only as theory or as legal standards but also as measures or variables in research. Of course, the problem in social equity analysis—as in the use of social equity in law or theory—is the compound character of equality.

At the level of the individual, we now have data and research findings that map, in at least a rudimentary way, personal views and preferences regarding equality. Jennifer Hochschield (1981) has determined that people have contradictory views of equality that are not determined so much by income level or political ideology as by more subtle distinctions. Individuals have varying opinions about equality depending on what domain of life is being considered and how equality is being defined. Hochschield based her findings on three different domains—*social*, including home, family, school, and community; *economic*, including jobs, wages, taxes, and wealth; and *political*, including voting, representation, and law—and used two conceptions of equality: (1) equal shares and equal procedures, and (2) differentiation as a combination of segmented equality and means-based equality of opportunity.

In the social domain, people strongly hold to norms of equal shares and equal procedures. Equal treatment of children, one spouse, equal sacrifice for the family, and equal treatment in the neighborhood mark the views of the poor, the middle class, and the rich. In schools, equal or fair procedures are important to fairly determine grades. In schools, families tend to move somewhat away from strict individual equality toward a differentiation based upon investment, such as the handicapped child needing more, an example of Rawlsian justice. And there is evidence of a differentiation of investment for the more gifted or those with greater potential. People are not, however, equally happy with the egalitarian character of social life. If they feel they have some control over their fate and are able to act on the principles of equality, they are more happy. If not, they are bitter and unhappy.

These same people endorse differentiation or means-based equality in the economic domain. In other words, people want an equal chance to become unequal. Productivity should be rewarded; poor people believe that doing so would produce a more equal income distribution, while wealthy people believe that it would result in less equal income. People also deeply support the notion of private property. Poor and rich alike do not oppose the accumulation of wealth, and both strongly oppose inheritance taxes. And both rich and poor partially abandon their views when it comes to poverty, feeling that "something should be done" about it.

In the political domain, as in the social domain, these people are egalitarian, feeling that political and civil rights should be distributed to everyone equally. "They want tax and social welfare policies mainly to take from the rich and give to the poor and middle classes. Their vision of utopia always includes more equality" (Hochschield, 1981, p. 181). Deep resentment looms over perceived unfairness resulting from loopholes in the income tax code, because it treats people unequally. People endorse tuition subsidies for the poor, housing subsidies, and even national health insurance.

Yet with all of these views, Hochschield found ambivalence. People recognize that they are sometimes inconsistent in their viewpoint. They sometimes feel helpless, angry, and confused about whom to blame for inequality, and they do not know how to make things better.

As the different domains of our lives best explain how we feel about equality, they also generally conform to the compound conception of social equity set out earlier in this chapter. Both in the theoretical model and in our minds, equality splits into equalities depending on domains, dimensions of time, jurisdictions, abilities, effort, and luck.

The field research on the distribution of local government service is filled with implications for social equity in public administration. Much of this research tests the *underclass hypothesis.* If one accepts this hypothesis, then the distribution of libraries and parks and of fire protection, water, sewer, police, and educational services would logically follow variations in power, wealth, and race.

The findings in this research generally indicate that the underclass hypothesis does not hold (Lineberry, 1977). Fixed services such as parks and libraries exhibit "unpatterned inequalities" that are not correlated with power, wealth, or race. These inequalities are more a function of the neighborhood's age and the condition of its housing. Mobile services such as police and fire protection tend to be distributed relatively equally, and the small variation that can be determined is not associated with race or wealth (Mladenka, 1978, 1981). On the burden or tax side, the evidence indicates that property tax assessments are unequal, with lower proportionate assessments for minorities and poor people and higher proportionate assessments for nonminorities and wealthier people (Lineberry, 1977).

Both interdistrict and intradistrict school-funding variations have tended, on the other hand, to confirm the underclass hypothesis. In the past twenty years, primarily as a result of court cases, more than half of the states have undertaken school finance reforms, all of which are designed to equalize funding between schools within or between districts. When compared to states without school finance reform, the reform states now provide greater equity in per-student funding, although not by much (Stiefel and Berne, 1981).

Why has the underclass hypothesis not been demonstrated in field research, except in the case of schools? Robert Lineberry and others argue persuasively that urban and state bureaucracies, following patterned decision or service delivery rules, have distributed public services in such a way as to ameliorate the effects of poverty and race. The effects of municipal reform, including the hiring of city managers, merit-based bureaucracies, and at-large and nonpartisan elections, have strengthened public service at the local level. Public services are routinized, patterned, incremental, and predictable, following understood or accepted service delivery or decision rules. Police and fire regulations require decentralization and wide discretion in deployment of staff and equipment. Social services tend to respond to stated demands. Each service has some basis for its service delivery rules (Lineberry, 1977; Jones, Greenberg, Kaufman, and Drew, 1978).

What is most significant here is that it is bureaucracy—professional public administration, particularly in larger cities—that distributes public services either in a generally equal way or in the direction of those especially in need. The point is that public administrators understand and practice social equity; like efficiency or economy, it is understood as a given in general public administration practice. We believe not just in the duty to serve but in the duty to serve equitably.

What, then, explains school-funding inequities? Public school bureaucracies have virtually no control over interdistrict funding levels. What explains Shaw, Mississippi, and other glaring examples of race-based service inequity? The answer is very often the lack of a genuinely professional public service.

Conclusions

We began this chapter by reviewing the argument that social equity should be the third pillar of public administration theory and practice. We then reviewed some theoretical, legal, and analytical developments of the last twenty years.

While we found the more abstract theories of distributive justice intellectually challenging, the theories that hold the most promise for both empirical verification and practical application to social equity and public administration are those that dissect the subject and illuminate the complexity of equality as both an idea and a guide. Those theories, coupled with the methodological tools of the policy analyst, enable us to examine the distribution of burdens and benefits so as to make informed and fair decisions. Legally, equality issues probably reached their zenith in the later stages of the U.S. Supreme Court under Earl Warren. The Court under both Burger and Rehnquist has narrowed the emphasis on affirmative action, equity in service distribution, and the like.

For social equity to become a standard for policy judgment and public action, the compound theory of social equity that details how alternative and sometimes competing forms of equality will serve to better inform our work. It will always be the task of the public servant to balance the needs for efficiency, economy, and social equity—but there can be no balance if the public servant understands the complexities of economy and efficiency but cannot plumb the details of fairness and equality.

We have presented here a nascent theory; a fully developed compound theory of social equity and public administration is our theoretical and research objective. Such a theory must be parsed by the policy field; informed by the effects of federalism; and able to define if not predict the effects of alternative policy, organizational structures, and management styles on the equity of public programs.

It is a great irony of our times that all of this has occurred during a period referred to as the age of the new individualism or the age of narcissism (Lasch, 1978). The dominant political ethos of the last twenty years has been probusiness—and antigovernmental, antitax, antiwelfare, and particularly antibureaucracy. This ideological consensus seems to indicate that the majority of people share this ethos.

Yet under the surface of majoritarian consensus, we see a significant shifting of the workforce from primary production to information and service jobs at lower net wages; a sharp increase in two-worker families; a profound discontinuity in income and ability to acquire housing, transportation, and food; and an increase in homelessness and poverty (Levy, 1987). Thus, while social equity was being developed as a theory and public administration has, following a social equity ethic, ameliorated inequality's effects, inequality has nevertheless increased as a fact (Wilson, 1987).

Most important in these conclusions is the research that indicates that public administrators tend to practice social equity. This will come as no surprise to those who are in public management at the local level. Public administrators solve and ameliorate problems, exercise judgment in service allocation matters, and use discretion in applying generalized policy. Fairness and equity have always been commonsense guides for action. Some are concerned that following the commonsense guides toward social equity seems to force bureaucracy into a political role (Hero, 1986). There is little doubt that public administration is a form of politics. The real issue is, which theories and beliefs guide the public administrator's action?

As it has evolved in the last two decades, social equity has served to order our understanding of the spirit of public administration and to give us the judgment we need to be both effective and fair.

Chapter Six

Intergenerational Concepts of Public Administration

We will ever strive for the ideals and sacred things of the city, both alone and with many; we will unceasingly seek to quicken the sense of public duty; we will revere and obey the city's laws; we will transmit this city not only not less, but greater, better and more beautiful than it was transmitted to us.

THE ATHENIAN CITIZEN'S OATH

Consider the oath taken by citizens of the city-state of Athens quoted above. With these words, citizens accepted the responsibility to effectively conduct the temporal affairs of Athens, and they pledged to pass the city on to the next generation in better condition than they received it. The Athenian public service ethic called for *more* than equality between the generations.[1] The purpose of this chapter is to consider issues of intergenerational equality and to ask the question, Do public officials have obligations to future generations?

It seems that issues of intergenerational fairness are all around us. The current debate over the national deficit rings with charges that the debt was incurred by a profligate generation and will be paid for by their children and their children's children (Aaron,

---

1. It is important to remember, however, that by modern standards equality was not practiced in Athens. Women were not citizens, for example, and the Greeks practiced slavery.

Bosworth, and Burtless, 1989). This debate is separate from the issue of which groups—the lower, middle, or upper classes—have benefited most from the runaway federal borrowing of the 1980s. Proposed solutions turn entirely on the question of who will pay if much of the deficit is not passed on to coming generations (Kotlikoff, 1991).

The health care finance issue is also mostly about fairness and equity between insured and uninsured people, between the elderly and those not yet old, between the medical and pharmaceutical professions, and between the various insurance companies. There is considerable evidence that unless health care costs are contained, the deficit cannot be reduced.

Much of the essential thrust of the environmental movement is to preserve the earth's resources for coming generations.

The social security system is by definition intergenerational.

These are but a few of the more visible policy issues that mostly hinge on questions of fairness and equity, both between groups in present generations and between present and future generations.[2]

The economic growth of the last half of the twentieth century, particularly in the United States, seemed to indicate that successive generations do better than their parents—and that successive generations have always lived better than those who came before them. In fact, in the longer sweep of history, intergenerational well-being has never been linear. Changes in human conditions such as nutrition, education, employment, and housing have been cyclical (Neustadt and May, 1986; Smith, 1988; Schlesinger, 1986; Kennedy, 1993; Strauss and Howe, 1991).

It is now clear that the generation born from the mid-1960s through the 1970s will likely do less well than their parents, at least

---

2. Note especially the organization of an interest group called Lead . . . or Leave that was established by people presently in their twenties. Lead . . . or Leave's slogan is "The deficit is our Vietnam." Jon Collins, one of the group's founders, states: "The nation went on a vast spending spree that didn't produce anything but bills. Now we not only have a financial deficit, but a social deficit, an environmental deficit, an infrastructure deficit. We're selling out the American dream. Whether you're a liberal and want a new War on Poverty, or you're a conservative and want a capital gains tax cut, you can't do any of it" (*New York Times,* Sunday, Mar. 7, 1993).

in terms of comparative income. Indeed, a recent review of social science research on generational differences concluded that the next generation will do worse psychologically, socially, and economically than its parents (Whitehead, 1993). Projections are that the differences between generations will widen as the baby-boom generation retires and the children born in the late 1970s and the 1980s start to enter the workforce.

There is no doubt that elected officials are now especially sensitive to intergenerational issues, particularly in regard to political rhetoric and symbols. But do public officials—including public administrators—have definable responsibilities to future generations?[3] If so, what are these responsibilities? Are theories or ethics available in the field to inform our thinking about future generations? Can there be social equity between generations?

This chapter deals with these questions in two ways. In the next section, we consider the philosophical and ideological perspectives on intergenerational equity. Then we present the compound theory of social equity as a tool for working with intergenerational issues, and we apply the compound theory of social equity to intergenerational questions of fairness and equity.

Future Generations as a Domain of Equity: Philosophical Perspectives

There are endless possible domains of equality. We think immediately of equal justice before the law, some level of equality in education, equality in voting, equal access to job opportunities, and other generally accepted domains of equality. Here we will not

---

3. The phrase *public officials* is taken to mean elected, politically appointed, and merit-based civil servants. The politics-administration dichotomy is rejected here (Waldo, 1949, 1980, 1990), and the practices of public administration are understood to legitimately include policy preferences and ethical or value preferences (Goodsell, 1995). If neutrality or neutral competence is also rejected (Frederickson, 1980), then it is appropriate to assess the policy and value preferences of public administrators (Rohr, 1989). It is assumed that elected and politically appointed public officials are pursuing policy and value preferences. For a contrary view—in which it is claimed that a nonneutral public administration will "steal the popular sovereignty"—see Victor A. Thompson (1975).

treat as domains specific fields of public policy (environment, education, health care) or spheres of individual or group interests. We are limiting this chapter to a treatment of the future (or future generations) as a broad and generalized domain. We ask: Can future generations be regarded as a domain, or part of a domain, of equality? How is this question answered philosophically and normatively?

Classical ideas of morality and ethics often include a consideration of future generations. In Plato's *eros* (desire, striving, life as an Idea), passion is a personal commitment to one's work—to a work that transcends the present for an uncertain future, for sacrifice not just to present others but to the concept of future others (Hartmann, 1981). The strength of the Platonic *eros* is the ethos of love—not just of one's neighbor but of the one who is to be, a love that cannot be returned. Aristotle asserted that men and women unite out of a "natural striving to leave behind another that is like oneself" (*Politics,* 1984 trans., 1252a30). Immanuel Kant's categorical imperative, as a set of principles that defines the general condition of human life, does not presuppose temporal limitations.

From this ethical perspective, time is irrelevant in moral philosophy (Rawls, 1971): if justice and equality are imperative principles of conduct in one place and at one time, they are imperative in another place and at another time. Edmund Burke accounted for a cross-generational community bound together by moral contracts. In 1690, John Locke described a state of nature in which we are moral equals, equally entitled to use the earth and its resources. In this condition, an individual may fairly possess land for his or her own use, provided that the land is used rather than wasted and that the person "leaves enough and as good for others" (Locke, [1690] 1965; p. 333). David Hume, while critical of Locke's contractarian notions, shared his view of future generations. In Hume's account of the virtues, we are "plac'd in a kind of middle station betwixt the past and the future [and] imagine our ancestors to be, in a manner, mounted above us, and our posterity to lie below us" (Baier, 1981, p. 19; Hume, [1739] 1968, p. 306).

Certainly, these philosophers regarded future generations to be in some general sense deserving of intergenerational justice, equity, and fairness. They described philosophically based domains of claims on the part of present generations toward future generations. But their considerations of morality and ethics were mostly temporal, with only very general conceptions of ethics between generations. It has been left to contemporary thinkers to fill in the details.

One might wonder why considerations of intergenerational morality are much more well developed in our time than they were in the past. We speculate that it has to do with the current issue of abortion, particularly in the United States, and with a wide range of contemporary environmental concerns (depletion of natural resources, endangered species, and global pollution) and technological issues (particularly nuclear energy and genetic engineering).

In modern moral philosophy and ethics, John Rawls is the leading advocate for including future generations in the domain of justice. His is a broadly based domain of claims (1971). Following social contract theory, Rawls has developed a principle of justice as fairness, in which "each person is to have an equal right to the most extensive basic liberty compatible with a similar liberty for all" (p. 250). He also developed a *difference* principle, in which "social and economic inequalities, for example, inequalities of wealth and authority, are just only if they result in compensating benefits for everyone, and in particular for the less advantaged members of society" (pp. 15–16).

In Rawlsian justice as fairness, choices are made behind a veil of ignorance that prevents one from knowing one's circumstances, rendering one unable to make self-advantageous preferences. Rawls's justice-as-fairness principle has been the dominant subject in philosophy and ethics for the past twenty years. Rawls's concept of intergenerational equity, however, is less well known and has seldom received consideration in the ethics literature.

When these concepts are applied to the problem of justice between generations, Rawls holds that once the difference principle is accepted, "the appropriate expectation in applying the difference principle is that of the long-term prospects of the least favored extending over future generations. Each generation must not only preserve the gains of culture and civilization, and maintain intact those just institutions that have been established, but it must also put aside in each period of time a suitable amount of real capital accumulation" (p. 285). This is the "just savings principle"— a capital accumulation in one generation for the next.

The criteria for justice between generations, according to Rawls, are those chosen from behind the veil of ignorance and in the original position. The parties do not know to which generation they belong, whether they are relatively rich or poor, whether their generation lives in wealth or poverty, and whether their society is agricultural or industrialized (p. 278). Behind this veil of ignorance, people would (and should) choose the difference principle and the principle of justice as fairness to guide their moral and ethical judgments, both in temporal and intergenerational circumstances. In Rawls's words,

> We can now see that persons in different generations have duties and obligations to one another just as contemporaries do. The present generation cannot do as it pleases but is bound by the principles that would be chosen in the original position to define justice between persons at different moments in time. In addition, men have a natural duty to uphold and to further just institutions and for this the improvement of civilization up to a certain level is required. The derivation of these duties and obligations may seem at first a somewhat farfetched application of the contract doctrine. Nevertheless these requirements would be acknowledged in the original position, and so the conception of justice as fairness covers these matters without any change in its basic idea [p. 293].

Rawls presents the most consistent and nuanced claim for an ethic of intergenerational fairness, although it is abstract and difficult to apply.[4] Circumstances seldom allow for a veil of ignorance; indeed, we prefer to be informed. Calculating the range of basic liberties, and the extent to which an individual falls above or below an acceptable range, is difficult. Finally, are Rawls's suggestions for procedural remedies enough? Is fairness achieved if the poor enjoy a kind of procedural due process of their circumstances, yet remain in poverty?

---

4. Brian Barry (1978) is a sharp critic of Rawls on matters of intergenerational justice. He nevertheless supports concepts of intergenerational justice based on his belief that "the overall range of opportunities open to successor generations should not be narrowed." It is asymmetric to attempt to make "successor generations better off, which is a nice thing to do but is not required by justice, and not making them worse off, which *is* required by justice" (pp. 243–244).

Many other contemporary theorists regard future generations as an appropriate domain for issues of equity, justice, and fairness, but they usually do so from a less demanding contractarian perspective than Rawls does. There is, for example, the argument that future generations are members of *our* moral community (Golding, 1981). As members of the extended moral community, we have obligations at the least to do no damage to the potential interests of future generations. We can do this better in the near term because our obligations are clearer. We are, according to Martin Golding, probably too ignorant to plan effectively for future generations that seem a remote notion to us. Daniel Callahan (1981) is more convinced of our longer-term obligations. He sets forth four principles that catalogue our obligations to future generations:

1. We should do nothing to jeopardize their existence.
2. We should do nothing to jeopardize their fundamental rights to a life of human dignity.
3. We should do this in such a way as to minimize jeopardy to the present generation.
4. We should use our moral commitment to our own children as the guide for intergenerational fairness.

A host of other modern thinkers, often for different reasons, agree that future generations are an appropriate domain for issues of morality such as equity (Jonas, 1981; Green, 1981; Hartshorne, 1981; Kavka, 1981; Dalattre, 1972; Baier, 1981; McKerlie, 1989; Partridge, 1981; Warren, 1981; Hardin, 1980). The language each uses is often different from the others'. Some speak of possible future persons (Baier, 1981); some speak of potential persons (Warren, 1981); some speak of being and nonbeing (Hardin, 1980). But all agree that there is a legitimate domain of morality between present and future generations.

Perhaps the most interesting arguments for intergenerational models of ethics are more empirical than philosophical. We have strong evidence of a long-standing domain of allocation to future generations. Humans commonly display a concern for the future; it is part of their moral psychology (Partridge, 1981). In this moral psychology, humans collectively establish moral institutions (governments, schools, and foundations) and trusts (local, state, and national parks; wildlife reserves; soil conservation programs; and pollution controls) that serve as evidence of an instinct toward future generations. There are, Ernest Partridge argues, as many examples of those in the present generation expressing positive moral instincts toward future generations as there are examples of jeopardizing institutions or conditions for future generations. Thomas Sieger Derr (1981) makes a similar point in claiming that people have a kind of "moral instinct" guiding them to take some responsibility for future generations. He writes that "we seem to be intuitively aware of the wrong in imposing the bad consequences of our acts on others without their acquiescence" (p. 40).

James Q. Wilson (1993) reviews the research literature on child development and identifies the emergence of a moral capacity in children. Two fundamental instincts in this moral sense are sympathy—a kind of natural, caring sociability—and fairness—a concern for just treatment that transcends individual interests. These natural characteristics are passed from generation to generation. Wilson points to recent Russian history for evidence: "After 75 years of cruel tyranny during which every effort was made to destroy civil society to create the New Soviet Man, we learn that people kept civil society alive, if not well. The elemental building blocks of that society were not isolated individuals easily trained to embrace any doctrine or adopt any habit; they were families, friends and intimate groupings in which sentiments of sympathy, reciprocity, and fairness survived and struggled to shape behavior" (p. 9). The irony is, of course, that state-imposed temporal equality is part of the logic of communism.

A stronger empirical case is found in the simple logic of *decision theory* (also called *action theory*). Charles Hartshorne (1981) points out that "it takes time for decisions to have their effect [therefore] all obligations in principle concern the future. Indeed, the entire rational significance of the present is in its contribution to the future good" (p. 103). In other words, if a decision—however instinctive or calculated—is the predicate of an action, then the process of decisions and actions is always inclined toward the future. The question is, How far into the future does this inclination extend? The next minute? The next day, year, generation?

Does it extend to remote generations of possible people? Decision processes, by definition, cannot affect the past.[5] We know that the cycle of decisions and actions is partly a process of informed predictions; as the future gets more distant, our predictions are less well informed and our decisions and actions are less reliable. In addition, we are not only more confident about the short term, we are more pressed to serve short-term interests (Simon, 1960; Harmon and Mayer, 1986; Harmon, 1989).

The contemporary challenge of intergenerational fairness appears to have taken most modern social scientists and policy analysts by surprise. On one hand, contemporary social science research and policy analysis have been heavily influenced by the teleological philosophy of utilitarianism particularly associated with John Stuart Mill and Jeremy Bentham. In this tradition, decisions and actions are judged by their temporal consequences, depending on the results to be maximized—security, happiness, pleasure, dignity, or the like. Presumably, results can be judged based on the utility of the individual, the family, the group, the neighborhood, the political jurisdiction, the nation-state, or even the world. In fact, much of the logic of the utilitarian perspective is individual, manifest these days by concepts such as empowerment and choice in politics and by techniques such as mathematical modeling in analysis. This work has been determinedly temporal. The tools and logic of utilitarian analysis have not yet been effectively applied to issues of intergenerational equity or fairness.

On the other hand, most contemporary scholarship and philosophy associated with issues of generational fairness tend to be deontological—based on fundamental principles of right and wrong. Much of this work is normative and exhortative. Only now are we beginning to see a fusion of these two approaches. Both Lawrence J. Kotlikoff's *Intergenerational Accounting* (1991) and Henry J. Aaron, Barry Bosworth, and Gary T. Burtless's *Can America Afford to Grow Old?* (1989) are good examples of the wedding of deontological norms and utilitarian tools. Derek Parfit, in *Reason*

---

5. Although decisions cannot affect the past, they can be based on ignorance of the past and therefore be badly informed. See especially *The March of Folly: From Troy to Vietnam*, by Barbara W. Tuchman (1984).

and Persons (1984), builds an ethic based entirely on reason (non-religious, with no absolute moral principles) in which he argues that in our concern for other people, including those in future generations, we often make mistakes based on false beliefs—especially the belief that the particular effects of individual acts can be calculated.

According to Parfit, we ignore what we do together that together "impose great harm on ourselves or others. Some examples are pollution, congestion, depletion, inflation, unemployment, recession, [and] overpopulation" (p. 444). To remedy this, Parfit suggests a more impersonal ethic in which we temper our concern for our own children with a broader commitment to all children. Parfit suggests a "unified theory" that reduces the disagreement between commonsense morality (primarily moral idealism, or the deontological perspective) and consequentialism (primarily a utilitarian and teleological perspective).

We return to the questions with which we began this chapter. Does evidence point to a domain requiring future allocations on the part of temporal public officials toward future people? The answer is yes. There is also, however, strong evidence—particularly in environmental and nutritional policy—of the failure to regard future generations as an appropriate domain. Can reasonable or justifiable domains of future intergenerational be claimed? Again, the answer is yes. These claims trace to the earliest statements of morality and ethics, and claims for the interests of future generations on the part of modern thinkers are especially well developed. We now turn to a construct for the more formal consideration of intergenerational equity.

The Compound Theory of Social Equity As a Model for Working with Intergeneration Issues

To build a model for the treatment of these issues, we use the concepts and theories of social equity, particularly in the fields of public administration and public policy. Issues of social equity are pervasive in every policy domain. A specific public policy that may be good in a general sense is seldom good or bad for everyone.

The terms *equity* and *social equity* were defined and developed back in Chapter Five. At the risk of repetition, let us reiterate that *equity* as the word is used here includes conceptual and philosophical treatments of fairness (Hochschield, 1981), justice (Rawls, 1971), and equality (Rae, 1981). Following the work of Jennifer L. Hochschield (1981), *fairness* is taken here to mean a more equal distribution of opportunities, costs, and benefits in social and political domains. In these domains, as compared with the economic domain, Hochschield found that Americans define equity as fairness and generally believe that the social and political domains are too often unfair (Page, 1983; Wilson, 1987). *Justice* is taken here to mean distributive justice. Following Michael Walzer (1983), we accept a pluralist conception of justice in which many spheres of justice and several acceptable criteria exist for determining what is just. And *equality,* as described here, is much more than political rhetoric or sloganeering; equality is not one thing but many things—in other words, *equalities* (Rae, 1981).

These treatments of fairness, justice, and equality have been brought together in the compound theory of social equity (Frederickson, 1990; Rae, 1981), which we defined in Chapter Five and which will be referred to here. In this theory, we find the nuanced concept of equalities rather than simpler forms or definitions of equality. In the compound theory of social equity, the terms *fairness, justice,* and *equality* are used interchangeably.

It is evident that in the compound theory of social equity's applied form, both elected and appointed public officials (not to mention judicial officials) practice both segmented and block forms of social equity in virtually every field of public policy (Lineberry, 1977; Frederickson, 1980, 1990). Public policy is also replete with examples of intergenerational social equity.

We determined earlier in this chapter that future generations, as blocks, are an appropriate domain of claims, although the claims are made by temporal generations on behalf of future generations. And we determined that future generations are an appropriate domain of temporal allocation of resources.

With this grounding, we return to the question of whether or not public officials have responsibilities to future generations for social equity. When applied to the question of intergenerational equity, block equalities are the most logical approach to the treatment of generations. Consider the three blocks and their definitions in Figure 6.1.

**Figure 6.1. Temporal, Near-Term Future,
and Future Generations.**

Temporal Generations	*Near-Term Future Generations*	*Future Generations*
Three generations of thirty years each	The children, grandchildren, and, in some cases, great-grandchildren of temporal generations	Those living beyond the great-grandchildren of temporal generations

Assume that each block is generally discrete and that our primary concern is with fairness or equity between the blocks, rather than with issues of fairness or equity within each block.

We now turn to matters of application.

Table 6.1 illustrates the logic of intergenerational social equity based on blocks. The horizontal axis depicts benefits, while the vertical axis depicts costs. Capital bonding for schools is the illustration. Temporal generations both benefit and pay, as do near-term future generations (although the benefits to the latter probably exceed the costs). And if the capital investment is done wisely, future generations will continue to benefit, being obliged only to pay the costs of maintenance.

Many excellent examples of both public policy and implementation of public administration conform to the logic of intergenerational social equity as illustrated in Table 6.1. Public research-and-development investments, particularly in health care, fit this model, as do virtually all public works investments. Environmental protection, historical preservation, and endangered species protection all fit this model. Public education—both K–12 and higher—fits the model, too, particularly if one accepts the Rawlsian concept of leaving "just institutions" in place for future generations.

One could argue that democratic constitutions, democratic institutions such as legislatures and laws, and judicial institutions are merely constructs left to us by the Founders that we will pass on to future generations. One could also argue for national defense as

**Table 6.1. Intergenerational Social Equity:
Capital Bonding for Schools.**

		Benefits		
		Temporal Generations	*Near-Term Future Generations*	*Future Generations*
	Temporal Generations	Strong	Moderate	Moderate
Costs	*Near-Term Future Generations*	Moderate	Moderate	
	Future Generations			

a form of commitment to maintaining such just institutions. All of these arguments conform to Rawls's "just savings principle" that defines justice and equity between generations.

The single most interesting aspect of intergenerational social equity is that it is so routinely and commonly practiced in policymaking and public administration. The evidence appears to support the philosophical arguments of Rawls and others that just institutions constitute a form of social equity between generations and that a general form of the just savings principle is at work in such cases. Many of the routine decisions made by policymakers and implemented by public administrators appear to support the existence of a vertical moral community in which present generations act favorably in behalf of both near-term and remote future generations.

If extensive examples of block equalities between generations can be found, then what about the segmentation of policy costs and benefits in both present and future generations? Temporal equality can be segmented, as in the case of a police department deploying a disproportionate share of its resources to high-crime locations in times of increased criminal activity in an attempt to make people living in such locations more equal to those living in safer areas. Temporal equity can also be block equality, as in the case of affirmation action or of military veterans' being preferred for governmental jobs. Intergenerational equality may be segmented or block, in present as well as future generations.

Consider, for example, environmental protection as a domain of equity. The people of present generations may invest in environmental protection measures such as eliminating landfills and controlling the dumping of toxic waste. However, extensive segmentation may occur among those in present generations regarding who pays for such policies, depending on tax structures, regulatory practices, incentives for business, or a combination of all of these factors. The distribution of costs will be uneven—that is, segmented: some will pay more than others for environmental protection. The benefits to future generations may also prove uneven, as in the case of a broadly based environmental protection policy stymied by the existence of particular locations (often associated with poverty) that cannot be cleaned up, at least in the short term.

The longest-standing form of intergenerational equity in public administration is associated with capital budgeting. At the state and local levels of government, it is simply assumed that the costs of buildings, roads, and other forms of capital should be borne by both present and near-term future generations (that is, two or perhaps three future generations). This assumption is based on the logic that the benefits of capital investments will be enjoyed by approximately the same temporal generations. At the national level, large-scale governmental debt was initially incurred to pull the country out of the Great Depression and to fight World War II—two policy decisions that presumed that the benefits of such activities would benefit near-term future as well as temporal generations.

The logic of research-and-development investments—particularly as they are associated with the National Science Foundation, the National Aeronautics and Space Administration, the National Institutes of Health, the Department of Energy, and the Department of Defense—assumes that temporal investments will benefit both temporal and future generations, but will benefit temporal generations often in a very segmented, uneven, and pork-barrel way.

Certainly, R&D is the key to several issues of intergenerational equity. Consider the case of oil, a nonrenewable natural resource. If some future generation consumes it to depletion—as is likely to happen—have subsequent generations then been deprived of their rights to oil? How many generations into the future are allowed to have rights to such a resource? "Obviously, if we push the generations into the unlimited future and divide the oil deposits by the number of people, we each end up with the right to a gallon or a quart or a teaspoon or a thimble full" (DeGeorge, 1979, p. 161).

We choose not to do that, assuming that we are entitled to use oil reserves—provided we invest in the research and development required to find an affordable substitute by the time the reserves are depleted. Still, present generations clearly are benefiting at a possible cost to future generations, and the investment in energy R&D probably does not match the temporal benefits of consuming, and depleting, the oil reserves.

We turn now to the opposite of intergenerational social equity: intergenerational social *inequity*.

Table 6.2 illustrates future generations paying for the benefits enjoyed by those in the present. The best examples have to do with depletion of natural resources and environmental degradation. Temporal generations benefit greatly by using timber, groundwater, hydroelectric capacity, oil, and minerals while leaving both near-term and long-term future generations to pay the costs. In the long term, temporal R&D investments will have to compensate for the imbalance between the generational costs and benefits of resource

**Table 6.2. Intergenerational Social Inequity:
Natural Resource Depletion.**

		Benefits		
		Temporal Generations	*Near-Term Future Generations*	*Future Generations*
Costs	*Temporal Generations*			
	Near-Term Future Generations	Moderate		
	Future Generations	Strong	Moderate	

depletion and environmental degradation. But no amount of R&D can re-create species that have been destroyed.

We can speculate that an intense preoccupation with temporal equality in the absence of a market economy, such as occurred in the industrialized Warsaw Pact nations between the 1930s and the 1980s, results in environmental degradation—a particularly pronounced form of intergenerational social inequity.

Table 6.3 illustrates *backloaded* intergenerational social equity, the best example of which can be seen in the operations of the American social security system. While investments were made in the system by individuals who are now retired and receiving benefits, those investments are on average much less than the benefits being paid out. Therefore, present working generations are paying disproportionately for the retirement benefits of present retired generations. The entire social security system is, of course, based on the promise that when temporal generations retire, they too will be supported by their working children.

As an illustration of backloaded intergenerational social equity, the most interesting feature of social security is the interaction of competing concepts of segmented and block equality. Retired individuals receiving social security are regarded as a block; they are all eligible for benefits. While some segmentation occurs, based

**Table 6.3. Intergenerational Social Equity:
Social Security Entitlement.**

		Benefits		
		Temporal Generations	*Near-Term Future Generations*	*Future Generations*
Costs	*Temporal Generations*	Moderate		
	Near-Term Future Generations	Strong		
	Future Generations			

on contributions and other factors, benefit recipients are thought of as a block. The current entitlement debate turns on the question of whether better-off benefit recipients—for example, those with retirement incomes totaling more than fifty thousand dollars per year—should receive lower benefits than low-income retired people.

This debate represents a most interesting twist on the question of intergenerational social equity, in which temporal generations normally must act on behalf of future generations—which are ordinarily regarded as a block—because they cannot speak for themselves. In backloaded intergenerational social equity, the most senior people among temporal generations turn out to be powerful voices in their own behalf. The irony in the debate over social security entitlements is that from the system's inception, better-off working people paid proportionately less to support their retired generation(s) than did the less well off of their working generation (Aaron, Bosworth, and Burtless, 1989; Kennedy, 1993; Kotlikoff, 1991).

Conclusions

We return now to our initial questions: Should the moral and ethical responsibility of public officials be extended to future generations, to potential or possible persons, to the remote? The answer is a cautious yes. The reasons are of two types—moral and applied, or practical.

In both philosophy and the practical affairs of people, there is a pervasive concern for fairness, justice, and equity; there can be no moral community without some agreed-upon arrangements for all three. These arrangements, most often manifest in government, may appear to be mostly temporal and horizontal. In fact, from the earliest practices of government the arrangements that sustained the moral order were also intergenerational and vertical. If, in the moral order and the arrangements that sustain it, we insist on some level of fairness and equity, such an insistence—particularly in the long term—is most probably as vertical as it is horizontal. We have illustrated here many examples of temporal policymakers and public administrators acting out obligations toward future generations.

The instincts and intuitions of the citizens of Athens toward their fellow citizens and toward their posterity are probably the moral norm. That we often fall short of this norm, both in our lifetimes and in our attitude toward future generations, does not invalidate it, nor does it indicate that transcendent moments of temporal fairness and equity, as well as ringing examples of intergenerational social inequity, have not occurred. They have.

Consider the American public school system—a remarkable institution designed to foster learning and to facilitate temporal social justice and pass the culture from generation to generation. Consider the institution of slavery—a huge lapse in morality; and its abolition—a courageous attempt to recompense that evil. Consider as well contemporary programs for sustainable development and ecological balance; they are attempts to ensure for future generations the resources of the earth. But also consider the extreme inequities in temporal affairs between the Northern and Southern hemispheres (Chase-Dunn, 1989; Pryer, 1975; Strange, 1988). The moral community is, then, both present and future—or as Annette Baier puts it, a "cross-generational moral community" (1981, p. 178).

This brings us to the point of seeking overarching moral or ethical principles to inform our public responsibilities to future generations. How shall we represent the future in the present? How can we tap the human instinct toward a moral community extended through time?

Following the logic of the compound theory of social equity, public officials should seek to adopt and implement policies that support intergenerational social equity. Short of that, they should adopt policies that are likely to have a neutral effect on future generations. They should *not* adopt policies that support intergenerational social inequity, as illustrated in the cost-benefit matrix in Table 6.2.

We recognize that we as human beings are ignorant of the distant future and that we can imagine only a little ahead. Still, we must act on what we know, even at the risk of making mistakes. The world of public policy is a world of creative problem solving. In the policy process, experts and specialists often define the problems and set the agendas. If problems are *defined* as both temporal and intergenerational, then through our creativity we will have to find policies that serve—at least to some extent—both ends. We are more knowledgeable now of the likely effects of toxic waste, pesticide overuse, overgrazing, strip-mining, groundwater depletion, and a host of other ecological problems. The informed and unexaggerated articulation of such effects on future generations can have a powerful influence on policy.

Many intergenerational ecological problems are only marginally related to present national boundaries. The World Commission on Environment and Development (1987), building on country-based studies and programs, is working to develop some regional programs and to find solutions, particularly in sustainable development, to ecological problems. Garrett Hardin (1980) and others have described the problem of population growth and the limited carrying capacity of the earth. Large-scale regional programs of education and access to birth control are imperative.

Technology, often the source of environmental problems, is also the source of many solutions. We know about miracle rice and the reduction of famine in Asia and the Indian subcontinent. We know about antibiotics. Many of our longer-range problems, such as population control, may be profoundly improved upon by technology. We now more clearly understand the limits of resources and the earth's probable inability to sustain the high levels of consumption associated with a high quality of life. Christopher Lasch (1990, 1995) and others suggest a return to definitions of well-being, moral worth, and happiness that are not linked to an acquisitive conception of success.

In the so-called global village, public officials can think of their own and other jurisdictions as laboratories for experimenting with and testing creative solutions to temporal and intergenerational social equity challenges. Once a solution is found in one setting, it may be suited to another, similar setting—resulting in a diffusion of innovation.

We know these things and more. In the spirit of public administration we hold some responsibility for social equity between generations; we must act as best we can, based on what we know. But what are the appropriate tools?

One argument is that most issues of distribution that affect future generations are the result of private market transactions, in which the interests of future generations are steeply discounted

(Arrow, 1983). A lack of intergenerational social equity is an example of private market failure. Government, through public policy, must intervene in the private market to regulate in favor of future generations. The problem is that government's attempts to either regulate the market or act directly in the interests of future generations have sometimes resulted in nonmarket failures, such as Defense Department–generated nuclear waste (Hardin, 1980).

Still, we act based on what we know, using—albeit in a clumsy way—the tools we have at hand. Whatever the weaknesses of market and nonmarket approaches, they represent a considerable improvement in the prospects of future generations whose interests are explicitly considered an obligation in the spirit of public administration.

Part Three

Ethics, Citizenship, and Benevolence in Public Administration

Chapter Seven

Ethics and Public Administration

*My experience is that many administrators have great
difficulty relating their democratic commitment to their
day-to-day activity. Though they are democratic in their
ideology, their need for achievement and high task
orientation make them very skeptical of any process that
accepts amateurism, is indulgent toward delay, and may
threaten the quality of the ultimate decision. It is not at
all unusual to find public leaders who will proclaim the
virtues of democracy at the voting and legislative level,
but practice the most outrageous authoritarianism in the
management of their own organizations.*
FRANK SHERWOOD, UNPUBLISHED SPEECH

The realm of ethics is a world of philosophy, values, and morals, while
administration is one of decisions and actions. Ethics will search for
right and wrong, while administration must get the job done. Ethics
is abstract, while administrative practices are irremediably concrete.
How can ethics inform administration? And how can administration
inform ethics? How can the ideas of administration—order, efficiency, economy, productivity—help define ethics? And how can the
ideas of ethics, of right and wrong, help define administration?

In the national, state, and city governments of the United States,
it was corruption that provided much of the impetus for the development of modern public administration. By the early years of the
twentieth century, the structures and policies of American governments were being changed for the purpose of reducing corruption.

These changes were of two types: (1) to reduce procedurally the potential for corruption, through the use of such management concepts as awarding contracts to the lowest bidder, pre- and postauditing, council-manager government, and prohibiting conflicts of interest, and (2) to bring into governmental service "better types" of people, through merit-based civil service systems for administrators and through concepts such as nonpartisan and at-large elections for politicians. The governmental reform movement, while not driven by what would today be described as a concern for ethics, was certainly driven by a concern for eradicating corruption.

The contemporary governmental ethics movement appears to serve essentially the same purpose as the reform movement of a century ago—that is, to reduce governmental corruption. The present ethics movement's emphases, however, are considerably different. Structures and programs—including whistle-blowing; telephone hot lines for reporting ethics abuses; ethics boards and commissions; ethics education programs for elected, politically appointed, and administrative officials; agency ethics officers; financial or other conflict-of-interest disclosure systems; and professional codes of ethics—all typify the modern approach to guarding against or reducing public corruption.

While the modern-day ethics movement may lack the fervor of the reform movement, it is nevertheless a self-conscious, visible, and growing governmental concern, with offices and officials who have ethics-related titles and responsibilities. Not only are issues of ethics pervasive in modern public life, but the implements of ethics enforcement are ubiquitous as well.

Much of the normative and philosophical leadership of the governmental reform movement was in the universities, and so it is today with the ethics movement. Virtually every major university boasts an institute or center devoted to the study of ethics or human values. There is, however, a difference between the role of universities in the reform movement and their role in the ethics movement. Academic programs, particularly in the public administration field of study, were influential in the governmental reform movement. Most leading universities offered such programs, which were almost all part of political science departments. In these programs, the perspective was historical, legal, philosophical, and deductive.

The development of political science as an empirically based social science; the emergence of public administration as an interdisciplinary, applied field of social science; and the more recent advent of policy studies all postdate the governmental reform movement. As a consequence, the contemporary study of ethics in universities, while still primarily steeped in a philosophical and deductive perspective, is now significantly informed by social and policy science research as well.

By applying research findings to the primary theories of governmental ethics, it should be possible—at least in a preliminary way—to indicate whether these theories work. Which applied theories of ethics are most effective? Are they uniquely effective in particular settings but not in others? Which of the theories, while compelling, seem incapable of application? When does ethical government come at too high a price in administrative effectiveness or political responsiveness? These and similar questions can be met, even in a preliminary way, by the results of research and analysis.

This is not to suggest that moral truths or human values are empirically testable. They are not. Human behavior as an expression of values can, however, be judged to be honest or dishonest as long as the concept of honesty is defined. Democratic government, including the U.S. Constitution and the country's laws, can be seen as a collective expression of agreed-upon values, or as the definitions of values. Other forms of pregovernmental or extragovernmental social agreement, such as personal honesty, are accepted as collective values. Individual and group behavior, when judged against social conventions, the laws, and the Constitution, can be said to conform and therefore be ethical, or not to conform and therefore be unethical. Given the tools of modern social science, it is possible to assess ethical behavior in this way.

In addition, governments institute policies, programs, and organizations designed to improve the prospects for individual and group ethics. The social sciences should help determine the extent to which such policies, programs, and organizations enhance ethics.

A second important difference between the governmental reform and ethics movements is that in the early 1900s, people knew what they did not like: governmental corruption. Many of the corrective policies adopted were administrative and managerial. By the mid-1930s, government began to grow dramatically. By the 1950s, it was routine to refer to the "administrative state" (Waldo, 1949) and to think of the civil service as "the fourth branch of government." By the 1980s, bureaucracy, especially as a symbol of big government, was the pivotal issue. "Bureaucrat bashing" and supposedly fighting waste, fraud, and abuse were the political weapons of choice. Governmental corruption was becoming an issue again—but this time it was an issue in and of the bureaucracy and served effectively to bring together public distaste for big government and high taxes on the one hand and concerns over corruption on the other.

During the governmental reform movement early in this century, corruption was generally understood to mean *political* corruption. In the present ethics reform movement, corruption is most often associated with bureaucracy. Does any evidence suggest that contemporary governmental ethics issues are primarily manifestations of big government and bureaucracy? Or is the bureaucratic machine, however inefficient, still more ethical than was prereform government and politics? Are contemporary problems of governmental ethics essentially political rather than administrative or bureaucratic?

The categories we use for this inquiry are purposely broad and generally conform to theoretical constructs in the ethics field. Research in governmental ethics, however, tends to be based in narrower categories and on more limited questions. It is, therefore, necessary to fit research findings into what appear to be the most appropriate theoretical categories. Even though ethics theorists and researchers may quarrel with the groupings used here, we are less concerned with perfecting the categories than we are with generally advancing what we know about governmental ethics.

Values are the soul of public administration (Cooper, 1990). The study and practice of public administration has never been regarded as only technical or managerial. Attempts to parse, on the one hand, the work of government into politics and policymaking as the expression of values and, on the other hand, administration as the mere technical and value-neutral carrying out of policy have not succeeded. That values inhabit every corner of government is a given. Whoever studies administration studies values, and whoever practices administration practices the allocation of values (Waldo, 1949).

In government administration, values are most often taken to mean those of politics or policy. Political values, such as who should hold elected office and who should exercise the sanctioned power of the state, connect to public administration because bureaucrats and civil servants often have extensive discretion. Policy values, such as choosing between spending on program A or program B, are influenced by administrators. Political and policy values and preferences like these are often connected to matters of ethics. It is an issue of policy ethics, for example, when a police department deploys its forces in such a way as to leave vulnerable neighborhoods without protection while other neighborhoods are covered. Policy ethics issues like this are seldom the focus of study in public administration.

Values such as individual adherence to the law, honesty, following professional codes of ethics, personal morality, commitment to constitutional principles (particularly of the Bill of Rights), and regime values most often characterize the study of ethics in public administration (Denhardt, 1988; Cooper, 1990; Rohr, 1986; Bowman, 1991; Lewis, 1991). This chapter emphasizes this perspective on administrative ethics.

Some Assertions

The following sections of this chapter summarize and synthesize research findings on particular aspects of public administration ethics.

The Nature of Humankind: Good or Bad?

Interesting parallels can be found between assertions in political philosophy about human nature and the evolution of the concept of administrative man. From Hobbes's perspective, humans struggle in a harsh and brutal world—a world in which base passions rule. Hobbes's Leviathan, the product of his "science of politics," would cause the people to covenant together, subjecting themselves to a single body of sovereign authority, so that they could maintain order and preserve peace. In this way, lawless and warlike natural passions could be controlled.

Following Locke, civil government is formed because humankind fails in the Law of Nature to exercise pure freedom responsibly, and therefore must make a compact with a sovereign to maintain peace and order. In modern political thinking, the works of Lowi (1969) seem to most nearly resemble the view of Hobbes and Locke. And, as we argued in Chapter Four, these views are also compatible with Plato's concepts of laws and of judging.

In Immanuel Kant's view, in contrast, humankind can only find morality in a state of freedom. This morality will be naturally and metaphysically derived, thus enabling free people—and presumably groups of free people—to reason together in the pursuit of order and peace. The contemporary work of Rawls (1971) and Dworkin (1985) seems similar to that of Kant.

Administrative man, following McGregor's Theory X framework (1960), practices management by control and through the hierarchy. McGregor's Theory Y framework, by contrast, favors the techniques of human relations and associated forms of collective or collegial management (Harmon and Mayer, 1986). That Theory X is to organization theory what Hobbesian man is to political philosophy, and that Theory Y is similar to the Kantian view of humankind is hardly a new observation. It is likely that the range of good and bad individuals found in politics is roughly comparable to the goodness and badness of those in administration. What may, however, be more important is whether political and administrative people are different, and whether this difference accounts for significant variations in the definition of ethics and ethical behavior in political compared with administrative settings.

Of course, it is not demonstrable that people in general are good or bad. It is, however, demonstrable that they are different from each other. That political man, absent the controls and enforced standards, will often pursue personal gain at public expense is clear (Holbrook and Meier, 1993). That professionals in different fields define ethics differently is also clear (Overman and Foss, 1993). For example, values such as empathy, fairness, ability to innovate, and concern for the public interest tend to be stronger among people preparing for or already engaged in public service careers than in those in potential or actual business careers (Nalbandian and Edwards, 1983).

Individuals who choose careers in public service tend to be more inclined toward job security and are more averse to risk than are people who engage in business careers (Bellanta and Link,

1981; Baldwin, 1991). Attitudes toward corruption and ethical conduct appear to be situationally determined; in other words, definitions of corruption and what constitutes ethical behavior vary depending on whether they pertain to a business, medical, legal, political, or public administration setting. Individuals in public service generally have a greater interest in power and influence, an inclination that seems to show that Machiavelli was right (Baldwin, 1991). Those in business and commerce have stronger acquisitive interests, seeming to indicate that Bentham was right (Baldwin, 1991).

It seems reasonable, therefore, to assume that people choose their field of work (when such choices are available) at least in part on the basis of personality characteristics and value preferences. And the attitudes of professionals toward ethical behavior are "higher," or more concerned with ethics, than those in the general population (Overman and Foss, 1993). All of this suggests that rather than asking whether humans are basically good or bad, it would be more useful to disaggregate the question into several: Is political man good or bad? Is business man good or bad? Is administrative man good or bad? Is medical or legal man good or bad? While we do not know whether humankind is good or bad in its entirety, we do know that people are different depending on their tasks and that the standards of goodness or badness are situational, depending on the setting and the task.

This contextual approach to dealing with the question is similar to two fundamental concepts of organization theory. The first is that organizations, professions, legislatures, businesses, and so on are "culture-bearing milieux" (Louis, 1983). The symbols, myths, metaphors, and language systems of various institutions—governmental agencies, houses of representatives, and businesses—are the artifacts of their organization culture. Second, organizations are systems of shared meanings as much as they are collectives of individuals working toward shared objectives.

The organization culture defines what is good and bad, and it attributes meaning or importance to goodness and badness (Smirich, 1983). Research on the contrasting response of Danish and German civil servants to the Holocaust bears this out. Chapter Nine describes how the culture and shared meanings of Danish civil servants did not allow them to accept the deportation and killing of the Jews, whereas it was accepted by most German civil servants. The differing structures of the Canadian and U.S. governments have led to different understandings of and approaches to conflict-of-interest laws in the public sector (Stark, 1993). And the facts of history and culture explain much of the variation in traditional corruption, such as graft among local contractors, in American cities (Holbrook and Meier, 1993).

In the governmental context, individuals are parsed into two general groupings—political and administrative. The political is meant to include both elected and politically appointed officials, while the administrative group includes the merit-based civil service and certain executives, such as city managers, who are appointed on the basis of professional rather than political criteria. In the federal government, the Civil Service Reform Act of 1978 called for a sharp increase in political (in this case presidential) appointees to provide for greater "policy responsiveness" on the part of the bureaucracy. During the Reagan presidency, these positions were filled with people who were generally loyal to the president's policy preferences. Few of the appointees had governmental experience; most came from business backgrounds. By any measure, policy responsiveness was based significantly on the president's preferences, even when it ran counter to both the Constitution and the law.

Significantly, the Reagan administration was also the most corrupt administration in recent memory (Welfeld, 1992; Pasztor, 1995). Did this happen primarily because bad people were brought into the administration? Did it happen because these new appointees found themselves in a governmental setting that they did not entirely understand and so engaged in practices that would have been either accepted or tolerated in business or professional settings? Or did the corruption occur because many of these appointees had little respect for government—because in their eyes the government was, after all, the problem? All three explanations may contribute to an understanding of corruption in the Reagan years, but the most salient explanation is probably that there are different standards for ethics in government than there are in business.

Governmental scandals such as Abscam and lesser examples indicate that some members of Congress and of state legislatures were willing to take bribes. Bribe-taking is a crime for which there should be no defense, even considering that the legislative setting is unique. The savings and loan fiasco—especially as it concerns the Keating Five—indicates that the close connection between political campaign contributions and legislative intervention in regulatory and administrative processes is laden with questions of ethics. Clearly, accepting bribes is understood to be unethical and illegal; intervening on behalf of a contributor, however, may be unethical—but it is legal.

The Ill Winds defense-contracting scandal involved primarily politically appointed public officials (Pasztor, 1995). But the laws and standards of ethics in defense procurement are clear, both for political appointees and for civil servants. The Ill Winds scandal was almost exclusively associated with political appointees. The scandals in the 1980s involving the Department of Housing and Urban Development (HUD) were also examples of high-level political wrongdoing rather than problems of bureaucratic "fraud, waste, and abuse" (Welfeld, 1992).

The point of mentioning these scandals is simple. Much greater evidence of scandal is associated with political appointees than with the merit-based civil service. Yet the general public has seldom distinguished between the behavior of political appointees and civil servants; all people see is corruption. The result has been a general decline in the legitimacy of government. The irony, of course, is that elected officials tend to blame the bureaucracy for fraud, waste, and abuse. The evidence shows, however, that it is *not* the bureaucrats who are practicing fraud—it is the appointees of elected officials. But when one public official sins—politician or not—all public officials are punished, at least in the court of public opinion.

One solution, of course, is to appoint "better types"—an argument that is widely used to explain how government can be improved. Better types can mean, in political terms, merely electing someone else to office. Indeed, the research of Holbrook and Meier (1993) shows that local governmental corruption is reduced by high levels of electoral competition and high voter turnout. But more often, better types means "types like us." The term as used by business executives means that individuals should be either elected or appointed to office who are from the business world or who share the values of business. The better types argument is used in the antibureaucratic sense, usually by politicians or business leaders, to suggest that public servants are lazy or unresponsive and that people with political or business backgrounds would be preferable.

In the governmental reform era, appointing better types meant replacing the spoils system with a merit-based civil service, and weakening political parties at the local level by structural changes that resulted in the election of business leaders and community-oriented individuals. In many ways the better types argument corroborates the view that the question of whether people are inherently good or bad is not nearly as important as whether persons are inclined toward political, bureaucratic, business, legal, medical, or other values and cultures.

The levels of moral reasoning perspective is an interesting cousin of the better types argument. According to Kohlberg, there are lesser to greater levels of moral reasoning depending on a variety of personality, demographic, contextual, and other factors. Therefore, different levels of moral or ethical development can be demonstrated (Kohlberg, 1980; Rest, 1986). Lesser or greater levels of moral reasoning are dependent on knowledge of the problem or situation, the time given to analysis and understanding, and the nature of the problem (Stewart and Sprinthall, 1993). Demography and organizational context among administrators does not influence levels of moral reasoning.

The point here is that careful and analytical approaches to problems improve the chances for moral or ethical solutions, at least in public administration settings (Stewart and Sprinthall, 1993). Implicit in much of this research is the possibility to improve the moral reasoning of public administrators by education, reasoning, and analytical processes (Lewis, 1991). Within a given context, therefore, people can be made better. That is certainly the message in much of the humanistic and group oriented decision-making perspective on public administration ethics (Denhardt, 1988).

What, then, can be concluded about the nature-of-man issue and the question of ethics in government administration? First, we can conclude that definitions of corruption vary by profession and setting, as do standards of ethical behavior. Second, the general bell curve of humankind from good to bad probably holds for each setting and profession. Third, it is in government that the most stringent standards and ethics expectations are found, especially in the administrative parts of government. Fourth, individuals from other settings, when placed in government, are more likely than are their governmental counterparts to breach standards of governmental ethics. Fifth, within government there are significant differences between the standards and ethics expectations of elected or political people and their appointed or civil service counterparts. And finally, it is possible to improve the moral reasoning of people in any organized context.

Making Ethical Decisions: Doing Right or Wrong

We shift from the question of whether people are inherently good or bad to the question of the rightness or wrongness of decisions. This suspends the question of contextual variation in definitions of good and bad and the nature of man in different contexts and simply asks whether a particular decision, set of decisions, or pattern of decisions is right or wrong, and why. The approach used here rests on two broad philosophical traditions. The first is the deontological tradition of decisions based on fundamental principles; the other is a teleological tradition of decisions based on calculations of their likely consequences or results (Lewis, 1991; Bok, 1978; French, 1983; Strauss and Cropsey, 1987).

In the deontological tradition, which is most particularly associated with Aquinas and Kant, decisions are based on duties or principles that are either right or wrong in themselves, the results being irrelevant to moral judgment. "Deontological reasoning comes in many shades, depending upon whether the rules of behavior are seen as permanent and universal; knowable or unknowable; derived from revelation, human law, or community norms; and so on. All permutations dictate that there are certain underlying rules according to which behavior is judged, and no matter how desirable the consequences, there are certain things managers (and government) may not do" (Lewis, 1991, p. 88).

The teleological tradition, which is most particularly associated with Mill and Bentham, is in the modern context often referred to as utilitarianism. In this tradition, decisions are judged by their consequences depending on the results to be maximized—security, happiness, pleasure, dignity, and the like. Results can be judged on the basis of the individual, the family, the neighborhood, the group or organization, the political jurisdiction, or the nation-state.

Explicit standards of right and wrong are a defining feature of American government. When taken together, the federal and state constitutions and laws and the charters and laws of the states' lesser jurisdictions are by any measure an impressive collection of definitions of right and wrong. In addition, countless administrative regulations have been adopted pursuant to laws and carrying the force of law. Add to this mix an entire branch of government established in part to interpret and protect the constitutions and laws. Although it may be trite to say, ours is a nation of laws and not of people. We certainly have an impressive deontological array of constitutions, laws, and regulations that codify our values and define the principles of right and wrong as we see them. Much of the study of ethics in American government is embedded in the constitutional-legal perspective (Rohr, 1989; Rosenbloom, 1983; Cooper, 1992).

Despite the law, citizens tend on one hand toward considerable tolerance for less egregious forms of corruption, such as conflicts of interest, blatant exercise of political influence, and small illegal monetary exchanges (Malek, 1993). On the other hand, citizens consider bribery, extortion, or the unlawful exchange of large sums of money ethically unacceptable. So regardless of the law, there is relatively widespread tolerance of petty corruption in American government (Malek, 1993). This would seem to indicate that absolute principles of ethics, in the deontological tradition, are usually malleable depending on the seriousness of the ethical breach.

If citizens express a considerable tolerance for petty corruption, is there also a problem of regime legitimacy? Is government generally held in low regard and therefore unable to sustain strong public support because of petty corruption? Probably not. But strong evidence suggests that people are much more inclined to obey the law if they believe it to be just and fair and if they believe that procedural justice exists in the administration of law (Tyler, 1990). Regime legitimacy is a function of fairness, equity, and some level of official benevolence in administering the law. To the extent to which both petty and grand corruption detract from fairness, equity, and official benevolence, they reduce regime legitimacy. The larger deontological issue here is the identification of fairness, equity, and benevolence as high-order ethical principles.

The current disquiet over the electoral advantage of incumbents further illustrates that issues of fairness and equity seem to be importantly connected to regime legitimacy. Efforts to limit the number of terms served by incumbents would presumably level the electoral playing field. That possibility seems more important to many voters than the experience or expertise of legislators.

Procedural controls established during the reform movement to reduce corruption were generally successful. Judged in any comparative way, American government is among the most clean or ethical. But these procedures are the "red tape" that causes government to be slow, non-risk-taking, bureaucratic, and nonresponsive. Perhaps the best evidence, however, that these anticorruption procedures work is the research that indicates that when such procedures are taken away to make government more businesslike, there is an increase in corruption (Henriques, 1986).

At the time of the reform movement, it was thought that elected officials worked in the realm of values in making laws and setting budgets. Administration was neutral, a value-free implementation of law and legislative intent. With the destruction of the policy-administration dichotomy, it became clear that values and political power are operative from the agenda-setting stage of the public policy process to the street-level implementation of policy (Waldo, 1949). The values and moral reasoning patterns of public administrators and civil servants became, then, almost as important as the values of elected officials (Cooper, 1990).

During this period, professional associations for public administrators rapidly developed codes of ethics and offered training programs and courses in ethics. Many jurisdictions adopted codes and standards. These codes and programs were primarily deontological—that is, they were statements of agreed-upon or settled values. The assumptions have been Kantian—that there are absolute principles of right and wrong, independent of results or consequences, and that public administrators will adhere to these values. Research on ethics for public administrators indicates that the Kantian assumption is essentially correct—that civil servants are significantly inclined to support values such as civic virtue, honesty, procedural fairness, equity, and human dignity (Menzel, 1993; Lewis, 1991). Good evidence also shows that citizens expect their government to be fair and equitable, even though these concepts are difficult to define (Hochschield, 1981).

On its face, this seems an odd finding, because public administrators live and work in a world that is unrelentingly teleological, a world in which policy and program results rule. In this world, the public administrator practices, to borrow from Simon (1947), "bounded ethics." In bounded ethics, the administrator functions within the limits of enabling legislation, with limited budgets, usually advocating or at least supporting the purposes of the agency. Questioning fundamentally the purposes and practices of the agency on the basis of morality issues is seldom found and rarely encouraged (Meltsner, 1979; Amy, 1984). Whistle-blowing is very risky to the whistle-blower and seldom results in fundamental organizational change (Perry, 1993; Glazer and Glazer, 1989; Johnson and Kraft, 1990; Jos, Tompkins, and Hays, 1989).

Following bounded ethics, the public administrator is—within the limits of organizational purpose and funding—almost always honest, virtuous, procedurally fair, and efficient. Indeed, many top public administrators have been and are examples of high morality in government (Cooper and Wright, 1992). To accept this conclusion, however, one must accept the boundaries within which the public administrator works.

There is another explanation for civil servants' apparent relative sense of right and wrong. Their work is embedded in rules, guidelines, inspections, forms, reports, and the other impedimenta of ethics enforcement. We have little doubt that these requirements are ethics enhancing, although it is likely that they inhibit workflow and creativity and reduce responsiveness. With all of these procedural guides, inspections, and oversight, what accounts for the occurrence of the HUD scandal, the Ill Winds scandal, the savings and loan scandal? The answer is that these scandals were primarily political rather than bureaucratic. Paul Light (1993a) describes how the impending HUD scandal was regularly reported to Congress by the HUD inspectors general: "As for the influence-peddling scheme at the top of the agency, the [inspectors general] simply were not equipped to pursue such high-level wrongdoing. Their task was primarily to look down for scandal, not *up*" (p. 112).

The antigovernmental, probusiness ethos of the last fifteen years has taken its toll on governmental ethics. Concepts of privatization and third-party government are especially in favor. Government, to use a word currently in vogue, is being reinvented to put together public-private partnerships, "empower" citizens with choices, and so on. In sum, it is now fashionable to degovernmentalize on the promise of saving money and improving services. If previously governmental functions are shifted to the private sector or are shared, it is a safe bet that corruption will increase. It is no small irony that government is moving in the direction of privatization at the same time that there is a rising concern for governmental ethics.

A similar paradox can be found in the universities. In public administration and public policy studies, the teleological perspective holds the high ground. The wholesale adoption of policy analysis based on the measurement of results in terms of efficiency is a factor, as is the popularity of the market model and theories of games, public choice, and cost-benefit analysis. What is right or wrong, what is moral or ethical, is to be judged in terms of utility of consequences. That such an approach is without a larger sense of absolute right or wrong is generally understood (Amy, 1984; Tong, 1986). In the presence of this utilitarian hegemony, the universities are rediscovering ethics. It is especially interesting that many of the leaders of the new ethics groups on campuses are neo-Kantians (Jennings, 1991).

What, then, can be concluded about ethical decision making in government and the doing of right and wrong? First, we can conclude that the ethics of decisions are often based in the constitution(s), regulations, and the law. Second, rules, regulations, reports, oversight, inspections, and the like do enhance the potential for ethical decisions, as do professional standards and codes of ethics. Third, public administrators practice a form of bounded ethics that generally accepts the agency's purposes and policies, and practices ethics within those bounds. Fourth, the most notable ethical breaches in recent years have been political rather than administrative. Fifth, citizens are concerned with issues of fairness, equity, and justice and are likely to view government as less legitimate when these issues are not met satisfactorily and when scandals occur. Sixth, as government moves in the direction of privatization, the potential for ethical breaches increases. Seventh, the study of public policy and the practice of policy analysis in American universities take a teleological and utilitarian perspective, while most of the theory associated with the new university centers for ethics study is deontological.

Democracy and Ethics: The Issue of Accountability

Central to the practice of government administration is the issue of accountability. Before the policy-administration dichotomy was rendered a myth, it was possible to beg the question of accountability, falling back on the rhetoric if not the substance of neutrality. No more. Beginning fifty years ago with Herman Finer (1941) and continuing to this day is a stream of scholarship that seeks forms of democratic control over the bureaucracy. In our time, Lowi (1969) argues for a juridical democracy in which laws are precise and bureaucratic latitude in carrying out those laws is nil. Gruber (1987) seeks bureaucratic control through both legislative and presidential actions. Burke (1986) looks for balance between democratic control through legislators and elected executives and informed discretion on the part of bureaucrats. In each of these perspectives, there is the assumption that there is a bureaucratic control problem.

Carl Friedrich (1940) counters Finer (1941) by arguing that effective administrative conduct requires bureaucratic expertise, along with the discretion to apply such expertise. A host of public administration scholars have over the years supported this position (Willbern, 1984; Long, 1949; Lilla, 1981). In recent years, the concept of taking personal responsibility for decisions and actions, especially associated with Dennis Thompson (1987), is put forth as a way to cope with the problems of "dirty hands" (that is, the fact that policy implementation requires one to get one's hands dirty) and "many hands" (the fact that all important actions are usually collective).

Public administrators cannot take personal responsibility unless they have some discretion, except in the case of refusing to act. John Rohr (1989) argues persuasively that there is a constitutional and legal basis for extensive bureaucratic discretion. Charles Goodsell (1995) claims that without bureaucratic discretion, government is ineffective.

The entire issue turns on the question of whether bureaucracy acts without controls or accountability, and the extent to which this occurs. Much of the discussion of bureaucratic controls and accountability simply assumes their absence. In fact, the question of controls and accountability is usually caught up in the political battle between the policy preferences of legislators (Congress, state legislatures, and city councils) and elected executives (president, governors, and strong mayors). Standard political rhetoric states that presidents or governors call for greater controls over bureaucracy when their administrations are carrying out the law and spending authorized appropriations on programs that the president or governor does not like. Legislators act in the same manner. Does this mean that the bureaucracy is out of control or unaccountable? No. Still, a surprising number of scholars accept this rhetoric as true and proceed to the question of controls and accountability.

Available research on the subject indicates the following: bureaucrats tend to be responsive—within the law and their appropriations—to executive direction (Seidman and Gilmour, 1986; Moe, 1982; Weingast and Moran, 1983; Wood and Waterman, 1991); in cases of the absence of accountability or a violation of the law or standards of ethics (such as occurred in the FBI under Hoover), both congressional and presidential oversight and controls failed (Hart and Hart, 1992); administrative agencies and their leaders are both experts and advocates for their tasks or missions and will seek support for those missions among legislators and elected executives (Kelman, 1987); interest groups and clients will support the programs and budgets of agencies supporting their interests (Thompson, 1967).

Simply put, there are very few examples of bureaucratic agencies operating outside the ordinary range of legislative and executive accountability. (The activities of Oliver North in the Reagan administration come to mind, but his was hardly a regularly established administrative agency with enabling legislation, a bureaucracy, or a budget approved by Congress.)

Perception is more important than reality. It is widely believed, particularly among elected officials, that government is rife with serious problems of bureaucratic control and accountability. Consequently, a wide range of legislation establishing prohibitions

against conflicts of interest has been enacted, and elaborate reporting procedures have been designed to prevent such conflicts—
such as designated ethics officers in federal agencies, inspectors
general in federal departments, agency codes of ethics, ethics hot
lines, ethics boards and commissions at the state and local levels,
and so on. Do they work? Yes. The inspector general system does
serve as an effective check against possible corruption (Light, 1993a,
1993b). And yes, codes of ethics "do less than everything and more
than nothing" (Lewis, 1991, p. 140). In addition, whistle-blowing is
a deterrent to possible agency misbehavior (Perry, 1993).

Most important, these steps have very likely increased democratic controls and decreased administrative discretion (Lewis,
1991). We may be close to Lowi's juridical democracy (1969). The
problem, of course, is that the effective administration of governmental affairs is diminished as a result.

Consider the opposite argument. Morgan and Kass (1993) discovered that local-level public administrators are experiencing a
role reversal in which elected officials will not or cannot decide issues and make policy. Under such circumstances, is it unethical for
bureaucrats to do nothing, especially if doing nothing would be
fundamentally harmful to the public? Should the civil servant take
responsibility when elected officials will not or cannot? Is the policy gridlock such that there can be no common ground on highly
charged emotional issues such as abortion or on especially complicated social issues such as health care policy? In circumstances
like these, do we have questions of role reversal? Can we turn the
policy-administration dichotomy on its head?

In this dichotomy, elected officials set policy and appointed officials carry it out—that is, they manage. We appear to be more
nearly able to agree on how to do certain things—to manage—
than we are on what should be done. Morgan and Kass call for a
revised moral framework that enables administrators to articulate
a complex ordering of moral claims compatible with our constitutional system of government. This is relatively close to Rohr's description (1989) of a constitutional basis for the administrative
role's legitimacy in American government.

There is no evidence, however, that Congress, state legislatures,
and city and county councils are inclined toward specificity in the
law, precise policy direction, or adequate funding to carry out policy

or to cease intervening in administrative affairs. The problems for administrators are still there—and now the administrators have less discretion to deal with the problems. As policy gridlock at the national level worsens, will we see a resurrection of the bureaucracy? Or is administration of the national government so diminished in latitude and so hamstrung with congressional micromanagement that we have the worst of both worlds—a Congress that cannot make policy and a bureaucracy that cannot manage?

What can be concluded about ethics and democracy and the issue of accountability? First, the perception that public bureaucracies are beyond control or unaccountable is widespread, although there is little evidence to support such a perception. Second, most evidence indicates that bureaucrats are accountable and controlled. But certain bureaucracies are powerful participants in the policymaking process and have influential protectors in the political world. Third, ethics controls on bureaucrats have been stepped up sharply, while administrative latitude and discretion have declined. Fourth, policy gridlock may possibly result in administrative role reversal, with an accompanying ethical dilemma.

Policy Ethics and Politics

The careful reader will have noticed that the *big questions* in ethics have not been addressed in this chapter of *The Spirit of Public Administration*. Indeed, some might regard the earlier parts of this chapter to be concerned mostly with petty ethics and governmental corruption. Because the book's main emphasis is on government administration, it offers virtually no treatment of legislative or electoral ethics, even though these too are often regarded as petty ethics. Bureaucracies do, however, connect to and sometimes influence larger matters of ethics—policy ethics—so we will briefly consider them here.

In a democratic polity, it would be correct to assume that the main venue for considering policy ethics is legislative. In fact, however, many policy ethics issues have become the province of the judicial branch. The issue of war is an exception; it has been left to the executive and legislative branches of government. War is perhaps the issue most laden with questions of morality. In comparing the attitudes of members of Congress and military officers toward war, Tamashiro, Secrest, and Brunk (1993) found that both groups agree on national self-protection and the moral authority of the state as appropriate justifications for war and the involuntary taking of life. But members of Congress are more willing than military officials to accept the risks of war, while those in the military are more inclined to view war as a policy tool. Certainly, the contrasting views of General Colin Powell and Secretary of Defense Richard Cheney on when and how to enter the Gulf War confirm these differing perspectives on the risks of war.

Many of the other big policy ethics issues, while belonging to the legislature(s), are decided by the courts. For example, the vexing issues of equity in per-student spending for public education is now in the courts in more than one-third of the states. The issues of property rights versus environmental protection are decided by the courts. Most states have had to increase their prison capacity sharply in response to court orders.

The point is clear: both elected executives and legislatures no longer wrestle with all of the great issues. They, along with the bureaucracy, often simply react to the courts' decisions. It is for this reason that proposed appointments to the Supreme Court receive as much attention and scrutiny as do senatorial or presidential candidates. It should also come as no surprise that scholars who study the big issues of ethics now tend to be professors of law. In public administration and political science, scholars tend to focus on smaller ethical issues; fortunately, philosophers still work on big questions.

The major policy ethics issues that remain the province of the legislative and executive branches often involve distributive justice (Frederickson, 1990). Examples include the morality of a health care system that fails to provide access for significant numbers of citizens; homelessness and low-quality housing; a transportation system that emphasizes highway construction and maintenance but does comparatively little to improve inner-city public transit; intergenerational inequity, as in the relatively favorable circumstances of the elderly compared with the children of the poor; the transferring of most of the costs of toxic waste disposal from this generation to the next; and the relative emphasis on funding research on one disease, such as AIDS, rather than another, such as breast cancer. It is clear that of all the moral or ethical issues faced by government, the issues most significant to the people have to do with fairness and justice.

Under conditions of majority rule, the distribution of taxes and benefits will likely favor the majority, or at least a coalition of influential minorities. There is maldistribution, sometimes on a massive scale. Where does the bureaucracy fit into this? At the service level, the evidence we have suggests both an ethic and the practice of forms of social equity that ameliorate some of the effects of majority rule (Lineberry, 1977).

What, then, can be concluded about policy ethics? First, we can conclude that many issues of policy ethics are handled by the courts. Second, legislatures, elected executives, and bureaucracies often react to judge-imposed policy. Third, both elected and appointed government officials often deal with issues of petty and midlevel ethics. Fourth, the major ethical issues faced by elected officials and public administrators have to do with distributive justice.

Issues of Business and Governmental Ethics

So why are problems with governmental corruption and with the ethics of public officials increasing? The answer: because we are losing our ability to think governmentally and to be governmental. To better understand this contention, consider two dimensions of contemporary government. The first is the structure and organization of activities done by or through government; the second is the set of beliefs, values, and experiences of individuals who function within the structures and organizations associated with government.

Consider a continuum with government at one end and business or enterprise at the other. To contrast the differences between structures and organizations that are primarily governmental in character rather than primarily enterprising, we use the following examples. Traditional governmental purchasing is done through bidding processes, elaborate specifications, and budget controls. In enterprise, purchasing is considerably flexible. In government, people are hired through a merit-based civil service system and are categorized, paid, and promoted in organized and routine ways— usually with grievance procedures to protect them. In enterprise, particularly where no union hiring is done, employment is often by managerial choice; job descriptions, equal pay for equal work, and similar procedures and notions may or may not be in place. In government, the tradition of checks and balances between those elected to represent the people, the executive and those who administer, and the courts is always operative. In enterprise, boards of directors are self-renewing and may have only a limited connection to either the primary stockholders or the clients—and are often only marginally connected with the enterprise itself. In government, particular bureaucrats carry out particular day-to-day administrative tasks. In enterprise, responsibility for carrying out duties may or may not be clearly defined. Governmental work is covered by extensive legislative and judicial oversight, as well as by considerable press attention. While enterprise may be subject to some regulation, it ordinarily receives little governmental oversight and minimal press attention. The biggest difference between enterprise and government is that enterprise is driven by the bottom line—the need to be profitable—while government operates on fixed budgets with service and regulatory measures of effectiveness.

These days it is popular to believe that many public functions can be more effectively carried out if they are operated more as an enterprise and less as a governmental organization. However, a review of the research and literature on the subject of corruption in government yields the following proposition:

Proposition One

The propensity for corruption and unethical behavior increases as organization and structure moves from the governmental model to the enterprise model.

As we increasingly privatize governmental activities—as we move from the direct carrying out of governmental services to contracting these services to free enterprise—we increase the propensity for corruption and unethical behavior.

The second continuum in this review would place individuals who are civically inclined at one pole and those who are privately inclined at the other. Individuals who work in organizations have a wide range of beliefs, values, and experiences with respect to government on one hand and private enterprise on the other. Those who are more civically inclined would generally have some interest in and respect for government; those who are privately inclined would generally be opposed to governmental regulation of business. People who are civically inclined tend to have some notion of the greater good or the public interest; those who are privately inclined tend to be more interested in the bottom line or in maintaining the economy through commerce. And finally, individuals interested in service would be regarded as more civically inclined and those interested in wealth as more privately inclined.

Research indicates that differences in individual beliefs, values, and experiences can significantly influence the careers that people choose, as well as their attitudes toward enterprise on the one hand and governance on the other. Consider, therefore, proposition two.

Proposition Two

The propensity for corruption and unethical behavior increases as the preponderance of individuals in an organization moves from the civically to the privately inclined.

If the dominant ethos or collective attitude in a governmental organization is civically inclined, then the emphasis on service, the greater good, the public interest, and effective government will be obvious. Conversely, if the governmental organization is increasingly served by those with private inclinations, who tend toward practices that in business are regarded as either acceptable or appropriate but that in government are considered unethical or corrupt, then corruption will result.

For purposes of the explication of these two dimensions consider the matrix illustrated in Figure 7.1.

The most significant problem that occurs when structures and organizations are matched with personal inclinations is listed in the lower right-hand box of the matrix. As privately inclined individuals move into positions of governmental responsibility, the evidence indicates that their beliefs, attitudes, and values are at odds with governmental and public definitions of ethical behavior. It is often for this reason that we find corruption and an absence of ethical behavior in government. Such behavior is not, however, primarily on the part of civil servants; rather, it occurs when individuals with privately inclined values come into governmental service.

**Figure 7.1. The Effects of Personal Inclinations
and Organization and Structure on Corruption and
Ethics in Government.**

| | | Personal Inclinations | |
		Civic	Private
Organization and Structure	Government	Likely to be least corrupt, most ethical	Likely to experience some corruption and unethical behavior, but within government
	Enterprise	As distance from government increases, chances for corruption and unethical behavior increase	Most likely to experience corruption and unethical behavior due to a lack of controls

The second most serious problem, as indicated in the lower left-hand box of the matrix, is the extent to which traditionally governmental activities have moved in the direction of privatization or contracting out. Diana Henriques's splendid analysis of public authorities, *The Machinery of Greed* (1986), illustrates the extent to which offering public services through the enterprise model has led to widespread corruption and an absence of ethics. Consider also Andy Pasztor's recent thorough analysis (1995) of the Ill Winds defense procurement scandal, which concluded that the enterprise model and careless political appointments resulted in enormous corruption. Welfeld (1992) found the same in the HUD scandals.

Certainly, no government is free of problems of ethics and corruption. The issue here is a matter of degrees. Based on research data, the two propositions presented here indicate that degrees of corruption and unethical behavior increase as more privately inclined people are appointed to governmental positions and as more governmental services are based on the enterprise model.

The conclusion one draws from this is that by attempting to adapt governmental practices to business, we pay a considerable price in ethics. In addition, we have little direct evidence that using so-called business practices or hiring people with strong private inclinations makes governmental services any more efficient or economical. Finally, as corruption and unethical behavior increase, citizens are inclined toward lessened respect for politics and government. Therefore, the legitimacy of government is reduced in the eyes of the public.

"A government ill executed," Alexander Hamilton wrote in *The Federalist* 70, "whatever it might be in theory, must be in practice a poor government" (Hamilton, Madison, and Jay, 1961, p. 423). The key to good execution of governmental affairs is *not* to try to make governments into businesses, but rather to make government work as the Founders intended.

Conclusions

The governmental reform movement of the early twentieth century has had a lasting effect on American government. Will the current push toward ethics reform have the same staying power and result in permanent changes? The answer is probably yes—especially if the incidence of governmental corruption continually decreases. But in the earlier movement, corruption was reduced by increasing administrative capacity and decreasing politics. In the present case, we are moving in the opposite direction—reducing administrative capacity and increasing political control—with the probability that more rather than less corruption will result. Today, of course, government provides more controls on political corruption than in the past. Whether they will work remains to be seen.

We end this chapter with a list of assertions—preliminary attempts to synthesize and summarize what is known about ethics in governmental administration. These assertions are meant to stimulate research and analysis and should be thought of as subject to testing and verification.

The future ethics research agenda should include the following six tasks.

First, standards of right and wrong vary significantly from context to context. Yet much of the literature on ethics (especially the deontological literature) sets out universal standards of behavior. This is a sensible approach for certain matters of right and wrong, such as for standards of human dignity, the sanctity of life, and adherence to the constitution(s) and law. But for many ethical issues, standards and expectations are situationally determined. Future research should focus on the settings, professions, and cultures in which ethical issues occur and measure behavior against the cultural expectations and professional standards appropriate to the research context.

Second, once this is done, researchers should compare ethical standards and behavior between settings, professions, and cultures. In this way, the richness and variety of the common ethical themes (and variations on those themes) can be described.

Third, researchers should assess the effect on the behavior of government officials, both political and administrative, of traditional procedural and managerial controls compared with modern approaches such as ethics officers, codes of ethics, inspectors general, and whistle-blowing.

Fourth, education and training are two of the most important modern techniques by which governments, professions, and universities attempt to enhance ethical behavior. Researchers should measure the actual results of education and training on behavior.

Fifth, researchers should assess the influence of privatization on governmental corruption and on ethics.

Sixth, researchers should measure the effects of reduced administrative discretion on both administrative effectiveness and ethics.

Chapter Eight

The Paradox of Distance and the Problem of Role Differentiation

with David G. Frederickson

> *[What] do Americans experience from bureaucracy? . . .*
> *Most clients of bureaucracy are satisfied most of the time*
> *with what happens to them, and often very satisfied.*
> *Bureaucrats are seen as usually helpful, honest, responsive,*
> *adaptive, efficient, dependable, fair, friendly, respectful,*
> *considerate, courteous. This is true at all levels of*
> *government and even in difficult low-reputation fields*
> *such as law enforcement, public welfare and the Postal*
> *Service.*
> CHARLES T. GOODSELL, *THE CASE FOR BUREAUCRACY*, P. 46

Public suspicion of government—and particularly the administrative features of government—is imbedded in our culture. As Stillman (1990) puts it, the "American Revolution was largely waged against the royal bureaucracy, and the administrative misdeeds of George III" (p. 20). And George III's colonial governors—his field staff—"were at the heart of the specific charges against the Crown cited in the Declaration of Independence" (p. 20).

Originally, the United States was an agrarian society that valued self-sufficiency more than it valued strong government. In 1835, Alexis de Tocqueville, reporting on his observations of the American character and of American attitudes toward government, found

183

that "a private individual [mediating] an undertaking however directly connected it may be with the welfare of society, . . . never thinks of soliciting the co-operation of the Government; . . . he publishes a plan, offers to execute it himself, courts the assistance of other individuals, and struggles manfully against all obstacles" (Tocqueville, [1835] 1970, p. 79).

Even during the nation's youth, presidential candidates used antibureaucracy as a main tenet of their platforms. Andrew Jackson, for example, thought that the duties of government officials were quite simple and that anyone of average intelligence could quickly learn them (Mosher, 1982). Bureaucrat-bashing fell out of fashion in the Progressive Era and during the great governmental reform movement at the beginning of the twentieth century; indeed, administrative expertise and executive power were seen as the answer to problems of corruption in government. By any measure, government is more ethical and less corrupt today than it was in the nineteenth century.

The considerable growth of government administration during the first half of the twentieth century is impressive. For example, approximately half of American cities use the council-manager form of local government, a system that did not exist in 1900 (Frederickson, 1995). In the 1950s and 1960s, it was common to refer to public administration—which included a merit-based civil service, a formal budgeting process, purchasing and bid controls, and a considerable deference for expertise—as the fourth branch of government.

Bureaucrat-bashing and a broad challenge to merit-based civil service, expertise, and professionalism in public administration began again in the 1970s and continues to this day. The most common form of contemporary criticism of the administrative parts of government is to associate them with "fraud, waste, and abuse," a phrase of particular usefulness to those seeking elective office (Downs and Larkey, 1986). This political mantra has had a profound effect on the public's perception of government in general and on public perception of government officials' ethics specifically.

We will treat two aspects of contemporary perceptions of these ethics. First, we will set out the paradox of distance, in which public opinion tends to be negative toward government and public officials in the abstract. But in their specific experiences with governmental programs and particular public officials, individual citizens tend to hold favorable views. Second, we will describe the absence of role differentiation in the public's perception of government official's ethics. The public tends not to distinguish between individuals who are elected to legislative bodies, those elected as executives, those who are politically appointed, and permanent civil servants. Finally, we connect the paradox of distance and the problem of role differentiation to explain why citizens hold negative views of public administrators. We also suggest that contemporary reforms, which are partly a response to criticisms of government and public officials, will result in more rather than less governmental corruption.

The Paradox of Distance

The prevailing sentiment of citizens of the United States is that government is ineffectual and corrupt and that government employees are incompetent and dishonest. In a recent poll, more than two-thirds of U.S. citizens thought that the federal government "creates more problems than it solves" ("Present Critique of Government," 1993, p. 89). Beyond the general question of the government's ability to solve problems is the question of efficiency. A 1992 survey found that 70 percent of Americans believed that "when something is run by government, it is usually inefficient and wasteful" ("Dissatisfaction with Our Government," 1994, p. 88). When asked whether the federal government's poor performance was due to the fact that the "problems are very difficult" or that "government is incompetent," a clear majority felt that governmental incompetence caused the poor performance. Twenty years ago, 60 percent of Americans felt that the government was run by a few big interests; today 75 percent hold that view.

This information seems to point to the public's belief that government is failing to perform the tasks it was set up to accomplish. These views, however, reflect how citizens feel about "the government" in the abstract, rather than how they view specific governmental functions or how they feel about encounters they have had with actual government officials. Most surveys and polls ask very general questions; they ordinarily do not ask about the provision of specific governmental services, the competence of specific civil servants, or even the effectiveness of specific governmental programs.

What is the level of satisfaction experienced by citizens who have actual encounters with bureaucrats? Are citizens satisfied or dissatisfied with the specific public services they receive?

In groundbreaking research in the mid-1970s, a group of scholars at the Survey Research Center of the University of Michigan discovered a fundamental paradox in the attitudes of citizens toward government. When asked how they felt about federal agencies in general, citizens usually responded negatively. But when asked for specific evaluations of how they were treated by a particular agency in a specific instance, they gave much more favorable responses (Katz, Gutek, Kahn, and Barton, 1975). In another study, Charles Goodsell (1980) interviewed the clients of three different welfare programs and discovered that "half to two-thirds of the clients interviewed perceived 'lots' of interest, effort, courtesy, and efficiency . . . the client[s] tended to perceive officials as interested and civil, but also businesslike and not gushy." He found somewhat similar results in a 1976 research study on postal clerks in different countries.

More recently, in *The Case for Bureaucracy* (1995), Goodsell presents the results of detailed surveys that collected information about Americans' attitudes toward specific governmental services with which they are familiar. These 1992 surveys were given to recipients of many of the most maligned agencies and service fields of government, including the Postal Service, public welfare, and law enforcement. The results are both surprising and encouraging: most people describe their encounters with public administrators as favorable experiences. The surveys report that "positive evaluation response rates tend to be at the two-thirds level at a minimum and often reach beyond 75 percent. Disapproval levels usually fall well below one-third" (p. 86). After a thorough review of all the surveys and research on the subject, Goodsell offers this conclusion:

> Bureaucrats are seen as usually helpful, honest, responsive, adaptable, efficient, dependable, fair, friendly, respectful, considerate, courteous. This is true on all levels of government and even in difficult, low-reputation fields such as law enforcement, public welfare and the Postal Service. . . . The "hard" data on bureaucracy, then, are like "soft" citizen opinions—overwhelmingly favorably. Bureaucracy works. To claim otherwise is either to ignore the evidence or

to assert that we are being totally fooled by the paradigm of rationality, with only a few critical theorists able to escape the charade.
Yet when these critics mail a letter or draw Social Security, bureaucracy will work for them too [p. 90].

Public education is the largest category of domestic spending
among all levels of government. The conventional wisdom over the
past twenty years is that the public schools are ineffective and that
many teachers are incompetent. But what the people *really* think
is considerably different. Highly reliable annual surveys of attitudes
toward and perceptions of schooling in America have been conducted since the early 1980s by Harris for the *Phi Delta Kappan,* a
national magazine on schooling and education. When asked to as-
sign a grade to the nation's public schools as a whole, only 18 percent of respondents give them an A or a B, while 48 percent give
them a C. When asked to grade the schools in their community, 40
percent give an A or a B, and 31 percent give a C. When asked to
grade the school that their child attends or attended, 64 percent
give an A or a B, and 24 percent give a C. The public's evaluation
of teachers follows the same pattern. These results have been consistent for many years ("Annual Survey of Education and Schooling," 1992, p. 45).

This is the *paradox of distance:* while people trust and even revere those government officials who are near at hand, they believe
that government officials who are far away are lazy, incompetent,
and probably dishonest. An individual may feel that the principal
of the neighborhood school and the police officer who lives
around the corner are exceptional but at the same time may believe that the educational and law enforcement systems are in
shambles.

The paradox of distance is partly a function of political
rhetoric. It is useful to those seeking and holding political office
to focus on the problems of government and to associate those
problems with government workers. Downs and Larkey (1986) describe this as the "wrong problems problem": "The roots of society's inability to reduce crime, make America energy-independent,
eliminate inflation and unemployment, or provide sufficient low-
income housing lie in an absence of technology, resources and political will. They are not products of bureaucratic ineptness or lazy

and indifferent government workers. The belief that government's incapacities are the product of such failings may make election rhetoric more colorful and protect us from dealing with difficult problems and hard choices, but it brings none of these goals any closer" (p. 241).

The paradox of distance is also a function of citizens' general disengagement from public life—a disengagement reflected in, for example, significantly lower participation in voting and in a lack of civics knowledge. In many ways, the modern communitarian movement is an attempt to reconnect citizens with their governments (Etzioni, 1991).

The contemporary term limits movement is an interesting reflection of the paradox of distance. Because the same politicians tend to get reelected, several states and cities have adopted term limits as a means of achieving political turnover. The evidence indicates that political incumbency is powerful not only because those already in office have name recognition and strong access to election campaign funding but also because people tend to favor the representatives of their own communities or states. Most Americans hold a generally negative perception of professional politicians in general, while those politicians representing *them* are seen as fine.

How can the public be so ambivalent? How can people hold such contradictory views? In many ways, our public life is a world of paradox. We support majority rule and minority rights; we want reduced taxes and yet want to preserve funding for the programs we like; we believe in both a general public consensus and individual freedom, in both centralization and decentralized federalism, in being both isolationist and interventionist, in idealism and materialism, and in being consensus minded and yet prone to conflict (Kammen, 1972). Certainly, to believe that government is generally ineffective and that public officials are usually incompetent—while favoring bureaucrats who are in close proximity and supporting near-at-hand governmental programs—is no greater paradox than we Americans are accustomed to.

This paradox of distance presents an enormous challenge to public management. In the absence of economic markets as mechanisms for measuring need and performance, public officials and public organizations struggle with the difficult questions of public preferences. One of the solutions has been to try making government act like a market, to empower citizens to make individual choices through payment of fees for services or through the use of vouchers. At the margins, such an approach may help resolve the paradox of citizens' demanding services yet not wanting to pay taxes. But it does not resolve the paradox of distance.

We were admonished in the New Testament to "love thy neighbor." As the great German theologian Dietrich Bonhoeffer wrote before he was executed by the Nazis at Flossenberg in 1945:

> Nietzsche, without knowing it, was speaking in the spirit of the New Testament when he attacked the legalistic and philistine misinterpretation of [the] commandment which bids us love our neighbor. He wrote: "You are assiduous in your attention to your neighbor and you find beautiful words to describe your assiduity. But I tell you that your love for your neighbor is a worthless love for yourself. You go to your neighbor to seek refuge from yourself and then you try to make a virtue of it; but I see through your [unselfishness]. . . . Do I advise you to love your neighbor? I advise you rather to shun your neighbor and love whoever is furthest from you!" If beyond his neighbor a man does not know this one who is furthest from him as his neighbor, then he does not serve his neighbor but himself; he takes refuge from free open spaces of responsibility in the comforting confinement of the fulfillment of duty [Koestler, 1971, p. 205].

Because of the paradox of distance, the danger for public officials—and especially for career public administrators—is to respond effectively to one's neighbors because that is the dominant sentiment of public opinion and to respond less effectively (or even fail to respond) to those farther away, in other neighborhoods. Certainly, it is moral for benevolent public administrators to love their neighbors and to act as their neighbors' deputies in providing effective service. But given the paradox of distance, the greater morality may be for public officials to love and serve equitably those who are farthest away.

The Absence of Role Differentiation

"Government isn't the solution," Ronald Reagan regularly declared. "It is the problem." Elected on the promise of a minimalist national government and a vow to stamp out fraud, waste, and abuse, the Reagan administration was in many ways prophetic. By 1987, actual waste, fraud, and abuse had become very serious problems in government.

> More than 100 members of the Reagan Administration have had ethical or legal charges leveled against them. That number is without precedent. While the Reagan Administration's missteps may not have been as flagrant as the Teapot Dome scandal or as pernicious as Watergate, they seem more general, more pervasive and somehow more ingrained than those of any previous Administration. During other presidencies, scandals such as Watergate seemed to multiply from a single cancer; the Reagan Administration, however, appears to have suffered a breakdown of the immune system, opening the way to all kinds of ethical and moral infections [*Time,* May 25, 1987; pp. 18–25].

There is an interesting irony here. One of the major accomplishments of the Carter administration was the Civil Service Reform Act of 1978, whose purpose was to make the civil service more responsive to the president. This was to be achieved by replacing hundreds of upper-level merit-based positions filled by permanent civil servants with nonpermanent positions appointed by the president. Ronald Reagan was the first to fully implement the new presidentially responsive civil service model. One of the many results of this change was an administration with many more ethical problems than previous administrations had experienced (Pfiffner, 1985). All but a few of the charges, indictments, and convictions for corruption during the Reagan administration had to do with political appointments—and politically appointed individuals constitute less than 2 percent of the personnel in the executive branch's departments and agencies.

Beginning with Watergate and continuing through scandals involving the Department of Housing and Urban Development (HUD), the savings and loan industry, and the Iran-Contra arms sales, as well as lesser scandals, the public has witnessed what appears to be an increasingly unethical and corrupt government. It is no wonder that citizens hold a negative view of governmental ethics. The problem is that these negative views tend to lump together all public officials—the political appointee along with the merit-based civil servant. And because the ordinary citizen may not understand in any detail the differences between these roles in government, if those who are politically appointed commit a sin, everyone gets punished, at least in terms of public opinion.

A 1992 Roper survey seems to support the absence of any important differentiation in attitudes toward types of public officials. When public officials were categorized as federal agency officials (merit-based civil servants as well as politically appointed executives), as U.S. senators, or as members of the U.S. House of Representatives, each category received an approximately similar score: 4 to 5 percent of survey respondents held them in "high" opinion, and 35 to 43 percent rated them as "fairly good." Using Roper data, Lipset and Schneider (1983) found a significant gap between public expectations of institutions such as business, labor, and government, and the public's confidence in those institutions. While government received fewer votes of confidence, none of these institutions was well regarded. Again, these surveys did not differentiate between roles in government and possible disparate opinions of individuals in those roles (Dalton, 1988).

Upon reviewing the HUD scandal, the House Government Operations Committee made the observation that "during the 1980s, HUD was enveloped by influence peddling, favoritism, abuse, greed, fraud, embezzlement and theft. In many housing programs objective criteria gave way to political preference and cronyism, and favoritism supplanted fairness. 'Discretionary' became a buzzword for 'giveaway'" (U.S. House of Representatives, 1990, p. 3).

In the late 1970s, the federal government created departmental inspector general positions designed to find and report any examples of governmental fraud or corruption. In his recent analysis of why HUD's inspector general failed to uncover corruption, Paul Light (1993a) states that "the [inspectors general] simply were not equipped to pursue such high-level wrongdoing. Their task was primarily to look down for scandal, not *up*" (p. 112). Under the provisions of the Civil Service Reform Act, dozens of new political appointments had been added to the top of the department, with high rates of turnover among the political appointments. Commitments and connections among political appointees seemed to be more important than commitments to the mission of HUD.

In this revolving-door setting, former HUD political appointees turned to their cronies for favors. And they received them. James Watt, the well-connected former secretary of the interior, received hundreds of thousands of dollars for talking to HUD secretary Franklin Pierce and others in an attempt to rig the granting of funds for housing rehabilitation. The administrative formula for the fair granting of these funds based on proper bids was simply ignored. Warnings to Congress by HUD's inspector general and by many HUD civil servants were ignored. Once the scandal was fully uncovered, those who were politically appointed were the ones charged and convicted (Light, 1993b; Welfeld, 1992).

This fine distinction is not understood by most citizens. They only know that there was corruption in HUD, and they likely frame their opinions about governmental ethics based on that limited knowledge.

One aspect of the absence of role differentiation in perceptions of governmental effectiveness may be a function of the general public disengagement from government. Part of the public's disillusionment and frustration with government, according to David Mathews (1994), is attributable to a general feeling of powerlessness or exclusion from governmental decision making. Mathews cites a 1991 study indicating that Americans feel they have "been pushed out of the political system by a professional political class of powerful lobbyists, incumbent politicians, campaign managers, and a media elite" (p. 12). The study also found that Americans feel that big interests and money play a much more important role in governmental decision making than do citizens' votes. In short, Americans "saw a system with its doors closed to the average citizen" (p. 12).

Note that the problem here is *not* with the bureaucracy or the permanent civil service. The problem is not with the schoolteachers or the police. Mathews's argument is that the electoral politics and policymaking aspects of government are what citizens find disempowering, *not* the work of those who implement policy—the bureaucrats.

Mathews argues that although the public feels left out of the established political system, people are still civic minded. While voting levels have declined, civic volunteering and participation has increased. Frustrated by politics as usual, people are participating in "citizen politics," taking matters into their own hands.

Examples of such endeavors include community watch and community involvement groups, nonprofit neighborhood organizations, and neighborhood-based special interest groups. While these activities are clearly political, participants seldom used the word politics to describe what they do.

To Mathews, the generalized public is indispensable to effective politics. But for a collection of individuals to become a *public,* there must be a forum for deliberation. Without deliberation, people cannot give direction to government, and government thereby loses legitimacy. Under these circumstances, citizens become clients or consumers rather than owners making policy. As jurisdictions have grown, government officials and public administrators have failed to develop forums and other means of collective deliberation.

Conclusions

One result of the constant negative opinions of government and public officials has been a new reform movement. Some of its tenets, such as more funding for schools and higher standards and better pay for teachers, are positive. But other tenets of this modern-day reform movement may eventually result in a less ethical government, for several reasons. First, a popular trend is to downsize the number of merit-based civil servants, but with this comes the loss of institutional memory and the "hollowing out" of government (Milward and Provan, 1994). Second, deregulation is especially popular. Hollowing out bureaucracy and eliminating regulations will make the seedbed for corruption and scandal; the savings and loan crisis should be seen as an early warning. Third, increased contracting out is also a popular reform, but people seem to forget that contracts have always made a tempting environment for kickbacks and fraud. Doesn't anyone remember why Spiro Agnew resigned as vice president? Fourth, establishing authorities and special districts that are two and sometimes three steps removed from direct electoral control by the public is another popular reform (Barns, 1994). The rationale is that these authorities need to be exempt from the red tape of regulations and insulated from politics so that they can be more businesslike in their operations. Many authorities and districts—such as airports, toll roads, and economic development units—are self-supporting and depend on fees for service. They are also very tempting settings for corruption (Henriques, 1986).

This brings us to our final point. One reason that these reforms achieve such popular support is the widely held view that government is ineffective and that public officials are unethical. It seems, therefore, that reform is in order. The reforms that are being adopted may, at the margins, make government more productive, but they will almost certainly result in less ethical government.

This being the case, in the years ahead we will eventually see another reform movement emphasizing administrative expertise, a merit-based civil service insulated from political meddling, and the use of regulations to control corruption. So in the short run, the country will pay an ethical price for political bureaucrat-bashing. In the long run, those of us in public administration should be of good spirit, because we can already hear the calls for administrative competence in government.

Chapter Nine

Patriotism, Benevolence, and Public Administration

with David Kirkwood Hart

> *When one sees one's fellows in danger, one's duty is to go to their aid; strongmen do much, the weak little, but being weak is no reason for folding one's arms and refusing one's cooperation.*
> ALEXIS DE TOCQUEVILLE, IN R. BOESCHE (ED.),
> *ALEXIS DE TOCQUEVILLE: SELECTED LETTERS ON POLITICS AND SOCIETY,* P. 95

In public administration circles, the widespread—and largely unjustified—disenchantment with public bureaucracies has contributed to the decimation of public programs and agencies. As a result, it is increasingly difficult for public administrators to meet their professional obligations in a responsible manner. Furthermore, a loss of purpose seems a common affliction among public-service professionals. Summarizing the work of the American Society for Public Administration (ASPA) Centennial Agenda Committee, James Carroll and Alfred Zuck (1983) wrote that "American public administration is acutely alienated from society, bedeviled by complexity, and guided by limited knowledge and understanding" (Newland, 1984, p. 6). These persistent situations must be rectified.

No small part of the problem results from public administration's excessive and uncritical reliance upon the value assumptions of business administration (Hartle, 1985). With some notable exceptions, too much of the literature about bureaucracy or the public service makes no significant distinction between the moral entailments of service in the public and private sectors. The most destructive effect of this equating public service with commerce has been the devaluation of public service to just another arena in which individuals can achieve essentially private ambitions. "Careerism" has been substituted for idealism.

Careerism, rooted in an egoistic, utilitarian philosophy, is considered to be the primary inducement in almost all American management theory (Barnard, 1938; Simon, 1947; March and Simon, 1958; Scott, 1982). Thus, the primary inducement for organizationally effective behavior is the advancement—through promotion or security, or both—of one's career. All organizational actions are considered as instrumental to one's career advancement; efficiency, product excellence, and even loyalty are sought because they contribute to one's career and not because they are valuable in themselves.

This tendency is particularly destructive in public administration, for it attacks the assumption that a special relationship should exist between public servants and citizens in a democracy (Frederickson, 1982; Frederickson and Chandler, 1984; Frederickson, 1972). A singularly baleful effect has been the reduction of citizens to "consumers"—simply customers of an agency that exist in "a mercenary exchange of good offices according to an agreed valuation" (Smith, 1982, p. 1759). The public expects something more from the bureaucracy, and rightly so. In truth, public administrators also expect more.

The ideal of American democracy assumes that a special relationship should exist between public servants and citizens. To put it briefly, this belief is that all public administration must rest upon and be guided by the moral truths embodied in the enabling documents of our national foundation. As Woodrow Wilson wrote in 1887: "Liberty cannot live apart from constitutional principle; and no administration, however perfect and liberal its methods, can give men more than a poor counterfeit of liberty if it rests upon illiberal principles of government" ([1887] 1941, p. 212).

But something more is necessary; Hannah Arendt alluded to it in her condemnation of Adolf Eichmann. According to Dossa (1984), "Fundamental to Arendt's political theory is the distinction between the public and the private. . . . The public realm is the laws of community distinguished by the disposition to care for fellow citizens. In contrast, the private realm is the domain of instinctual individualism marked by the disposition to advance self-interest. . . . Public life characterized by an excessive and almost exclusive concern for the private self and its interests is a precondition of evil: it is a necessary though not a sufficient condition" (p. 165).

Along with the commitment to correct principles, public servants must genuinely care for their fellow citizens. In this regard, Eichmann had defaulted on his moral obligation as a public servant. For him, as for most of the Nazi bureaucracy, the public service was simply a place for the achievement of personal ambitions. No special relationship with the public existed.

We contend that this special relationship lies in a conception of political community marked by a pervasive patriotism based on benevolence. To illustrate this concept, we will contrast the actions of public servants and citizens toward the Jews in Germany and Denmark during World War II, because the Danes' conduct stands as a paradigmatic example of the patriotism of benevolence.

The Bureaucrat: Careerist or Moral Hero?

To rid Europe of all Jews, the Nazis concluded—with no pangs of conscience—that the most effective method would be "administrative genocide" (Hilberg, 1967; Dawidowicz, 1975). While it was necessary to enlist many organizations in Germany for the murder of the Jews (Arendt, 1963), the most essential organization was the bureaucracy. Hilberg (1967) wrote that "the destruction of the Jews was . . . no accident. When in the early days of 1933 the first civil servant wrote the first definition of a 'non-Aryan' into a civil service ordinance, the fate of European Jewry was sealed" (p. 662). We do not contend, as Hilberg puts it, that "every last *Wachtemeister* and *Brieftrager* knew about the 'Final Solution'" (p. 662). But the evidence supports the fact that bureaucrats in reasonably significant positions knew that something wretched was happening to the Jewish people (Hilberg, 1971; 1967, pp. 662–669).

Thus, by the time that the vast killing centers had been devised in Eastern Europe, all of the significant bureaucrats knew what was happening to the Jews. Yet almost without exception, they continued to do their jobs, and the slaughter went on unabated. As Yahil (1969) writes: "What is surprising . . . is the number of 'veterans' in the ministry—in the main respectable and enlightened persons steeped in tradition and culture—who faithfully served Hitler's interests. This phenomenon was not peculiar to the Foreign Ministry; it was characteristic of the whole political and administrative system and to a great extent of the military in the Third Reich" (p. 402).

After the war, with few exceptions, those same bureaucrats excused their complicity by claiming that as bureaucrats, they had no option but to obey their leaders, since the prime duty of the bureaucrat is obedience. But "administrative neutrality" is scarcely an acceptable excuse for abetting unmitigated evil. Sensing this, most of the bureaucrats fell back to their next line of defense: self-preservation. But the record does not support their claim in that regard. Individuals within that ubiquitous complicity were seldom forced to assist in the processes of the Final Solution. They could resign or seek a transfer (and some did). The only reprisal would have been the dead-ending of their careers—and that appears to have been their decisive consideration. They were committed above all else to their careers. It would seem that, except for the most fanatical Nazis, these bureaucrats were driven by no ideology beyond the desire for career advancement.

By contrast, the Danish people gave us an example of bureaucratic moral responsibility. After the German invasion of April 9, 1940, Denmark became a model protectorate, its government intact and watched over by a minister plenipotentiary from the German Foreign Office. From the outset, Berlin pressured the Danish government to disenfranchise the country's Jewish citizens and to deport them to the concentration camps with the stateless Jews then living in Denmark. To the Germans' considerable surprise, the orders were met with immediate and complete refusal from every segment of Danish society: politicians and ministers, business and labor leaders, teachers and ordinary citizens.

The pressure to deport Danish Jews continued to build and finally came to a head in the late summer and fall of 1943. The Danish armed forces were disbanded, martial law was imposed, and the Danish government was dropped into limbo. Because of this crisis, the constitutional monarch, Christian X, asked the heads of the bureaus to take over (Yahil, 1969, pp. 125–126). Thus, during the critical events of October 1943, when the Nazis moved against the Danish Jews, Denmark was being led by its bureaucrats.

We do not have adequate space to describe the nearly unbelievable rescue operation that ensued. Suffice it to say that the Danish people, in both their public and private capacities, set new parameters for what people can and should do (Flender, 1963; Bertelsen, 1954). Furthermore, the bureaucrats performed with exemplary courage, albeit after a somewhat shaky start. They found finances, guaranteed the sanctity of Jewish homes and properties, protected Jewish funds, and dealt with innumerable other responsibilities. For the small number of Jews who were captured in the Nazi roundup, the Danish government provided oversight. The bureaucrats watched after the Jews in the concentration camp at Theresienstadt, eventually assisting in their release and transfer to Sweden.

While the Danish people as a whole were heroic in their defense of their fellow citizens, we must be especially aware of the moral courage shown by the bureaucrats. They refused to compromise on the rights of the Jews, whether citizens or not. Their professional careers were secondary to their primary professional obligation—the guarantee of the rights of all. "Above all differences of opinion, however, the people and its leaders were conscious of a number of basic values, which were not merely subscribed to by everyone, but for which every Dane who associated himself with the essentials of the constitution was prepared to fight. These were the basic principles of freedom, equality, law, and justice" (Yahil, 1969, p. 33).

The bureaucracy steered its course by an unwavering commitment to the democratic values of the Danish nation. As Arendt (1963) wrote of the entire population of Denmark, it "was the result of an authentically political sense, an inbred comprehension of the requirements and responsibilities of citizenship and independence" (p. 179).

As a final note, some might think that the example of the Danes and the Nazis is too dramatic. But the drama must be separated from the context of the war. The routine activities of the Nazi bureaucrats were quite similar to their peacetime activities: they performed small, everyday tasks that aided in the realization of state policy. Thus, their example is not dramatic, even though the state policy was hideous beyond comprehension.

There was, however, real drama in the actions of the Danish bureaucrats. But would the drama be any less real had American local government officials simply refused to discriminate against black people in the 1950s? And is there not real drama in the moral heroism of Marie Ragghianti, the woman who blew the whistle on the sale of pardons by Tennessee Governor Ray Blanton, who was subsequently sent to prison for his deeds (Maas, 1980; Hejka-Ekins, 1992)? We do not discredit our own examples of bureaucratic heroism, and we must not discredit those of other nations. If nothing else, they demonstrate that the moral truths and obligations of democracy are not limited by national boundaries.

Careerism Versus the Patriotism of Benevolence

Thus, we have two radically different examples of the public service's moral responsibilities. In Denmark, the actions of the bureaucrats were distinguished by moral heroism in the service of democratic values. In Germany, the bureaucrats' actions were distinguished by an obsession with career success that ultimately abetted monstrous evil. What accounts for the difference? Our purpose here is not to discuss the cultural differences between the nations, as important as they are. Rather, we believe that the difference can be understood by considering the relationship between *patriotism* and *benevolence.*

A significant reason why people enter the public service is some feeling of patriotism. Bureaucrats in Germany and Denmark believed in their respective nations and considered themselves patriots. The difference between them lies in contrasting perceptions of the moral obligations of patriotism. In Denmark, the bureaucrats considered their moral obligations to be at the heart of career service, while those in Germany placed governmental careers above their moral obligations to the people (Arendt, 1963; Yahil, 1969; Speer, 1970). In other words, the Nazi bureaucrats were state careerists, while the Danish bureaucrats were patriots of the people.

For the Nazi bureaucrats, patriotism meant accepting a supreme leader whose will was the foundation of the nation's laws and participation in the pageantry of nationalism. But their moral responsibilities ended in the charade of uniforms, salutes, and rallies. By limiting the morality of patriotism to display, the German bureaucrats were relieved of any necessity for moral thought—or more important, of any need to love the people within their political areas of responsibility. This allowed them to concentrate all of their efforts on their careers.

By contrast, patriotism for the Danes consisted of a profound commitment to the democratic values of their nation and a genuine love of the people. As Yahil (1969) observes, "What is significant here is that for the Danes national consciousness and democratic consciousness are one and the same. Only as a free citizen in a lawful and democratic state can the Dane behold his patriotism. . . . Equality, freedom, the rights assured to every Dane, and the duties incumbent upon him as laid down in the constitution are valid for all citizens without exception, and all citizens constitute a mutual guarantee to one another that these principles will be maintained" (p. 402).

Thus, the Danish bureaucrats coupled ideological commitment with a politically significant love of one another, which was the guarantee of those democratic rights being extended to all. The Danes were, of course, correct in their understanding of their moral obligations and of the patriotism of benevolence as the prior and necessary condition for public service in a democracy. The Danes were uncomfortable with that claim, however, as Yahil (1969) observes: "Perhaps the most astonishing phenomenon, and the very element in which greatness lay, was the fact that the Danes regarded their deed as not in the least extraordinary or worthy of praise and admiration. In their opinion they merely did the natural and necessary, and never for a moment considered the possibility of abandoning the Jews to their fate" (pp. xi–xii).

In the United States, we define the primary moral obligation of the public service as the *patriotism of benevolence:* an extensive love of all people within our political boundaries and the imperative that they must be protected in all basic rights granted to them by the enabling documents. If we do not love others, why should we work to guarantee the regime values to them? The special relationship that must exist between public servants and citizens in a democracy is founded on the citizens' conscious knowledge that they are loved by the bureaucracy.

The Recovery of Benevolence

It is not our purpose here to discuss in detail the concept of benevolence, but we do intend to emphasize the singular importance of the patriotism of benevolence as an ideal for the public service. The essence of political idealism, as envisioned by the Founders and typified by Thomas Jefferson, was the embodiment of the ideal in the present. According to Flower and Murphey (1977), "Jefferson's political theory is fundamentally a moral—i.e., normative—theory. It is not a theory about how people, or nations, actually behave, but about how they should and can behave. . . . But Jefferson also believed that a moral political order could really be created in the world, and that such an order was approximated by the United States. Thus, it is a highly practical morality which is being espoused, for men can so design their political structure as to realize the moral order" (pp. 337–338).

This, then, is the model for the public service—the combination of patriotism (the love of the regime values) with benevolence (the love of others) realized in action. That linkage was summarized by Adam Smith in 1759:

> The love of our country seems, in ordinary cases, to involve in it two different principles; first, a certain respect and reverence for that constitution or form of government which is actually established; and secondly, an earnest desire to render the condition of our fellow citizens as safe, respectable, and happy as we can. He is not a citizen who is not disposed to respect the laws and to obey the civil magistrate; and he is certainly not a good citizen who does not wish to promote, by every means in his power, the welfare of the whole society of his fellow-citizens [(1759) 1982, p. 231].

Since the extension and protection of the regime values to all citizens is the purpose of our government, then benevolence becomes the necessary condition of that purpose. The problem, however, lies not as much with the entailments of patriotism as it does with the entailments of benevolence. The eighteenth-century meaning of benevolence required not only the love of others, but disinterested love at that: "From the standpoint of the agent, he acts morally when he seeks to bring about a state of affairs which constitutes the happiness of another and does this not from motives of self-interest nor from any other motive save that of seeking the good of another, the good being understood in terms of his happiness" (Roberts, 1973, p. 7).

In contemporary literature, benevolence is given at best a cursory nod as an oddity of intellectual history, but seldom is it suggested that we should take the idea seriously or try to put it into practice. We have almost completely lost the belief that benevolence is essential to democracy. But to the political philosophers of the eighteenth century who influenced the Founders, benevolence was of vital importance for any meaningful democracy (Becker, 1942; Lovejoy, 1961; White, 1978; Wills, 1978; Bryson, [1945] 1968). They looked upon benevolence, along with self-love, as the two major motivations for action.

Certain affections or feelings can motivate action, but self-love and benevolence are the most important. Thus benevolence was not just a theoretical concept—it was something to be practiced (Jensen, 1971; Hume, [1739] 1968). In the contemporary United States, we have reduced that duality to the single motivation of a self-love rooted in a hedonic egoism, as summed up in the unpleasant Mandevillean phrase, "Private vices, public virtues." It does not matter that the notion was generally rejected by the most significant of our country's Founders; it dominates today.

The concept of benevolence is the key to understanding the aspirations of the Founders for how democracy could be achieved in the nation. Certainly, they understood human frailty and did not rest everything upon the voluntary benevolence of the individual. James Wilson acknowledges the problem: "According to some writers, man is entirely selfish; according to others, universal benevolence is the highest aim of nature. One founds morality upon sympathy solely; another exclusively upon utility. But the variety of human nature is not so easily comprehended or reached. It is a complicated machine; and is unavoidably so, in order to answer the various and important purposes for which it is formed and designed" (McCloskey, 1967, p. 200).

The *Federalist* papers—while unfortunately one-sided—are certainly evidence of the Founders' concern with creating a system that would compensate for such human frailties. But even as they made provisions for human weakness, they also stressed the importance of human strength. They were quite clear about the importance of benevolence, and they included it in their prescriptions for government. Writing about the foundations of Jefferson's moral philosophy, Koch ([1943] 1957) observes: "Jefferson considered . . . benevolence, or active affection for others, as the true expression of our natural, instinctive moral equipment. Any moral system which should attempt to ground morality on self-interest was foredoomed to failure, in Jefferson's eyes" (p. 30). A significant number of the other Founders were of a similar opinion (Howe, 1966; Koch, 1966).

For Jefferson and the others, the success of the governmental system depended on the prior acceptance, by both public servants and citizens, of the regime values' truth (and this is still the case today). But that immediately raised another problem. Even if everyone believed, people still had no reason to exert themselves by extending those values to others—especially if doing so entailed personal loss or inconvenience. In the jargon of today, why not just maximize one's own utility and let the others fend for themselves? Whenever altruism is necessary, it will be predicated on its utility to self and achieved through bargaining.

The Founders debated this issue extensively. They were aware of the problems of self-interest, of course, but they also believed that the necessary element for realizing a true democracy was that citizens and public servants alike be possessed of an extensive and active love for others—in other words, that they possess a sense of benevolence. Without it, there remains only a careerist, egoistic motivation to guarantee the regime values to all of the people. And that, as our recent history so sadly demonstrates, is insufficient.

The Patriotism of Benevolence and the Spirit of Public Administration

How might the patriotism of benevolence be realized in the spirit of public administration today? The first step in the process must be to rid ourselves of the notion that idealism has no place in the bureaucracy. Conventional wisdom has it that the very nature of bureaucratic organization precludes significant moral action on the part of public servants toward their citizen clients, unless directed by policy. In an excellent essay, Mainzer (1964) argues: "Does not bureaucracy, embodying obedient, routinized, joint, anonymous action, destroy the possibility of personal responsibility for the deed? Does it not destroy, thereby, the possibility of personal honor? If so, the dominance of bureaucracy in our day may require that old virtues be re-examined or that we reconcile ourselves to the impossibility of living a worthwhile life within a large organization" (p. 71).

It must be noted that the negatives Mainzer cites are much more the function of large-scale organization than of anything intrinsic to the public service. Unfortunately, his pessimism reflects a consensus about public service—that due to the nature of bureaucratic organization, public administrators get scant opportunity for honor and moral heroism.

Nevertheless, it was the Founders' intent that all public servants should view the processes of government as a moral endeavor; theirs is not just to administer but to assist in bringing the ideals of democracy into existence. Thomas Jefferson set the model, as Parrington (1927) wrote about the Declaration: "The words were far more than a political gesture to draw popular support; they were an embodiment of Jefferson's deepest convictions, and his total life thenceforth was given over to the work of providing such political machinery for America as should guarantee for all the enjoyment of those inalienable rights" (p. 350).

For that reason, public servants must be both moral philosophers and moral activists, which would require (1) an understanding of and belief in the American regime values; and (2) a sense of extensive benevolence for the people of the nation. Therefore, the primary duty of public servants is to act as guardians and guarantors of the regime values for the American public. This does not mean that public administrators should usurp the policy responsibilities of elected officials. Those officials must articulate such policies that in the light of changing events will be most effective in realizing the regime values for all people. The bureaucrats must, of course, administer such policies as effectively, efficiently, and equitably as possible. But we must distinguish between the regime values and public policy. The regime values are the absolute values that all elected officials and public administrators are sworn to protect. They are the touchstone. In this area, public administrators can accept no compromise, either in law or in practice.

For example, if a public policy depends on racial or sexual discrimination, it offends the regime values and is automatically forfeit.

Public administrators are then bound, by the oath of office implied in their employment, to refuse to implement such policies. This is, of course, what the Danish public servants did during World War II—and what most American public servants failed to do during the years of sanctioned racial discrimination. Obviously, decisions of conscientious refusal must never be taken lightly nor used for simple partisan reasons. But the honorable bureaucrat must be fully capable of conscientious refusal at any point at which the regime values are violated.

But why should this be a responsibility of the public administrator? Is it not the responsibility of the courts to watch after the regime values? Certainly it is. But even if the courts ameliorate injustice, they can be circumvented. For instance, *Brown* v. *Board of Education* was decided in 1954, but to this day we have not achieved racial equality in education. Furthermore, racial and sexual discrimination still persists within the governments of the United States, sometimes with official approval and bureaucratic compliance.

Others will argue that it is the responsibility of elected officials to watch after the regime values. They certainly do have that responsibility, but they must also be aware of the flow of political events and the ceaseless movement of public opinion. Also—and this is most important—politicians come and go, bracketed by periodic elections and subject to the whims of their constituencies. Their minds must necessarily be in other places. Bureaucrats, however, are responsible for the day-to-day implementation of public policy. It is precisely because of such permanence that bureaucrats' political obligation to the regime values is greater—for they must superintend the realization of those values in the everyday lives of citizens.

Conclusions

Finally, some will argue that the patriotism of benevolence is too idealistic, as if idealism had no place in the public service. They see the demands of practicality as all-consuming and idealism as a waste of time. But this glorification of practicality cuts at the essential idealism that should guide the public service. While practicality is essential, our government was also intended to achieve the ideal. To abandon idealism in favor of practicality is to violate a central purpose of our government. Furthermore, an obsession with practicality above all else does not allow us to meet the challenges we face. Eric Hoffer (1951) caught the situation eloquently: "The tangibility of a pleasant and secure existence is such that it makes other realities, however imminent, seem vague and visionary. Thus it happens that when times become unhinged, it is the practical people who are caught unaware and are made to look like visionaries who cling to things that do not exist" (p. 72).

We are not without contemporary examples of such patriotism, and even moral heroism, in the American public service. In the countless day-to-day processes of administering cities, counties, states, and the national government, public servants weigh issues of justice, equality, fairness, and common human dignity. When they function with honor and benevolence, all citizens benefit; and when they do not, citizens become alienated from their government and hostile to the public service (Frederickson, 1980). Our argument is that the demands of the patriotism of benevolence are such that the question of what the public servant should do under such circumstances would never come up.

Some contemporary scholars of public administration are reemphasizing a return to the idealism of our nation's origins. Too often, these scholars limit their conceptions of idealism to an ethic that defines what a bureaucrat should not do. For a rebirth of the spirit of public administration, such an ethic is necessary but not sufficient. We must define what public administration should do—and that brings us to the singular importance of benevolence. Gawthrop (1984b) has addressed the problem, reminding us of both the importance and the difficulties of benevolence. In the ethics of public administration, the commandment to "love thy neighbor" is comparatively easy. The great difficulty is in extending benevolence beyond the family and the neighborhood to include the unseen others of the nation and of the world.

John Rawls (1971) has also acknowledged the importance of benevolence; unfortunately, he argues that it is a morality of "supererogation" and thus is not for ordinary people. This was not the belief of the Founders, however. While the love of proximate others may be reasonably attainable, the love of humankind does require a form of moral heroism that is not easy to come by but is nonetheless achievable if people commit themselves to its attainment.

Therefore, public servants must inculcate the patriotism of benevolence into their work. Idealistic though this charge may be, we are bound by the covenants of our inception to be both idealistic and practical. It is within the patriotism of benevolence that the ideal and the practical are fused. As Parrington (1927) wrote of Jefferson, so should we aspire: "That Jefferson was an idealist was singularly fortunate for America; there was need of idealism to leaven the materialistic realism of the times" (p. 350).

Chapter Ten

The Public Administrator as Representative Citizen

with Ralph Clark Chandler

> *We must have magistrates, for without their prudence
> and watchful care a state cannot exist. In fact, the whole
> character of a republic is determined by its arrangements
> in regard to magistrates. Not only must we inform them of
> the limits of their administrative authority, we must also
> instruct the citizens of the extent of their obligation to obey
> them. For the man who rules efficiently must have obeyed
> others in the past, and the man who obeys dutifully
> appears fit at some later time to be a ruler. Thus he who
> obeys ought to expect to be a ruler in the future, and he
> who rules should remember that in a short time he will
> have to obey.*
> CICERO, *LAWS*, III, 2

In this chapter we propose an entirely new role for the American public administrator—that of representative citizen. Intentional ambiguity and tension exists between the ideas of *representative* citizen and representative *citizen*. The former carries with it something akin to the patriotism of benevolence described in Chapter Nine, while the latter addresses the public administrator's commitment to social equity.

If public administrators are *representatives* of the people, they are trustees of the public good in the same way that the Roman tribune protected the interests of the citizens of Rome against the patrician class, or the dispensers of the king's justice under English common law protected the rights of citizens against the lords of the manor and the king himself. In this view, civil servants are sworn to uphold the same constitution as are other officers of government, and they may in fact be competent to define the public interest on their own authority. Administrators may be as close to citizens as elected representatives. In fact, legislators may be far removed and preoccupied with the legislative processes or captured by special interests. Under such conditions, frontline public administrators can and ought to act as the agents of citizens bewildered by the complexity of modern government.

If public administrators are representative *citizens,* there are subtle but important distinctions in the role's definition; the model becomes less elitist and presumptuous and more democratic and fiduciary. In this view, public administrators are first and foremost citizens themselves. As Terry L. Cooper (1991) argues, public administrators are employed by their fellow citizens to carry out the work of citizenship on their behalf. As citizens in lieu of the rest of us, public administrators are the primary contact between the citizen and public organizations.

When this contact is effectively carried out, following Cooper, public administration contributes to an ongoing renewal and reaffirmation of the social contract. Public administrators can assist the people in the covenanting process begun when our Puritan forebears sat off the coast of New England in 1620 and wrote the Mayflower Compact. That would make William Brewster the Younger, who drafted the compact, the first American public administrator. As his "descendants," we regularly engage in readjusting or reconstructing the mutual expectations of citizens in a democratic polity. Public administrators therefore occupy the office of citizen.

Public administrators have often been surrogates for the rest of the citizenry. If civil servants are indeed servants, one must ask servants of whom or for what? Are they merely servants of political figures elected by varying fractions of the populace, or of certain ideas usually summarized as justice and equity? Aristotle defined the citizen as one who is capable of both ruling and obeying. We endorse the position that the public administrator, as representative citizen, must find the legitimate personal and institutional authority both to rule and to obey.

The Problem of Low Citizenship and Low Administration

An obvious problem with the representative citizen concept is that both trustees and servants are self-interested. If government is administered by men and women who are not unlike the citizens whom the Founders said would constantly assault the reasonable bounds of selfishness, why not be content with a public service ethic that is procedural in nature? Why should public administration presume to define morality, ethics, citizenship, benevolence, justice, or equity?

The concept of representative citizen competes with a clearly defined American preference for low citizenship. John A. Rohr (1986) has pointed out that as early as *The Federalist* 63, James Madison explicitly rejected the ancient idea of an active role for citizens in government largely because of the problem of self-interest. Madison maintained that the major difference between the republics of Europe and the government that took root in America "lies in the total exclusion of the people in their collective capacity from any share in the latter" (Hamilton, Madison, and Jay, 1961, p. 387). Madison declared that this attractive aspect of American political development would be reinforced in the new Constitution.

Alongside low citizenship, stood low administration. In his administrative histories, Leonard D. White (1951) emphasizes again and again the low profile assumed by administrative officers in the new republic. Even the centralizing and interventionist federalists, remembering that they won ratification of the Constitution by the narrowest of margins, gathered civil servants of modest and gentlemanly demeanor who would not stir up the riffraff. Roughly 65 percent of the highest-level federalist appointments came from the landed gentry, merchant, and professional classes.

When the states rights oriented antifederalists came to power with Thomas Jefferson, he replaced seventy-three of the ninety-two top federalist appointments with his own brand of guardian. The democratization of the public service under Andrew Jackson did nothing to increase professionalism within it. Power was transferred from one group, the gentry, to another, political parties, but never to the people as a whole. Citizenship kept its low profile.

During the birth of American public administration, no administrative class or "permanent undersecretaries" on the British and European models were established. In the reform period of the early twentieth century, political neutrality and professionalism were upheld, and citizen participation and social responsiveness were sacrificed to efficiency. As we near the end of the twentieth century, Americans find themselves with the worst of public service worlds, for in the long run not only has the federalist view of low citizenship triumphed but so has the antifederalist view of low administration.

Low Citizenship–Low Administration Compared with Other Models

A four-cell matrix elaborating the citizenship versus administration model would include the following combinations:

- High citizenship–low administration
- High citizenship–high administration
- Low citizenship–high administration
- Low citizenship–low administration

Perhaps historical examples of governmental design of public organizations other than the American low-low model could give us perspective on the restructuring task awaiting American public administration. It is probably better for the examples to come from antiquity than from current history, because the results of the early experiments are in. Thus, we use ancient Athens rather than the Swiss cantons as an example of high citizenship–low administration, ancient Rome rather than the Scandinavian democracies as a high citizenship–high administration model, and ancient Egypt rather than the former Soviet Union for low citizenship–high administration. Figure 10.1 illustrates the composite model.

High Citizenship and Low Administration in Ancient Athens

Proponents of high citizen participation in government would find themselves at home in fifth-century Athens, especially if they were fortunate enough to be citizens (see Figure 10.1). The Athenian popular assembly included all citizens of the state. A council of five hundred served as the executive committee of the popular assembly, and under it was an administrative apparatus consisting of what

**Figure 10.1. A Model for
Citizen Versus Administrative Participation in Government.**

High Citizenship

High Citizenship *Low Administration* Ancient Athens	*High Citizenship* *High Administration* Ancient Rome
Modern America *Low Administration* *Low Citizenship*	Ancient Egypt *High Administration* *Low Citizenship*

Low   High

Administration   Administration

Low Citizenship

William C. Beyer (1982) has called "amateur boards." The committee had a separate board for each of the less technical functions of government, such as inspecting weights and measures, purchasing grain, and staging public games. The only concessions that the Athenians made to high administration were sole executives in charge of manpower, finance, springs, and architecture.

So dedicated were the Athenians to citizen participation that they took special steps to keep board members from becoming experts through experience. Board members were chosen from the citizenry by lot—rather like Ben Barber's conception (1986) of strong democracy. If a citizen possessed special qualifications for the assigned tasks of a board, it would be by chance. The term of office was only one year, and members could not be reelected to the same board. Also, the board positions were unpaid except for meals. As Beyer has observed, the Athenians were less interested in making their government efficient than in keeping it responsive to their wishes.

Public administrators in ancient Athens did not need to be efficient. There were no public lands to oversee, no agricultural empire to regulate, and no social welfare system to administer.

Government was confined largely to a defensive military role. Education was left to private schools, only minimal police protection was provided, and public buildings and other public works were constructed under contract to private builders. Even tax collection was put in the hands of individual entrepreneurs.

Such individualism produced artists, sculptors, architects, rhetoricians, poets, dramatists, philosophers—and Athens's unquestioned cultural and intellectual leadership of the ancient world. So the amateurish Athenian government should not be regarded as belonging necessarily to a less advanced stage of human development. Yet someone had to do the chores. Someone had to teach the children, keep the accounts, and enforce the laws.

It was the slaves.

One of the most striking features of ancient Athens's public administration is the extent to which state slaves were used in governmental service. They constituted a corps of permanent workers in the offices and on the streets. They were teachers, accountants, policemen, soldiers, prison attendants, bailiffs, and mint workers. They served in a hundred occupations matching the classification systems of today's personnel manuals. The fact that their overseers were chosen by lot to keep factionalism out of public administration was political genius at work.

Let us not be misled, however, by the Athenian government's reputation for citizen participation. Although the role of citizen did far outweigh the role of administrator even in the small-scale Athenian democracy, permanent and competent executives were employed at critical levels in the hierarchy. These executives were supported by a cadre of able public servant slaves. The Athenians could afford a high citizenship model because someone else—the slaves—paid the price, just as the United States could afford the same model through most of its history for a similar reason. As long as there was bounty in the land, as long as waste could be absorbed, and as long as open spaces, empty jobs, and unmade fortunes were the real conditions of American life, people could talk high citizenship without really meaning it—especially the part about justice and equity.

Americans cannot do that anymore. Any idealization of the benefits of citizen participation in American government—or any romanticized retreat to a yeoman-citizen past that never was—will run aground on hard reality and the unavoidable task of modern public administrators to define probity and manage scarcity.

If abundance was the natural soil of competitive individualism in America, scarcity is the soil of mutualism and the practice of administrative statecraft. Now it appears that American public administrators must parcel out the settled land. The high citizenship model of ancient Athens will not work in the new century if high administration does not turn out to conserve our limited resources.

Low Citizenship and High Administration in Ancient Egypt

If proponents of high citizenship would find themselves at home in ancient Athens, proponents of high administration would feel equally at home in ancient Egypt. The Egyptian administrative class participated in the unique relationship that existed between the king and his subjects, and the Egyptians experienced authority as a personal relationship. The Pharaoh was god as well as king, and the people related to him and his representatives as a national family. The massive public works projects—building the pyramids and harnessing the Nile—that the king, his engineers, and the people participated in together were seen not so much as examples of the powerful exploiting the weak, but as common labor employed to raise monuments to the common self. Everyone could see how grand the king was. When under the Ptolemies this personal relationship was translated into Greek terms, and the god translated into the absolute authority of the state, the Egyptian civilization crumbled.

The prestige of the Egyptian civil service was such that it was the most sought-after vocation in society. Royal schools were established to train civil servants in the techniques of statecraft; higher-level officials were the instructors. But the instructional programs in these so-called stables of education were not limited to teaching students about the practical work of governmental departments. They were also designed to provide for the liberal education and intellectual development of Egypt's future administrators. Graduates could look forward to well-paid positions with regular bonuses for meritorious service, clear lines of promotion, and a high degree of professional stability.

Moses, who was reared as a prince of Egypt, was probably a graduate of such a royal school. The organizational skills he learned can be seen in the records as he led the Israelite exodus from Egypt in about 1290 B.C. E. N. Gladden (1972) notes that "the nomadic movements of such a large body of people together with their livestock and effects, harried for part of the way by the Egyptians, involved feats of organization and informal administration of no mean order" (p. 38). Later in his career, Moses put into practice what would later be called the science of administration, which included span of control, management by exception, and delegation of authority.

A more direct view of the techniques of high administration in ancient Egypt is seen in the Biblical novella about Joseph. The story, in Genesis, gives us precise knowledge of Egyptian affairs and customs as known from Egyptian sources, and it is a parade example of administrative fiction.

The story itself is well known. Joseph, who was the favorite of his father, Jacob, was sold into slavery by his eleven jealous brothers. Joseph eventually became the property of Potiphar, the captain of the guard in Pharaoh's household. Joseph's reward for spurning the advances of Potiphar's wife was to be thrown into prison, where he successfully interpreted the dreams of two fellow inmates. One of them, the chief butler of the royal household, was later released and had occasion to recommend Joseph to Pharaoh as a soothsayer. Pharaoh was so pleased with Joseph's talents that he inducted him into the high office of vizier (prime minister) by exercise of despotic power.

What Joseph accomplished as prime minister of Egypt is an extended analogy of what all successful Egyptian public administrators did. He steered the country through difficult times, conserving and storing excess produce during years of good harvest for use in the years of famine that inevitably came. He enlarged the public domain and arranged with cultivators of the fields to receive a fifth of their crops, which would be sold to increase the king's treasury. He made Egypt's agricultural goods an instrument of foreign policy. He consolidated his position by marrying Asenath, the daughter of the high priest of Heliopolis. And always he busied himself with training the next generation of professionals in the ethics of Egyptian public service (Wildavsky, 1988).

The art of Egyptian statecraft did not develop full-blown from a commitment to administrative energy. It came from a process of education and continuing education; from reading, thinking, listening, reflecting, becoming; and from a set of holistic relationships represented in modern management by Theory Z, or by the governance concept. According to Frederick C. Mosher (1982):

> As in our culture in the past and in a good many other civilizations, the nature and quality of the public service depends principally upon the system of education. Almost all of our future administrators will be college graduates, and within two or three decades a majority of them will probably have graduate degrees. Rising proportions of public administrators are returning to graduate schools for refresher courses, mid-career training, and higher degrees. These trends suggest that university faculties will have growing responsibility for preparing and for developing public servants both in their technical specialties and in the broader social fields with which their professions interact. The universities offer the best means of making the professions safe for democracy. At least one may hope [p. 219].

High Citizenship and High Administration in Ancient Rome

The representative citizen role finds its best analogue in the high citizenship–high administration model of ancient Rome. The model was worked out differently in republican and imperial Rome, but its essential characteristics remained the same. In both periods, the Roman civil service was a magnificent professional body for administering the affairs of state, and the status of the Roman citizen was the envy of the civilized Western world.

Citizenship was understood in reference to legal standards in ancient Rome. Originally the law of Rome applied only to residents of the city, a very limited body of citizens who were born to it as part of their civic heritage. As Roman political power and wealth grew, however, a larger and larger body of alien residents came to Rome. They had to transact business both with Romans and among themselves. The Romans met the problem of legally recognizing these foreign doings by creating a special judge, the *praetor peregrinus*, whose function was to piece together formal law by considerations of justice and equity. The effective body of Roman law that grew from this was based simply on requirements of fair dealing, common sense, and what good business practice regarded as honesty and fairness. It was called the *jus gentium,* the law common to all peoples.

The *jus gentium* promoted equality before the law at the same time that the Stoic view of the *jus naturale* was promoting the idea of a worldwide human brotherhood. The Stoics declared that men (and presumably women) are by nature equal, despite differences of race, rank, and wealth. These two ideas coalesced in republican Rome to establish a view of citizenship that undermined rigid distinctions between citizens and foreigners and rejected the Greek idea that citizenship should be limited to those who can actually have a share in governing. Rather, citizenship should be based on belief in a community of civic friendship, in which bonds of friendship rather than mutual self-interests were a source of unity.

For Aristotle, citizenship could hold only between equals. But because men were not equal in Aristotle's view, he inferred that citizenship must be restricted to a small and carefully selected group. By contrast, Cicero inferred that because all men—and all fellow citizens—are subject to one law, they must therefore be equal. For Cicero, high citizenship was a moral requirement rather than a fact. The political deduction of the Roman republicans was that a state cannot exist permanently unless it recognizes the mutual obligations and rights that bind its citizens together. In their view, the state is a moral community, a group of people who in common possess the state and its law. It can be defined then as the *res publica,* the affair of the people. Hence the citizens of Rome could, and often did, veto acts of the Senate.

It is understandable that Roman citizenship was a valuable possession. As R. H. Barrow (1949) notes, "As [citizenship] increased in value, Rome granted it more sparingly, the citizens of the capital jealously guarded its extension, and for years Italian resentment smoldered" (p. 165). Still, all Italians were made Roman citizens by 89 B.C., and the emperor Caracalla bestowed citizenship on the entire population of the Roman Empire in A.D. 212.

Roman administrative practice was rooted in the same understanding of law that citizenship was. Administrative power was the corporate power of the people. The magistrate's warrant was the law, and he was a creature of the law. Cicero said, "For as the laws govern the magistrate, so the magistrate governs the people, and it can truly be said that the magistrate is a speaking law, and the law a silent magistrate" (1928 trans., III, 1).

As an administrator of the law in ancient Rome, the magistrate was often called "a priest of justice." He had considerable discretion to define justice and equity as he was being faithful to the laws. The administrator was said to have a duty to obey the moral law—or else, as Augustine later observed, the state would represent nothing but highway robbery on a large scale (Barrow, 1949, p. 174).

Marcus Porcius Cato (95–46 B.C.) was a typical Roman administrator whose character and habits Plutarch described in some detail. Cato worked hard to ensure that he knew a good deal about his duties, Plutarch said. In their dealings with experienced clerks, ponderous public records, complicated laws, and precedent accumulated upon precedent, Roman administrators wanted to maintain the tradition that support staff were their servants and not their masters. "Cato's assiduity and indefatigable diligence won very much upon the people. He always came first of any of his colleagues to the treasury, and went away last. He never missed any assembly of the people, or sitting of the senate, being always anxious and on the watch for those who lightly, or as a matter of interest, passed votes in favor of this or that person" (Plutarch, 1951 trans., p. 42).

Under the Roman Empire, there were five executive departments of state, all activist and interventionist in the best tradition of high administration. (Alexander Hamilton would have been pleased.) The administrative energy that characterized the system transformed the power of the tribune in republican Rome to the power of the legate in imperial Rome. The formal power of citizen veto became the informal power of citizen participation. Officials of the central government would do no more than the legates told them would be tolerated in the provinces. How much could Gaul be taxed this year? How many recruits to the legions could Dalmatia supply? What part of the grain quota could Carthage provide? Local populations were continually being consulted in a *jus gentium* application of the Pax Romana.

The Roman civil service's degree of standardization in positions, titles, and salaries approached that of a military organization. Modern computer technology would have suited nicely the Roman penchant for system and order. But whereas standardization seemed to enhance the dignity and prestige of the Roman civil service, in the United States it tends to produce bureaupathology. The reason for this curious difference does not lie in the form of government, for both American and ancient Roman polities are mixed constitutions. Perhaps it lies in the expectations of the civil servants themselves. Roman civil servants expected to participate in the grandeur of the republic and the empire, while their American counterparts expect to deal with criticism and to be preoccupied with rules and procedures.

These differing expectations may in turn be a function of the philosophical bases of the two civil services. The Roman system was rich in civic tradition, while the American system is poor. For the American administrative system to move from a low citizenship–low administration model to the high citizenship and high administration of the Roman model, it must appropriate the Stoic roots of Roman civility.

Conclusions: A Few Kind Words for Bureaucrats

The task of redefining the role of American public administrators in the twenty-first century does not mean we have to learn Greek or Latin and become classics scholars. It would serve us well, however, to know what was known in classical times and to try to make that knowledge relevant to our own needs. The doctrines of justice and equity that Stoic philosophers translated into Roman jurisprudence and laid into our common store of values formed the foundation of the ideas of community, patriotism, and benevolence. The secularization and fragmentation of community, and the loss of civic capital after the Reformation, does not make these ideas any less valuable now; it only makes them more obscure and difficult to gather into the modern *res publica*. To illustrate this, we will set out four alternative relationships between citizenship and administration, as shown in Figure 10.2 and Figure 10.3.

If anyone is in a position to renew communal values, it is the public administrator who must deal with communal problems every day. Whether those problems have to do with *communi*cations, *commu*ters, *commu*nicable diseases, *commu*nism, or a dozen other aspects of *commu*nity, the mutual interdependence of the American citizenry is plain to see. The public administrator's task

**Figure 10.2. A Model for Relating Citizenship
to Professional Public Administration.**

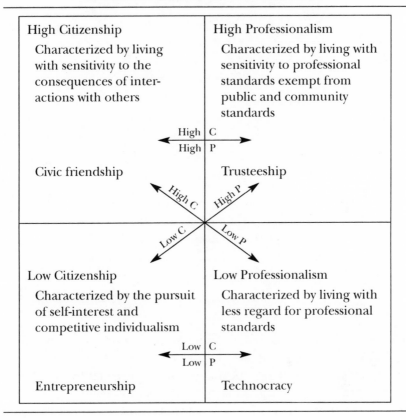

is to take unapologetic leadership in making American public institutions more reflective of the communal values of justice and equity that are our heritage. The factionalized and fractional political system cannot do it. The judicial branch has carved out another role for itself. Private institutions and their managers have a totally different agenda. Such an energetic view of bureaucracy is in the spirit of Hamiltonian public administration.

Public managers in the United States still have the widespread respect of the American people. For all the negative talk about bureaucrats, the fact is (as Chapter Eight describes) most clients of American bureaucracies are pleased with the services they receive.

**Figure 10.3. A Model for Combining Selected Views
of Citizenship and Professionalism.**

High Citizenship

High Citizenship *Low Professionalism* Civic Friendship and Technocracy	*High Citizenship* *High Professionalism* Civic Friendship and Trusteeship
Technocracy and Entrepreneurship *Low Professionalism* *Low Citizenship*	Trusteeship and Entrepreneurship *High Professionalism* *Low Citizenship*

Low
Profesionalism

High
Professionalism

Low Citizenship

The bureaucracy is less a monolith than a composite of many small and diverse agencies not far removed from the citizens they serve. Many citizens know that underneath the required antibureaucracy rhetoric of politics is the demonstrable fact that public organizations do both stimulate and implement change. Certainly, the private sector does not do administration any more efficiently or at a higher rate of productivity than does the public sector (Wamsley and others, 1990).

Some degree of trusteeship is currently being practiced in American public administration and has been for some time. Americans' rhetoric needs to catch up to our conduct. Our real need, however, is to stop denigrating the role of authority; doing so only debilitates the process of governance. All mature societies have secular "priesthoods" in which institutional wisdom is preserved. The real politics-administration dichotomy is not that public servants should be passively obedient to political authority; it is that the representatives occupying the office of citizenship will be among the custodians of justice and equity. Those communal values are beyond any ruler's transient political advantage.

The temptation in modern American public administration is to move from our low-low position in the model shown in Figure 10.1 to either the high citizenship position (the Athenian example) or the high administration position (the Egyptian example). The Athenian movement marches under the banner of citizen participation, the Egyptian under the banner of professionalism. If each movement is independent of the other, there will be problems in the American system. High citizenship alone might work if interest-group forces were less centrifugal and if the need to manage scarce resources intelligently were not so pressing. Certainly, the engaged citizenship envisioned in the communitarian movement would strengthen a democracy defined as the collective pursuit of the common good (Mathews, 1994).

The problem, of course, is in balancing the needs and interests of individuals and groups on the one hand with the community on the other—and this is precisely why high administration is essential. American democratic government is responsive to the interests of organized and well-financed forces, but the needs and rights of individuals, and particularly of poor people, are the special responsibility of a benevolent public administration. Where low public administration is the norm (as is presently the case in many American jurisdictions), public organizations lack the capacity to make the laws fair and just. High administration alone might work if there were a wider consensus about what professionalism means and if its definition included obedience to codified professional standards as well as the power to rule. But with the possible exception of some cities, particularly relatively homogeneous suburbs that employ an orthodox council-manager form of government, Americans tend to resist high administration.

The idea of the public administrator as representative citizen attempts to bridge the chasm of self-interest that has characterized the American experiment from the beginning. Thus far, Americans have proved highly adaptive to the changing requirements of their environment and institutions. This time, however, practical need requires theoretical sophistication at a nontechnical level. It remains to be seen whether American public administration has the vision and spirit to move in the direction of high citizenship with high administration and to realize the moral unity of a society come of age.

Chapter Eleven

Pushing Things Up to Their First Principles

*I see public administration professionally and,
especially, academically as distinguished by concern
with the generality of the conduct of the public business
in pursuit of the public interest. If it is to be distinguished
it must be profoundly related to the whole content of
political and social theory; its practitioners must have not
knowledge alone, but the understanding that is wisdom—
eminently human, thoroughly earthly, and at the same
time highly aspiring.*
PAUL H. APPLEBY, *PUBLIC ADMINISTRATION AND
DEMOCRACY,* P. 346

This book is about a search for the soul and spirit of public administration. The purpose of this closing chapter is to condense the many ideas in *The Spirit of Public Administration* into a brief list of first principles. In this chapter, we ask the question, Of the concepts, ideas, and arguments used here, which are the most important?

The first question we should ask is one of *domain*. Throughout most of public administration's history, our domain has been government—that is, the state. The work of public administration was based on national and state constitutions, on city charters, and on enabling legislation. Although we called our work public administration, we were in fact practicing *government administration*.

Many scholars in the field—including Bozeman (1987), Mathews (1994), Stillman (1990), and Putnam, Leonardi, and Nanetti (1993)—have reminded us that the words *public* and *government* do not have the same meaning. Government means the state. Public is a pregovernmental concept that broadly describes the full range of human collective activities taking place outside of people's private homes and distinct from the market, or the private pursuit of gain.

What does *public* in public administration mean? Some of us are accustomed to, and primarily committed to, a public administration that is state-based—the law in action—and therefore equate public administration with government administration. Others define our domain differently to include nonprofit, third-party, volunteer, contract, parastatel, utilities, and authorities as well as a wide range of governmental, quasi-governmental, and essentially private-governmental organizations.

In the earlier traditions of public administration, the state was generally held in a favorable view. In much of contemporary public administration, however, the focus is on the limitations of the state. This is another version of the domain question.

An additional version of the domain question is manifest in the word *governance*. It is assumed that governance comprehends the full range of public activity—governmental, quasi-governmental, and nongovernmental. This use of governance as a word and concept is wholly compatible with the following first principle:

> Our founders wisely chose to label the field *public administration* rather than *government administration*. Public administration includes the state; indeed, it is rooted in the state. But it is—and should be—more broadly defined to include the administration or implementation aspects of all forms and manifestations of collective public activity.

This description of the domain of public administration is filled with implications for the details of our work. Much of non-state public administration is not "democratic" or is one, two, or even three steps removed from citizen or legislative control. This situation may result in problems of ethics, oversight, inequality, and the like. But these nongovernmental public organizations are managed, by public administrators who should both understand and have the spirit of public administration. This description of public administration is both empirically informed and conceptually sound, and it leaves a wide space for discussion as to *which* public activities are better done governmentally, quasi-governmentally, or nongovernmentally.

The second question we should ask is one of *task*. How should we define or describe the *administration* part of public administration?

In the modern origins of the field, the emphasis was on a science of management and on developing the principles of administration, with a focus on staff functions, particularly budgeting and personnel. Concepts of organization such as hierarchy and coordination were important.

Beginning in the 1950s, the *academic* focus of public administration shifted in two ways: (1) toward a science of decision making and (2) toward human relations theory and practice. By the 1970s, decision science had been transformed into a rational choice theory that borrowed heavily from economics. At about the same time, the emphasis shifted from organization and management to policy analysis and policymaking.

Throughout this period the *practices* of public administration remained rooted in concepts of organization and management. By the 1970s, the reform progressive period had ended, and the period of bureaucrat-bashing and downsizing had begun. Slowly, starting with the shift toward policy implementation, the field began to move back to earlier issues of organization and management. In the mid-1990s, we are witnessing the almost complete return to this earlier focus, albeit in a somewhat different language. Consider these contemporary concepts and phrases:

- The new principles of public administration (Hood and Jackson, 1991)
- An organizational design science
- "Leadership counts" (DiIulio, 1994; Behn, 1991; Doig, 1983)
- "Institutions matter" (March and Olsen, 1995)
- Managers as entrepreneurs (Osborne and Gaebler, 1992)
- The National Performance Review (1993; DiIulio, Garvey, and Kettl, 1993; Kettl, 1994)
- *Results-oriented*
- *Mission-driven*
- Total Quality Management (Cohen and Brand, 1993)

Organizational and managerial issues are again central to academic perspectives in the field. This is especially good news because these modern aspects of public administration are much nearer actual field practice than were (and are) decision theory and notions of rational choice.

We have also witnessed a healthy return to issues of efficiency and economy, particularly following the notion that rules, regulations, and red tape may not be as productive to efficiency and economy as simple good management. Issues of equity and fairness are now deeply rooted in the field as well.

All of this suggests the following second principle:

The task of public administration is to efficiently, economically, and equitably organize and manage the full range of public (governmental, quasi-governmental, and nongovernmental) institutions.

While such a principle sounds terribly traditional and rather obvious, public administration, like most endeavors, is at its best when it stays on task. This principle is broad enough to encompass all the theories of organizing, from hierarchy to matrix to loose-coupling to the garbage can to empowerment. It also encompasses the full range of management theories, from leadership to human relations.

We should boldly assert that the effectiveness of public agencies, organizations, and institutions is dependent on the theories and practices of modern public administration. This brings us to issues of public administration's scope.

At the high point of the reform-progressive period, it was not uncommon to hear public administration referred to as the fourth branch of government. Now, after more than twenty years of antibureaucracy rhetoric, cutbacks, and downsizing, such a phrase sounds absurd. The lessons of the last two decades indicate that we should be circumspect in defining the scope of our work.

At the risk of employing a somewhat sanitized version of the policy-administration dichotomy, public administration is best served when it emphasizes implementation, management, and the day-to-day operations of public institutions. When circumstances require that we engage in policymaking, we should be a part of governing. But when we do so, we must acknowledge that we risk moving past the legitimate scope of our work.

Listen to elected officials—particularly elected executives. They believe that *they* make policy. They believe that *they* govern. (Do public administrators have "policy envy"? one may ask. The answer is yes—and we may even have "governing envy.")

In the implementation of policy, public administrators have a responsibility to effect principles of efficiency, economy, and equity. We have a responsibility to implement policy in the spirit of the patriotism of benevolence. It is beyond question that policymakers rely on us for expertise, and because of that, we influence policy. We know that we are not neutral, and we should not be neutral. We should be nonpartisan advocates of our task (good and fair organization and management) for our agency's mission and for the guarantees of American regime values.

Entrepreneurial policy leadership is currently fashionable and is certainly suited to a governor or mayor or maybe even a president. When public administrators engage in entrepreneurial leadership, they should be especially sensitive to the distinctions between the roles of those who are elected and those who are appointed civil servants.

The third principle of public administration is as follows:

> The scope of public administration is the implementation of public policy, the effective organization and management of public agencies, the nonpartisan advocacy of public agencies' missions, and the maintenance of regime values for all citizens.

In public administration, we wrestle with the issues of discretion. Some scholars of the field, including Lowi (1969) and Gruber (1987), argue that the discretion of bureaucrats is too great. Others such as Osborne and Gaebler (1992) use the words *empowerment* and *entrepreneurial* essentially to argue an expansionist view of the proper range of discretion in public administration. The third principle set out above urges some caution in taking an expansionist view of administrative discretion. In policy implementation, we have more than enough responsibility to serve the citizens. We should never forget that we have the responsibility to vouchsafe the principles and practices of direct electoral democratic government, and in doing so, we recognize and support the powers of elected officials to enact binding law and policy.

If we combine the issue of task and the issue of scope, we come to this question: Can even the best management (some may be inclined to say Total Quality Management) overcome the problems of flawed policy? While the perspective presented here urges a circumspect definition of public administration's scope, we should insist that we *cannot* solve the problems of contradictory, incoherent, and intentionally vague policy by better management alone. It follows, then, that even such a circumspect definition would include our responsibility to inform, to urge, and to insist that elected officials face up to policy dilemmas rather than suggesting that such problems can be somehow ameliorated by better management. Perhaps one definition of the scope of public administration could suggest that we be "boldly circumspect." (Do these qualities seem inconsistent or oxymoronic? Never mind. We can be both: in confronting flawed policy we can be bold, and in the scope of our work we can be circumspect.)

In trendy versions of public administration, we often find the "wrong problems problem" (Downs and Larkey, 1986), which gives management answers to policy questions. We see aspects of the wrong problems problem in the reinventing government movement.

Although they will tend to resist our efforts, we should continually press our political masters to make tough policy choices. And we should encourage our political masters to make available the resources required for us to effectively implement public policy. This is what we mean by a "boldly circumspect" public administration.

When we are obliged to implement flawed public policy, we must work to enhance the positive and just aspects of the policy. We also must work to ameliorate its weaknesses, contradictions, and overreaching goals. We must work to make the policy we implement as just and compassionate as possible. And we must resist, thwart, or refuse to implement policy that runs counter to the founding documents or to American regime values.

In the American federal system, the issues of *level* arise continually. The practices of public administration are balanced between the national government and its roles and responsibilities on one hand and American subgovernments and their roles and responsibilities on the other.

Academic public administration, however, has had a long preoccupation with the national government. Our literature and our teaching are heavily oriented toward the national government. This is partly because the national government is now involved in a broad range of issues that were traditionally thought to belong to the state and local levels. But this orientation is also partly due to status: it is regarded as prestigious to study, write about, consult for, or take positions in the national government. Many more scholars strive to be heard on the national stage than on the state or local level.

The media's preoccupation with the national government also pushes public attention to the national level. As a result, citizens have more knowledge about a remote federal government than about governments that are closer at hand. To put it more strongly, Americans know more and more about the national government— the level that probably affects us least—and less and less about government at the state level (universities, highways, health care) and local level (public safety, schools, public works, recreation)—which affects us more.

Public administration, particularly as a field of study, is a part of this issue. To regain balance in our perspective, here is the fourth principle:

> Public administration, as both a field of study and a field of practice, should
> be equally focused on the federal, state, and local levels of government in
> American federalism.

Next, we come to the issues of *change*. Change is always a difficult challenge for public administrators. The context of public organizations is very dynamic. We usually face this paradox: the environment of organizations changes rapidly and sometimes unpredictably. The very essence of organization, however, is to be orderly and predictable. Our organizations tend to be orderly, stable, predictable—indeed, they are generally static and resistant to change. But we must be able to respond to change.

Consider these generalizations about administrative and organizational change:

1. We know how to do things, and with sufficient resources, we do some things very well (La Porte and Thomas, 1995; Landau, 1991). Other tasks—for example, prisons and welfare—are considered "impossible jobs," and even their best management results in only limited success (Hargrove and Glidewell, 1990). The problem lies not in *how* to do things but in determining what *ought* to be done.

2. In the traditions of public administration, we have assumed that it was important to set sensible goals and then to institutionalize to achieve them. In difficult or turbulent times, a more logical approach is often to commit to sensible actions so that we can understand and achieve sensible overall objectives (Harmon and Mayer, 1986).

3. Public administrators once thought that the challenge of reform was to put things right. Recognizing that things put right are unlikely to stay right, we now know that the real challenge is to institutionalize change procedures. The key is to seek agreement around the criteria by which organizational effectiveness is judged.

4. Both institutional growth and decline are respectable forms of change. The challenge for both political leaders and public administrators is to know when such increments or decrements make sense.

5. Responsiveness to citizens (consumers, clients, customers) was once thought to be a function of fostering widespread participation (cooptation) and eliciting greater information about preferences. This often results in goal displacement and resistance to change (Wilson, 1989). We now understand that being responsive means enhancing the capacity of *clients* (customers, citizens) to facilitate or elicit institutional adaptation to *their* needs.

Of course, a total reconciliation of the static characteristics of institutions and the dynamics of institutional context cannot occur. The contemporary study of change indicates, however, that the prospects for institutional responsiveness will improve if we follow the logic set out in this chapter.

We come, then, to the fifth principle:

> We should manage public organizations and institutions in such a way as to enhance the prospects for change, responsiveness, and citizen involvement.

The current emphasis on innovation and creativity in public administration is very good news. Attempting to broaden the range of administrative discretion and citizen choices, trying to build organizational cultures that encourage creativity and risk taking, and developing systems for the diffusion of innovation are all goals that make for effective contemporary practice.

In applying innovation and creativity to our administrative tasks we should, however, avoid the perils of political manipulation. Even the most creative administrator cannot increase organizational performance after the second or third cycle of downsizing. Simply put, every innovation has its limitations.

Our final three principles have to do with responsibility, accountability, and service. We move from issues of task, domain, and level to issues of ethics and morality in public administration.

To whom are public administrators responsible? To the elected executive? To the Constitution and the laws? To the elected legislators or their subordinates? To professional standards and codes of ethics? The answer, of course, is that we are responsible to all of these. But this answer is contingent on the issue at hand; it is a necessary but not sufficient answer.

The broader and more serviceable answer is that public administrators are responsible to the citizens. We are responsible for weighing and balancing constitutional and legal issues with political issues and for making decisions that reduce to our best understanding of policy implementation in a democratic context. We are responsible for a kind of moral agency to the citizens (Morgan and Kass, 1993; Wamsley and others, 1990).

Many will argue that such a level of responsibility is impossibly vague. Certainly, it is abstract and imprecise—but so are our ultimate responsibilities. We cannot know the range of citizen opinions, attitudes, needs, and preferences, but we can know the importance of an ultimate responsibility to the people.

Many will also argue that we must merely follow the national and state constitutions, the laws, and the directives of the chief executive. To go beyond that is to steal the popular sovereignty (Thompson, 1975). But in an era of vague and contradictory laws, co-management (Gilmour and Halley, 1994), and shared power (Kettl, 1993a), public administrators are finally left to decide. Without a broader responsibility to the public, we have a weak rudder. If we assume that we work for the people and that we are representative citizens, or citizens twice, we have a stronger rudder. This view of the spirit of public administration is what ennobles our work.

In the early days of modern public administration, the founders of the field were reformers and linked the field to broad issues of civics and citizenship in the management of public organizations. This made public administration special and unique— it was not just a job to be done. To rediscover the spirit of public administration, we must rediscover the field's link to civics and citizenship.

This is the sixth principle of public administration:

In the democratic context, public administrators are ultimately responsible to the citizens. It is this responsibility that ennobles our work.

The careful reader will know that such a principle begs the question of responsibility to *which* citizens, because citizens differ greatly in their preferences and needs. For a long time, the field ignored this question, assuming that if a public organization was generally efficient or economical, it was efficient or economical for everyone. Although we know that this is not true, it nevertheless has always been easy to hide behind managerial symbols of efficiency, economy, effectiveness—and, these days, performance.

In the modern spirit of public administration, we have a responsibility to be fair, just, and equitable. Trying to achieve these qualities has always been one of the goals of democratic government, particularly in the context of market capitalism. It is often the public administrator's job, in both governmental and third-sector public organizations, to level the playing field of opportunity and to manage the safety net under the competitive private market.

Issues of fairness and equity are central to the working of democratic government, particularly in a system that separates its powers. But these issues do not belong solely to legislators and elected executives; while they may settle the broader questions of distribution and of costs and benefits, it is left to public administrators to wrestle with the smaller questions of fairness and equity. This responsibility brings dignity and nobility to our work. It is often more comfortable, however, for us to talk and act as if we manage only to standards of efficiency, economy, and effectiveness. In the spirit of public administration, we must insist that we also manage public affairs to standards of fairness and equity. It is simply a part of our ethic—part of the moral tools of our work.

This, then, brings us to the seventh principle:

> Public administration's commitment, in theory and practice, to standards of equity and fairness is as important as its commitment to efficiency, economy, and effectiveness. Following standards of equity and fairness can bind the citizens together in our own time and also bind us to future generations.

Finally, the work of public administrators is guided by a deeper moral current. To be fully in the spirit of public administration, we must genuinely care for and work with the citizens, we must care for and believe in the constitutions and the laws, and we must feel passionately about good management as well as justice. We choose to call this *benevolence,* a word taken to mean a broad and unashamed love of the people, the citizens. We also take benevolence to mean a commitment both to serve a greater collective good and to fairly minister to the individual needs of citizens. It is the spirit of benevolence that binds together the public school teacher and the student, the police officer and the threatened, the regulator and the citizen who needs protection.

Without benevolence, public administration is merely governmental work. With benevolence, our field has a meaning and purpose beyond just doing a good job; the work we do becomes noble—a kind of civic virtue. Not all benevolent public administration is understood or appreciated, and when public administrators are subjected to repeated bureaucrat-bashing, it is easy for us to feel alienated (Lipsky, 1980). When this happens, the spirit of public administration weakens. Still, the benevolence of public administration is what constitutes the bedrock of our field and sustains the spirit of our work.

The eighth and final principle is as follows:

> The spirit of public administration is dependent on a moral base of benevolence to all citizens.

In summary, the spirit of public administration is found in (1) defining our domain broadly; (2) setting our task to be the efficient, economical, and equitable management of public organizations and institutions; (3) limiting the scope of our field to the effective and fair implementation of public policy and the nonpartisan advocacy of our organizations' missions; (4) focusing equally on federal, state, and local government; (5) managing public organizations and institutions so as to enhance the prospects for change and responsiveness; and (6) serving the citizens fairly and benevolently. If we strive to do this, modern public administration can meet the aspirations of the guardians of Athens and leave our cities and our nation better and more beautiful.

References

Aaron, H. J., Bosworth, B., and Burtless, G. T. *Can America Afford to Grow Old?* Washington, D.C.: Brookings Institution, 1989.

Allison, G. T. *Essence of Decision: Explaining the Cuban Missile Crisis.* Boston: Little, Brown, 1971.

Amy, D. J. "Why Policy Analysis and Ethics Are Incompatible." *Journal of Policy Analysis and Management,* 1984, *3,* 573–591.

"Annual Survey of Education and Schooling." *Phi Delta Kappan,* Sept. 1992, *74*(1), 45.

Appleby, P. H. *Big Democracy.* New York: Knopf, 1945.

Arendt, H. *Eichmann in Jerusalem: A Report on the Banality of Evil.* New York: Viking Penguin, 1963.

Aristotle. *Nicomachean Ethics.* (M. Ostwald, ed. and trans.) New York: Bobbs-Merrill, 1962.

Aristotle. *Politics.* (C. Lord, trans.) Chicago: University of Chicago Press, 1984.

Arrow, K. *Social Choice and Justice.* Cambridge, Mass.: Belknap Press, 1983.

Baier, A. "The Rights of Past and Future Persons." In E. Partridge (ed.), *Responsibility to Future Generations.* Amherst, N.Y.: Prometheus, 1981.

Baldwin, N. J. "Public Versus Private Employees: Debunking Stereotypes." *Review of Public Personnel Administration,* 1991, *11,* 1–27.

Barber, B. *Strong Democracy: Participatory Politics for a New Age.* Berkeley: University of California Press, 1986.

Barnard, C. I. *The Functions of the Executive.* Cambridge, Mass.: Harvard University Press, 1938.

Barns, N. *The Formation of American Local Governments: Private Values in Public Institutions.* New York: Oxford University Press, 1994.

Barrow, R. H. *The Romans.* New York: Penguin Books, 1949.

Barry, B. "Circumstances of Justice and Future Generations." In R. I. Sikora and B. Barry (eds.), *Obligations to Future Generations.* Philadelphia: Temple University Press, 1978.

Becker, C. *The Declaration of Independence.* (Rev. ed.) New York: Vintage Books, 1942.

Behn, R. D. *Leadership Counts: Lessons for Public Managers from the Massachusetts Welfare, Training, and Employment Program.* Cambridge, Mass.: Harvard University Press, 1991.

Bellah, R. N., and others. *Habits of the Heart: Individualism and Commitment in American Life.* Berkeley: University of California Press, 1985.

Bellanta, B., and Link, A. N. "Are Public Sector Workers More Risk Averse Than Private Sector Workers?" *Industrial and Labor Relations Review,* 1981, *34,* 408–412.

Bensen, A. A., II. "The Liability of Missouri Suburban School Districts for the Unconstitutional Segregation of Neighboring Urban School Districts." *University of Missouri at Kansas City Law Review,* 1985, *53*(3), 349–375.

Bentham, J. *The Principles of Morals and Legislation.* Riverside, N.J.: Hafner Press, 1948. (Originally published 1789.)

Berry, F. S., Chackerian, R., and Weschler, B. "Reinventing Government: Lessons from a State Capitol." Paper delivered at the Third National Public Management Research Conference, Lawrence, Kansas, October 1995.

Bertelsen, A. *October '43.* (M. Lindholm, trans.) New York: Putnam, 1954.

Beyer, W. C. "The Civil Service of the Ancient World." In J. W. Fesler (ed.), *American Public Administration: Patterns of the Past.* Washington, D.C.: American Society for Public Administration, 1982.

Bok, S. *Lying: Moral Choice in Public and Private Life.* New York: Vintage, 1978.

Bowman, J. L. (ed.). *Ethical Frontiers in Public Management: Seeking New Strategies for Resolving Ethical Dilemmas.* San Francisco: Jossey-Bass, 1991.

Bozeman, B. *All Organizations Are Public: Bridging Public and Private Organizational Theories.* San Francisco: Jossey-Bass, 1987.

Brown, D. B. *When Strangers Cooperate.* New York: Free Press, 1995.

Brown v. Topeka Board of Education, (I) 3/4/47 U.S. 483, 1954.

Bryson, G. *Man and Society: The Scottish Inquiry of the Eighteenth Century.* New York: Kelley, 1968. (Originally published 1945.)

Bryson, J. M., and Crosby, B. C. *Leadership for the Common Good: Tackling Public Problems in a Shared-Power World.* San Francisco: Jossey-Bass, 1992.

Buchanan, J. M., and Tullock, G. *The Calculus of Consent: Logical Foundations of Constitutional Democracy.* Ann Arbor: University of Michigan Press, 1962.

Burke, J. P. *Bureaucratic Responsibility.* Baltimore, Md.: Johns Hopkins University Press, 1986.

Burns, J. M. *The Deadlock of Democracy.* Englewood Cliffs, N.J.: Prentice Hall, 1963.

Burns, N. *The Formation of American Local Governments: Private Values in Public Institutions.* New York: Oxford University Press, 1994.

Callahan, D. "What Obligations Do We Have to Future Generations?" In E. Partridge (ed.), *Responsibility to Future Generations.* Amherst, N.Y.: Prometheus, 1981.

Carroll, J. D., and Zuck, A. M. *The Study of Administration Revisited.* Washington, D.C.: American Society for Public Administration, 1983.

Carroll, L. *Through the Looking Glass: What Alice Found There.* New York: Grosset & Dunlap, 1960. (Originally published 1871.)

Chase-Dunn, C. K. *Global Formation: Structures of the World Economy.* Cambridge, Mass.: Basil Blackwell, 1989.

Cicero. *Laws.* (C. W. Keyes, trans.) Cambridge, Mass.: Harvard University Press, Loeb Classical Library, 1928.

City of Richmond v. J. A. Croson Company, 109 S. Ct. 706, 1989.

Cleveland, H. *The Future Executive: A Guide for Tomorrow's Managers.* New York: HarperCollins, 1972.

Cohen, S., and Brand, R. *Total Quality Management in Government: A Practical Guide for the Real World.* San Francisco: Jossey-Bass, 1993.

Cooper, P. *Hard Judicial Choices.* New York: Oxford University Press, 1992.

Cooper, T. L. *The Responsible Administrator: An Approach to Ethics for the Administrative Role.* (3rd ed.) San Francisco: Jossey-Bass, 1990.

Cooper, T. L. *An Ethic of Citizenship for Public Administration.* Englewood Cliffs, N.J.: Prentice Hall, 1991.

Cooper, T. L., and Wright, N. D. (eds.). *Exemplary Public Administrators: Character and Leadership in Government.* San Francisco: Jossey-Bass, 1992.

Dahl, R. A. *A Preface to Democratic Theory.* Chicago: University of Chicago Press, 1956.

Dalattre, E. "Rights, Responsibilities, and Future Persons." *Ethics,* Apr. 1972, *82,* 254–258.

Dalton, R. J. *Citizen Politics in Western Democracies: Public Opinion and Political Parties in the United States, Great Britain, West Germany and France.* Chatham, N.J.: Chatham House, 1988.

Dawidowicz, L. S. *The War Against the Jews: 1933–1945.* Austin, Tex.: Holt, Rinehart & Winston, 1975.

DeGeorge, R. T. "The Environment, Rights and Future Generations." In K. E. Goodpaster and K. M. Sayer (eds.), *Ethics and Problems in the 21st Century.* Notre Dame, Ind.: University of Notre Dame Press, 1979.

Denhardt, K. G. *The Ethics of Public Service: Resolving Moral Dilemmas in Public Organizations.* Westport, Conn.: Greenwood Press, 1988.

Derr, T. S. "The Obligation to the Future." In E. Partridge (ed.), *Responsibility to Future Generations.* Amherst, N.Y.: Prometheus, 1981.

Derthick, M. "American Federalism: Madison's Middle Ground in the 1980's." *Public Administration Review,* Jan./Feb. 1987, *47,* 66–74.

Dewey, J. *Individualism, Old and New.* New York: Minton, Balch, 1930.

Dewey, J. *The Public and Its Problems.* Chicago: Swallow Press, 1954.

DiIulio, J. J. "Principled Agents: The Cultural Bases of Behavior in a Federal Government Bureaucracy." *Journal of Public Administration Research and Theory,* 1994, *4,* 277–320.

DiIulio, J. J., Garvey, G., and Kettl, D. F. *Improving Government Performance: An Owner's Manual.* Washington, D.C.: Brookings Institution, 1993.

"Dissatisfaction with Our Government." *The Public Perspective,* Mar./Apr. 1994, *5*(3), 88.

Doig, J. W. "To Claim the Seas and Skies: Austin Tobin and the Port of New York Authority." In J. W. Doig and E. C. Hargrove (eds.), *Leadership and Innovation: A Biographical Perspective on Entrepreneurs in Government.* Baltimore, Md.: Johns Hopkins University Press, 1983.

Dossa, S. "Hannah Arendt on Eichmann: The Public, the Private and Evil." *Review of Politics,* Apr. 1984, *46,* 165–166.

Downs, A. *Inside Bureaucracy.* Boston: Little, Brown, 1967.

Downs, G. W., and Larkey, P. D. *The Search for Government Efficiency: From Hubris to Helplessness.* New York: Random House, 1986.

Dworkin, R. *A Matter of Principle.* Cambridge, Mass.: Harvard University Press, 1985.

Edelman, M. J. *Political Language: Words That Succeed and Policies That Fail.* Orlando, Fla.: Academic Press, 1977.

Etzioni, A. *A Responsive Society: Collected Essays on Guiding Deliberate Social Change.* San Francisco: Jossey-Bass, 1991.

Evans, K. G., and Wamsley, G. L. "Where's the Institution? Neo-Institutionalism and Public Management." Paper delivered at the Third National Public Management Research Conference, Lawrence, Kans., Oct. 1995.

Finer, H. "Administrative Responsibility in Democratic Government." *Public Administration Review,* 1941, *14,* 335–350.

Flathman, R. E. *The Public Interest: An Essay Concerning the Normative Discourse of Politics.* New York: Wiley, 1966.

Fleishman, J. "Self-Interest and Political Integrity." In J. Fleishman, L. Liebman, and M. H. Moore (eds.), *Public Duties: The Moral Obliga-*

tions of Government Officials. Cambridge, Mass.: Harvard University Press, 1981.

Flender, H. *Rescue in Denmark.* New York: Simon & Schuster, 1963.

Flower, E., and Murphey, M. G. *A History of Philosophy in America.* (Vol. 1.) New York: Putnam, 1977.

Frederickson, H. G. "Toward a New Public Administration." In F. Marini, *Toward a New Public Administration: The Minnowbrook Perspective.* Scranton, Pa.: Chandler, 1971.

Frederickson, H. G. (ed.). "Curriculum Essays on Citizens, Politics and Administration in Urban Neighborhoods." *Public Administration Review,* Oct. 1972, *32* (special issue), 565–738.

Frederickson, H. G. (ed.). "Symposium on Social Equity and Public Administration." *Public Administration Review,* Jan./Feb. 1974, 34(*1*), 1–51.

Frederickson, H. G. *The New Public Administration.* Tuscaloosa: University of Alabama Press, 1980.

Frederickson, H. G. "The Recovery of Civism in Public Administration." *Public Administration Review,* Nov./Dec. 1982, 42(*6*), 501–509.

Frederickson, H. G. "Citizenship, Social Equity, and Public Administration." In R. G. Denhardt and E. T. Jennings Jr. (eds.), Frederickson, H. G. "Public Administration and Social Equity." *Public Administration Review,* 1990, *50*(2), 228–237.

Frederickson, H. G. (ed.). *Ideal and Practice in Council-Manager Government.* (2nd ed.) Washington, D.C.: International City/County Management Association, 1995.

Frederickson, H. G., and Chandler, R. C. (eds.). "Citizenship and Public Administration." *Public Administration Review* (Special issue on citizenship and public administration), Mar. 1984, *44*, 97–209.

French, P. A. *Ethics in Government.* Englewood Cliffs, N.J.: Prentice Hall, 1983.

Friedrich, C. J. "The Nature of Administrative Responsibility." *Public Policy,* 1940, *1*, 3–24.

Fukuyama, F. *Trust: The Social Virtues and the Creation of Prosperity.* New York: Free Press, 1995.

Fullilove v. Klutznik, 448 U.S. 448, 1980.

Garvey, G. *Facing the Bureaucracy: Living and Dying in a Public Agency.* San Francisco: Jossey-Bass, 1993.

Gaus, J. "Trends in the Theory of Public Administration." *Public Administration Review,* 1950, *10*, 161–168.

Gawthrop, L. C. "Civis, Civitas and Civilitas: A New Focus for the Year 2000." *Public Administration Review* (Special issue on citizenship and public administration, H. G. Frederickson and R. C. Chandler, eds.), Mar. 1984a, *44*, 101–107.

Gawthrop, L. C. *Public Sector Management, Systems and Ethics.* Bloomington: Indiana University Press, 1984b.

Gilmour, R. S., and Halley, A. A. (eds.). *Who Makes Public Policy: The Struggle for Control Between Congress and the Executive.* Chatham, N.J.: Chatham House, 1994.

Gladden, E. N. *A History of Public Administration.* (Vol. 1.) London: Frank Cass, 1972.

Glazer, M. P., and Glazer, P. M. *The Whistleblowers: Exposing Corruption in Government and Industry.* New York: Basic Books, 1989.

Glendon, M. A. *Rights Talk: The Impoverishment of Political Discourse.* New York: Free Press, 1991.

Golding, M. P. "Obligations to Future Generations." In E. Partridge (ed.) *Responsibility to Future Generations.* Buffalo, NY: Prometheus Books, 1981, 61–72.

Goodsell, C. T. "Cross-Cultural Comparison of Behavior of Postal Clerks Toward Clients." *Administrative Science Quarterly,* Mar. 1976, *12,* 140–150.

Goodsell, C. T. "Client Evaluation of Three Welfare Programs." *Administration and Society,* Aug. 1980, *12,* 123–136.

Goodsell, C. T. *The Social Meaning of Civic Space.* Lawrence: University Press of Kansas, 1988.

Goodsell, C. T. *The Case for Bureaucracy: A Public Administration Polemic.* (3rd ed.) Chatham, N.J.: Chatham House, 1995.

Green, R. M. "Intergenerational Distributive Justice and Environmental Responsibility." In E. Partridge (ed.), *Responsibility to Future Generations.* Amherst, N.Y.: Prometheus, 1981.

Green v. School Board 391 U.S. 430, 437–438, 1968.

Griggs v. Duke Power Company, 401 U.S. 424, 1971.

Gruber, J. E. *Controlling Bureaucracies: Dilemmas in Democratic Governance.* Berkeley: University of California Press, 1987.

Gusfield, J. R. *Symbolic Crusade: Status Politics and the American Temperance Movement.* (2nd ed.) Urbana: University of Illinois Press, 1986.

Haar, C. M., and Fessler, J. W. *Fairness and Justice: Law in the Service of Equality.* New York: Simon & Schuster, 1986.

Hamilton, A., Madison, J., and Jay, J. *The Federalist Papers.* New York: New American Library, 1961.

Hardin, G. *Promethean Ethics.* Seattle: University of Washington Press, 1980.

Hargrove, E. C., and Glidewell, J. C. *Impossible Jobs in Public Management.* Lawrence, Kans.: University Press of Kansas, 1990.

Harmon, M. M. "'Decision' and 'Action' As Contrasting Perspectives in Organization Theory." *Public Administration Review,* 1989, *49*(2), 144–149.

Harmon, M. M., and Mayer, R. T. *Organization Theory for Public Administration.* Boston: Little, Brown, 1986.

Hart, D. K. "The Virtuous Citizen, the Honorable Bureaucrat and Public Administration." *Public Administration Review* (Special issue on citizenship and public administration, H. G. Frederickson and R. C. Chandler, eds.), Mar. 1984, *44,* 111–119.

Hart, D. K., and Hart, D. W. "George C. Marshall and J. Edgar Hoover: Noblesse Oblige and Self-Serving Power." In T. L. Cooper and N. D. Wright (eds.), *Exemplary Public Administrators: Character and Leadership in Government.* San Francisco: Jossey-Bass, 1992.

Hartle, T. W. "Sisyphus Revisited: Running the Government Like a Business." *Public Administration Review,* Mar./Apr. 1985, *45,* 341–351.

Hartmann, N. "Love of the Remote." In E. Partridge (ed.), *Responsibility to Future Generations.* Amherst, N.Y.: Prometheus, 1981.

Hartshorne, C. "The Ethics of Contributionism." In E. Partridge (ed.), *Responsibility to Future Generations.* Amherst, N.Y.: Prometheus, 1981.

Hawkins v. Town of Shaw, 303 F. Supp. 1162, 1171, N.D. MISS. 1969.

Heclo, H. "Issue Networks and the Executive Establishment." In A. King (ed.), *The New American Political System.* Washington, D.C.: American Enterprise Institute, 1978.

Hejka-Ekins, A. "Marie Ragghianti: Moral Courage in Exposing Corruption." In Cooper, T. L., and Wright, N. D. (eds.), *Exemplary Public Administrators: Character and Leadership in Government.* San Francisco: Jossey-Bass, 1992.

Henriques, D. B. *The Machinery of Greed: Public Authority Abuse and What to Do About It.* Lexington, Mass.: Lexington Books, 1986.

Hero, R. E. "The Urban Service Delivery Literature: Some Questions and Considerations." *Polity,* Summer 1986, *18,* 659–677.

Hilberg, R. *The Destruction of the European Jews.* (Rev. ed.) Chicago: Quadrangle, 1967.

Hilberg, R. (ed.). *Documents of Destruction.* Chicago: Quadrangle, 1971.

Hirschman, A. O. *Shifting Involvements: Private Interest and Public Action.* Princeton, N.J.: Princeton University Press, 1982.

Hochschield, J. L. *What's Fair? American Beliefs About Distributive Justice.* Cambridge, Mass.: Harvard University Press, 1981.

Hoffer, E. *The True Believer.* New York: HarperCollins, 1951.

Holbrook, T. M., and Meier, K. J. "Bureaucracy and Political Corruption: Patterns in the American States." In H. G. Frederickson (ed.), *Ethics and Public Administration.* Armonk, N.Y.: Sharpe, 1993.

Hood, C., and Jackson, M. *Administrative Argument.* Brookfield, Vt.: Dartmouth, 1991.

Howard, P. K. *The Death of Common Sense: How the Law Is Suffocating America.* New York: Random House, 1995.

Howe, J. R., Jr. "A Virtuous People." In J. R. Howe (ed.), *The Changing Political Thought of John Adams.* Princeton, N.J.: Princeton University Press, 1966.

Hume, D. *Treatise on Human Nature.* New York: Oxford University Press, 1968. (Originally published 1739.)

Hume, D. "Of Goodness and Benevolence." *Enquiry Concerning the Principles of Morals.* (Sec. 11.) New York: Liberal Arts Press, 1957. (Originally published 1751.)

Ingraham, P. W., and Rosenbloom, D. H. "The New Public Personnel and the New Public Service," *Public Administration Review,* Mar./Apr. 1989, *49,* 116–124.

Jefferson, T. *The Writings of Thomas Jefferson.* (Vol. 15, A. A. Lipscomb and A. E. Bergh, eds.) Washington, D.C.: Thomas Jefferson Memorial Association, 1905.

Jenkins v. State of Missouri, 593 F. Supp. 1485, W.D. MO, 1984.

Jenkins v. State of Missouri, 855 Fed. R. 8th Circuit 1297–1319, 1984.

Jennings, B. "Taking Ethics Seriously in Administrative Life: Constitutionalism, Ethical Reasoning and Moral Judgement." In J. S. Bowman (ed.), *Ethical Frontiers in Public Management: Seeking New Strategies for Resolving Ethical Dilemmas.* San Francisco: Jossey-Bass, 1991.

Jensen, H. *Motivation and the Moral Sense in Francis Hutcheson's Ethical Theory.* The Hague: Martinus Nijhoff, 1971.

John, D. J., Kettl, D. F., Dyer, B., and Lovan, W. R. "What Will New Governance Mean for the Federal Government?" *Public Administration Review,* Mar./Apr. 1994, *54*(2), 170–175.

Johnson, R. A., and Kraft, M. E. "Bureaucratic Whistleblowing and Policy Change." *The Western Political Quarterly,* Dec. 1990, *43*(4), 849–874.

Jonas, H. "Technology and Responsibility: The Ethics of an Endangered Future." In E. Partridge (ed.), *Responsibility to Future Generations.* Amherst, N.Y.: Prometheus, 1981.

Jones, B. D., Greenberg, S. R., Kaufman, C., and Drew, J. "Service Delivery Rules and the Distribution of Local Government Services: Three Detroit Bureaucracies." *Journal of Politics,* 1978, *40,* 333–368.

Jos, P. H., Tompkins, M. E., and Hays, S. W. "In Praise of Difficult People: A Portrait of the Committed Whistleblower." *Public Administration Review,* 1989, *49,* 552–561.

Kammen, M. *People of Paradox: An Inquiry Concerning the Origins of American Civilization.* New York: Knopf, 1972.

Katz, D., Gutek, B. A., Kahn, R. L., and Barton, E. *Bureaucratic Encounter: A Pilot Study of the Evaluation of Government Services.* Ann Arbor: Survey Research Center, Institute for Social Research, University of Michigan, 1975.

Kaufman, H. *Time, Chance, and Organization: National Selection in a Perilous Environment.* Chatham, N.J.: Chatham House, 1985.

Kavka, G. "The Futurity Problem." In E. Partridge (ed.), *Responsibility to Future Generations.* Amherst, N.Y.: Prometheus, 1981.

Kelman, S. *Making Public Policy: A Hopeful View of American Government.* New York: Basic Books, 1987.

Kemmis, D. *Community and the Politics of Place.* Norman: University of Oklahoma Press, 1990.

Kennedy, P. M. *Preparing for the Twenty-First Century.* New York: Random House, 1993.

Kettl, D. F. "Public Administration: The State of the Discipline." In A. W. Finifter (ed.), *Political Science: The State of the Discipline II.* Washington, D.C.: American Political Science Association, 1993a.

Kettl, D. F. *Sharing Power: Public Governance and Private Markets.* Washington, D.C.: Brookings Institution, 1993b.

Kettl, D. F. *Reinventing Government? Appraising the National Performance Review.* Washington, D.C.: Brookings Institution, 1994.

Kingdon, J. W. *Agendas, Alternatives and Public Policies.* (2nd ed.) New York: HarperCollins, 1995.

Koch, A. *The Philosophy of Thomas Jefferson.* Gloucester, Mass.: Peter Smith, 1957. (Originally published 1943.)

Koch, A. "Liberty." In *Madison's "Advice to My Country."* Princeton, N.J.: Princeton University Press, 1966.

Koestler, A. "Beyond Holism and Atomism—The Concept of the Helon." In A. Koestler and J. R. Smythies (eds.), *Beyond Reductionism.* Boston: Beacon Press, 1971.

Kohlberg, L. *The Meaning and Measurement of Moral Development.* Worcester, Mass.: Clark University Press, 1980.

Kotlikoff, L. J. *Intergenerational Accounting.* New York: Free Press, 1991.

Krislov, S. *Representative Bureaucracy.* Englewood Cliffs, N.J.: Prentice Hall, 1974.

La Porte, T. R., and Thomas, C. W. "Regulatory Compliance and the Ethos of Quality Enhancement: Surprises in Nuclear Power Plant Operations." *Journal of Public Administration Research and Theory,* 1995, 5, 111–139.

Lan, Z., and Rosenbloom, D. "Public Administration in Transition." *Public Administration Review,* 1992, 52(6), 535–539.

Landau, M. "Multiorganizational Systems in Public Administration."

Journal of Public Administration Research and Theory, Jan. 1991, *1*(1), 5–18.

Lasch, C. *The Culture of Narcissism: American Life in an Age of Diminishing Expectations.* New York: Norton, 1978.

Lasch, C. *The True and Only Heaven: Progress and Its Critics.* New York: Norton, 1990.

Lasch, C. *The Revolt of the Elites: And the Betrayal of Democracy.* New York: Norton, 1995.

Lehane, R. *The Quest for Justice: The Politics of School Finance Reform.* White Plains, N.Y.: Longman, 1978.

Lerner, N. W., and Wanat, J. "Fuzziness and Bureaucracy." *Public Administration Review,* 1983, *47,* 500–509.

Levy, F. *Dollars and Dreams: The Changing American Income Distribution.* New York: Russell Sage Foundation, 1987.

Lewis, C. W. *The Ethics Challenge in Public Service: A Problem-Solving Guide.* San Francisco: Jossey-Bass, 1991.

Leys, W.A.R. *Ethics for Policy Decisions.* New York: Prentice Hall, 1952.

Liddell v. State of Missouri, 731 F. 2D 1294, 1323, 8 Cir., 1984.

Light, P. C. "Federal Ethics Controls: The Role of Inspectors General." In H. G. Frederickson (ed.), *Ethics and Public Administration.* Armonk, N.Y.: Sharpe, 1993a.

Light, P. C. *Monitoring Government: Inspectors General and the Search for Accountability.* Washington, D.C.: Brookings Institution, 1993b.

Lilla, M. "Ethos, 'Ethics,' and Public Service." *Public Interest,* 1981, *63,* 317.

Lindblom, C. E. "The Science of Muddling Through." *Public Administration Review,* 1959, *19,* 79–88.

Lindblom, C. E. *The Intelligence of Democracy: Decision Making Through Mutual Adjustment.* New York: Free Press, 1965.

Lineberry, R. L. *Equality and Urban Policy: The Distribution of Urban Public Services.* Thousand Oaks, Calif.: Sage, 1977.

Link, A. S. *The Higher Realism of Woodrow Wilson, and Other Essays.* Nashville, Tenn.: Vanderbilt University Press, 1971.

Lippmann, W. *Essays in the Public Philosophy.* Boston: Little, Brown, 1955.

Lipset, S. M., and Schneider, W. *The Confidence Gap: Business, Labor and Government in the Public Mind.* New York: Free Press, 1983.

Lipsky, M. *Street-Level Bureaucracy.* New York: Russell Sage Foundation, 1980.

Lipsky, M. "Advocacy and Alienation in Street-Level Work." In C. T. Goodsell (ed.), *The Public Encounter: Where State and Citizen Meet.* Bloomington: Indiana University Press, 1981.

Locke, J. *Two Treatises of Government.* (2nd Treatise, sect. 4, P. Laslett, ed.) New York: NAL/Dutton, 1965. (Originally published 1690.)

Long, N. E. "Power and Administration." *Public Administration Review,* Autumn 1949, *9,* 257–264.

Long, N. E. "Bureaucracy and Constitutionalism." *American Political Science Review,* 1952, *46*(3), 808–818.

Louis, M. R. "Organizations As Culture-Bearing Milieux." In L. R. Pondy and others (eds.), *Organizational Symbolism.* Greenwich, Conn.: JAI Press, 1983.

Lovejoy, A. O. *Reflections on Human Nature.* Baltimore, Md.: Johns Hopkins University Press, 1961.

Lowi, T. J. *The End of Liberalism: Ideology, Policy and the Crisis of Public Authority.* New York: Norton, 1969.

Lynn, L. E. *Managing Public Policy.* Boston: Little, Brown, 1987.

Lynn, L. E. "Assume a Network: Reforming Mental Health Services in Illinois." *Journal of Public Administration Research and Theory.* Apr. 1996, 6(*2*), 297–314.

Maas, P. *Marie: A True Story.* New York: Random House, 1980.

Mainzer, L. C. "Honor in the Bureaucratic Life." *Review of Politics,* Jan. 1964, *26,* p. 71.

Malek, K. "Public Attitudes Toward Corruption: Twenty-five Years of Research." In H. G. Frederickson (ed.), *Ethics and Public Administration.* Armonk, N.Y.: Sharpe, 1993.

March, J. G., and Olsen, J. P. *Democratic Governance.* New York: Free Press, 1995.

March, J. G., and Simon, H. A. *Organizations.* New York: Wiley, 1958.

Marini, F. *Toward a New Public Administration: The Minnowbrook Perspective.* Scranton, Pa.: Chandler, 1971.

Marone, J. A. *The Democratic Wish: Popular Participation and the Limits of American Government.* New York: Basic Books, 1990.

Mathews, D. "The Public in Theory and Practice." *Public Administration Review* (Special issue on citizenship and public administration, H. G. Frederickson and R. C. Chandler, eds.), Mar. 1984, *44,* 122–123.

Mathews, D. *Politics for People: Finding a Responsible Public Voice.* Urbana: University of Illinois Press, 1994.

McCloskey, R. G. (ed.). *The Works of James Wilson.* (Vol. 1.) Cambridge, Mass.: Harvard University Press, 1967.

McDowell, G. L. *Equity and the Constitution.* Chicago: University of Chicago Press, 1982.

McGregor, D. *The Human Side of Enterprise.* New York: McGraw-Hill, 1960.

McKerlie, D. "Equality and Time." *Ethics,* Apr. 1989, *99*(3), 475–491.

Meier, K. J. *Regulation: Politics, Bureaucracy, and Economics.* New York: St. Martin's Press, 1985.

Meltsner, A. *Policy Analysis in the Bureaucracy.* Berkeley: University of California Press, 1979.

Menzel, D. C. "The Ethics Factor in Local Government: An Empirical Analysis." In H. G. Frederickson (ed.), *Ethics and Public Administration.* Armonk, N.Y.: Sharpe, 1993.

Milliken v. Bradley, 418 U.S. 717, 1974.

Milward, H. B., and Provan, K. G. "The Hollow State: Provision of Public Services." In H. Ingram and S. R. Smith (eds.), *Public Policy for Democracy.* Washington, D.C.: Brookings Institution, 1994.

Milward, H. B., Provan, K. G., and Else, B. "What Does the Hollow State Look Like?" In B. Bozeman (ed.), *Public Management: The State of the Art.* San Francisco: Jossey-Bass, 1993.

Missouri v. Jenkins, 115 S. Ct. 2573, June 14, 1995.

Mladenka, K. R. "Organizational Rules, Service Equality, and Distributional Decisions in Urban Politics." *Social Science Quarterly,* 1978, *59,* 192–201.

Mladenka, K. R. "Responsible Performance by Public Officials." In C. T. Goodsell (ed.), *The Public Encounter: When States and Citizens Meet.* Bloomington: Indiana University Press, 1981.

Moe, T. M. "Regulatory Performance and Presidential Administration." *American Journal of Political Science,* 1982, *26,* 197–224.

Morgan, D., and Kass, H. D. "The American Odyssey of the Career in Public Service: The Ethical Crises of Role Reversal." In H. G. Frederickson (ed.), *Ethics and Public Administration.* Armonk, N.Y.: Sharpe, 1993.

Mosher, F. C. *Democracy and the Public Service.* (2nd ed.) New York: Oxford University Press, 1982.

Murchland, B. "Thinking About the Public." *Kettering Review,* Winter 1984, 11–17.

Nalbandian, J. "The U.S. Supreme Court's 'Consensus' on Affirmative Action." *Public Administration Review,* Jan./Feb. 1989, *49*(1), 38–45.

Nalbandian, J., and Edwards, J. T. "The Values of Public Administration: A Comparison with Lawyers, Social Workers and Business Administrators." *A Review of Public Personnel Administration,* 1983, *4,* 114–129.

Nathan, R. P. *The Administrative Presidency.* New York: Wiley, 1983.

National Performance Review (Vice President Albert Gore). *From Red Tape to Results: Creating a Government That Works Better and Costs Less.* Washington, D.C.: U.S. Government Printing Office, 1993.

Neustadt, R. E. *Presidential Power.* New York: Wiley, 1960.

Neustadt, R. E., and May, E. R. *Thinking in Time: The Uses of History for Decisionmakers.* New York: Free Press, 1986.

New York Times. Jan. 24, 1989, pp. 1, 12.

Newland, C. A. *Public Administration and Community: Realism in the Practice of Ideals.* McLean, Va.: Public Administration Service, 1984.

Newland, C. A. "Public Executives: Imperium, Sacerdotium, Colloquium? Bicentennial Leadership Challenges." *Public Administration Review,* 1987, *47,* 45–56.

Niskanen, W. A. *Bureaucracy and Representative Government.* Hawthorne, N.Y.: Aldine de Gruyter, 1971.

Osborne, D., and Gaebler, T. *Reinventing Government.* Reading, Mass.: Addison-Wesley, 1992.

Ostrom, V. *The Intellectual Crisis in American Public Administration.* University: University of Alabama Press, 1973.

Overman, E. S., and Foss, L. "Professional Ethics: An Empirical Test of the 'Separatist Thesis.'" In H. G. Frederickson (ed.), *Ethics and Public Administration.* Armonk, N.Y.: Sharpe, 1993.

Page, B. *Who Gets What From Government.* Berkeley: University of California Press, 1983.

Palmer, P. J. *The Company of Strangers.* New York: Crossroads, 1981.

Parfit, D. *Reason and Persons.* Oxford, England: Clarendon Press, 1984.

Parrington, V. L. *Main Currents in American Thought: The Colonial Mind—1620–1800.* (Vol. 1.) Orlando, Fla.: Harcourt Brace Jovanovich, 1927.

Partridge, E. "Who Cares About the Future." In E. Partridge (ed.), *Responsibility to Future Generations.* Amherst, N.Y.: Prometheus, 1981.

Pasztor, A. *When the Pentagon Was for Sale: Inside America's Biggest Defense Scandal.* New York: Scribner, 1995.

Perry, J. L. "Whistleblowing, Organizational Performance, and Organizational Control." In H. G. Frederickson (ed.), *Ethics and Public Administration.* Armonk, N.Y.: Sharpe, 1993.

Peters, B. G., and Savoie, D. J. (eds.). *Governance in a Changing Environment.* Montreal: McGill-Queens University Press, 1995.

Pfiffner, J. P. "Political Public Administration." *Public Administration Review,* Mar./Apr. 1985, *45,* 352–356.

Plato. *The Laws.* (T. J. Saunders, trans.) New York: Penguin Books, 1970.

Plato. *The Republic.* (G.M.A. Grube, trans.) Indianapolis: Hackett, 1974.

Plessy v. Ferguson, 163 U.S. 537, 1896.

Plutarch. *The Lives of the Noble Grecians and Romans.* (J. Dryden trans.) New York: Modern Library, 1951.

"Present Critique of Government." *The Public Perspective,* Mar./Apr. 1993, *4*(3), 89.

Pressman, J. L., and Wildavsky, A. *Implementation: How Great Expectations in Washington Are Dashed in Oakland: Or, Why It's Amazing That Federal Programs Work at All, This Being a Saga of the Economic Development*

Administration As Told by Two Sympathetic Observers Who Seek to Build Morals on a Foundation of Ruined Hope. (3rd ed.) Berkeley: University of California Press, 1984.

Pryer, C. *The Debt Trap: The IMF and the Third World.* New York: Monthly Review Press, 1975.

Putnam, R. D., Leonardi, R., and Nanetti, R. Y. *Making Democracy Work: Civic Traditions in Modern Italy.* Princeton, N.J.: Princeton University Press, 1993.

Pye, L. W. "The Myth of the State: The Reality of Authority." In R. K. Arora (ed.), *Politics and Administration in Changing Societies: Essays in Honor of Professor Fred W. Riggs.* New Delhi: Associated Publishing House, 1992.

Rae, D., and Associates. *Equalities.* Cambridge, Mass.: Harvard University Press, 1981.

Rawls, J. *A Theory of Justice.* Cambridge, Mass.: Belknap Press, 1971.

Redford, E. S. *Democracy in the Administrative State.* New York: Oxford University Press, 1981.

Rest, J. *Moral Development: Advances in Research and Theory.* New York: Praeger, 1986.

Roberts, T. A. *The Concept of Benevolence: Aspects of Eighteenth Century Moral Philosophy.* Old Tappan, N.J.: Macmillan, 1973.

Rohr, J. A. *To Run a Constitution: The Legitimacy of the Administrative State.* Lawrence, Kans.: University Press of Kansas, 1986.

Rohr, J. A. *Ethics for Bureaucrats: An Essay on Law and Virtue.* (2nd ed.) New York: Dekker, 1989.

Romzek, B. S., and Dubnick, M. J. "Accountability in the Public Sector: Lessons from the Challenger Tragedy." *Public Administration Review,* May-June 1987, *47,* 227–238.

Rosenau, J. N., and Czempiel, E. *Governance Without Government: Order and Change in World Politics.* New York: Cambridge University Press, 1992.

Rosenbloom, D. H. *Public Administration and Law: Bench v. Bureau in the United States.* New York: Dekker, 1983.

Rourke, F. E. *Bureaucracy, Politics and Public Policy.* Boston: Little, Brown, 1984.

Rourke, F. E. "Bureaucracy in the American Constitutional Order." *Political Science Quarterly,* 1987, *102,* 217–232.

Salamon, L. M. *Beyond Privatization: The Tools of Government Action.* Washington, D.C.: Urban Institute Press, 1989.

Scharr, J. "Some Ways of Thinking About Equality." *Journal of Politics,* 1964, *26,* 867–895.

Scharr, J. "Equality of Opportunity and Beyond," in Rowland Pennock and John W. Chapman, (eds.) *NOMOS IX: Equality.* New York: Atherton, 1967, 226–252.

Schervish, P. G., Hodgkinson, V. A., and Gates, M. *Care and Community in Modern Society: Passing on the Tradition of Service to Future Generations.* San Francisco, Jossey-Bass, 1995.

Schlesinger, A. M. *The Cycles of American History.* Boston: Houghton Mifflin, 1986.

Schubert, G. A. *The Public Interest: A Critique of the Theory of the Political Concept.* New York: Free Press, 1960.

Schultze, C. *The Public Use of Private Interest.* Washington, D.C.: Brookings Institution, 1976.

Scott, W. G. "Barnard on the Nature of Elitist Responsibility." *Public Administration Review,* May/June 1982, *42,* 197–201.

Seidman, H., and Gilmour, R. *Politics, Position and Power: From the Positive to the Regulatory State.* (4th ed.) New York: Oxford University Press, 1986.

Selznick, P. *Leadership and Administration.* New York: HarperCollins, 1957.

Sennett, R. *The Fall of Public Man.* New York: Knopf, 1977.

Serrano et al. v. Ivy Baker Priest, 5 Cal. 3d 584, 1978.

Shapiro, M. A. "The Presidency and the Federal Courts." In Arnold J. Meltsner (ed.), *Politics and the Oval Office.* San Francisco: Institute for Contemporary Studies, 1981.

Simon, H. A. *Administrative Behavior: A Study of Decision-Making Processes in Administrative Organizations.* New York: Free Press, 1947.

Simon, H. A. *The New Science of Management Decision.* New York: HarperCollins, 1960.

Skowronek, S. *Building a New American State.* Cambridge, England: Cambridge University Press, 1982.

Smirich, L. "Organizations as Shared Meanings." In L. R. Pondy and others (eds.), *Organizational Symbolism.* Greenwich, Conn.: JAI Press, 1983.

Smith, A. *The Theory of Moral Sentiments.* (D. D. Raphael and A. L. Macfie, eds.) Indianapolis: Liberty Classics, 1982.

Smith, S. R., and Lipsky, M. *Nonprofits for Hire: The Welfare State in the Age of Contracting.* Cambridge, Mass.: Harvard University Press, 1993.

Smith, T. A. *Time and Public Policy.* Knoxville: University of Tennessee Press, 1988.

Speer, A. *Inside the Third Reich: Memoirs.* (R. Winston and C. Winston, trans.) Old Tappan, N.J.: Macmillan, 1970.

Stark, A. "Public-Sector Conflict of Interest at the Federal Level in Canada and the U.S.: Differences in Understandings and Approach." In H. G. Frederickson (ed.), *Ethics and Public Administration.* Armonk, N.Y.: Sharpe, 1993.

Statistical Abstracts. Washington, D.C.: U.S. Government Printing Office, 1993.

Stewart, D. W., and Sprinthall, N. A. "The Impact of Demographic, Professional and Organizational Variables and Domain on the Moral Reasoning of Public Administrators." In H. G. Frederickson (ed.), *Ethics and Public Administration*. Armonk, N.Y.: Sharpe, 1993.

Stiefel, L., and Berne, R. "The Equity Effects of State School Finance Reform: A Methodological Critique and New Evidence." *Policy Sciences,* 1981, *13*(1), 75–98.

Stillman, R. J. *Preface to Public Administration: A Search for Theories and Directions.* New York: St. Martin's Press, 1990.

Strange, S. *States and Markets.* London: Pinter, 1988.

Strauss, L., and Cropsey, J. (eds.). *History of Political Philosophy.* Chicago: University of Chicago Press, 1987.

Strauss, W., and Howe, N. *Generations: The History of America's Future, 1584–2069.* New York: Morrow, 1991.

Sullivan, W. M. *Reconstructing Public Philosophy.* Berkeley: University of California Press, 1982.

Swann v. Charlotte-Mecklenburg Board of Education 402 U.S. 1, 1971.

Tamashiro, H., Secrest, D., and Brunk, G. "Ethical Attitudes of Members of Congress and American Military Officers Toward War." In H. G. Frederickson (ed.), *Ethics and Public Administration*. Armonk, N.Y.: Sharpe, 1993.

Thompson, D. *Political Ethics and Public Office.* Cambridge, Mass.: Harvard University Press, 1987.

Thompson, J. D. *Organizations in Actions.* New York: McGraw-Hill, 1967.

Thompson, V. A. *Without Sympathy or Enthusiasm: The Problem of Administrative Compassion.* University: University of Alabama Press, 1975.

Time. (Several stories on cover topic of corruption in the Reagan administration.) May 25, 1987, pp. 14–29.

Tocqueville, A. de. *Democracy in America.* (Part 1.) New Rochelle, N.Y.: Arlington House, 1970. (Originally published 1835.)

Tocqueville, A. de. "Alexis de Tocqueville to Louis de Kergorlay, January 1835." In R. Boesche (ed.), *Alexis de Tocqueville: Selected Letters on Politics and Society.* Berkeley: University of California Press, 1985.

Tong, R. *Ethics in Policy Analysis.* Englewood Cliffs, N.J.: Prentice Hall, 1986.

Truman, D. B. *The Governmental Process.* New York: Knopf, 1957.

Tuchman, B. W. *The March of Folly: From Troy to Vietnam.* New York: Ballantine, 1984.

Tucker, R. C. *Politics as Leadership.* Columbia: University of Missouri Press, 1983.

Tyler, T. R. *Why People Obey the Law.* New Haven, Conn.: Yale University Press, 1990.

U.S. House of Representatives. Committee on Government Operations, Abuse and Mismanagement at HUD, 101st Congress, 1st Session. Washington, D.C.: U.S. Government Printing Office, 1990.

University of California Regents v. Bakke, 438 U.S. 265, 1978.

Ventriss, C. "The Current Dilemmas of Public Administration: A Commentary." *Dialogue,* Summer 1984, *6*(4), 3–11.

Waldo, D. *The Administrative State.* Somerset, N.J.: Ronald Press, 1949.

Waldo, D. *The Enterprise of Public Administration: A Summary View.* Novato, Calif.: Chandler and Sharp, 1980.

Waldo, D. "A Theory of Public Administration Means in Our Time a Theory of Politics Also." In N. B. Lynn and A. Wildavsky (eds.), *Public Administration: The State of the Discipline.* Chatham, N.J.: Chatham House, 1990.

Walster, E., and Walster, G. W. "Equity and Social Justice." *Journal of Social Issues,* 1975, *31*(3), 2–43.

Walzer, M. *Spheres of Justice: A Defense of Pluralism and Equality.* New York: Basic Books, 1983.

Wamsley, G., and others. *Refounding Public Administration.* Thousand Oaks, Calif.: Sage, 1990.

Warren, M. A. "Do Potential Persons Have Rights?" In E. Partridge (ed.), *Responsibility to Future Generations.* Amherst, N.Y.: Prometheus, 1981.

Weingast, B. R., and Moran, M. J. "Bureaucracy, Discretionary Congressional Control? Regulatory Policy Making by the Federal Trade Commission." *Journal of Political Economy,* 1983, *91,* 756–800.

Welfeld, I. H. *The HUD Scandals: Howling Headlines and Silent Fiascos.* New Brunswick, N.J.: Transaction, 1992.

White, L. D. *The Jeffersonians: A Study in Administrative History, 1801–1929.* New York: Free Press, 1951.

White, M. *The Philosophy of the American Revolution.* New York: Oxford University Press, 1978.

White, O. "The Citizen of the 1980's." In C. T. Goodsell (ed.), *The Public Encounter: Where State and Citizen Meet.* Bloomington: Indiana University Press, 1981.

Whitehead, B. D. "Dan Quayle Was Right." *The Atlantic Monthly,* Apr. 1993, *271*(4), 47–84.

Wildavsky, A. "Ubiquitous Anomie: Public Service in an Era of Ideological Dissensus." *Public Administration Review,* 1988, *48*(4), 753–755.

Wilensky, P. "Efficiency or Equity: Competing Values in Administrative Reform." *Policy Studies Journal,* 1981, *9,* 1239–1249.

Will, G. F. *Statecraft as Soulcraft: What Government Does.* New York: Simon & Schuster, 1983.

Willbern, Y. "Is the New Public Administration Still with Us?" *Public Administration Review,* July-Aug. 1973, *33*(4), 376.

Willbern, Y. "Types and Levels of Public Morality." *Public Administration Review,* 1984, *44*(2), 102–108.

Wills, G. *Inventing America.* New York: Doubleday, 1978.

Wilson, J. Q. *Bureaucracy: What Government Agencies Do and Why They Do It.* New York: Basic Books, 1989.

Wilson, J. Q. "The Moral Sense." *American Political Science Review,* 1993, *83*(1), 1–10.

Wilson, W. "The Study of Administration." *Political Science Quarterly,* Dec. 1941, *56*(2), 197–222. (Originally published 1887.)

Wilson, W. J. *The Truly Disadvantaged: The Inner City, the Underclass and Public Policy.* Chicago: The University of Chicago Press, 1987.

Wood, B. D., and Waterman, R. W. "The Dynamics of Political Control over the Bureaucracy." *American Political Science Review,* 1991, *85,* 801–828.

World Commission on Environment and Development. *Our Common Future.* New York: Oxford University Press, 1987.

Yahil, L. *The Rescue of Danish Jewry.* (M. Gradel, trans.) Philadelphia: Jewish Publication Society of America, 1969.

Yates, D. *Bureaucratic Democracy: The Search For Democracy and Efficiency in American Government.* Cambridge, Mass.: Harvard University Press, 1982.

Name Index

Subject Index

CPSIA information can be obtained at www.ICGtesting.com
Printed in the USA
BVOW07*0150160614

356394BV00003B/28/A